The Essence of
Statistics for Business

PUBLISHED TITLES

The Essence of Total Quality Management
The Essence of Small Business
The Essence of Strategic Management
The Essence of International Money
The Essence of Financial Accounting
The Essence of Management Accounting
The Essence of Marketing Research
The Essence of Change
The Essence of Industrial Relations and Personnel Management
The Essence of Information Systems
The Essence of Competitive Strategy
The Essence of Statistics for Business
The Essence of Operations Management
The Essence of Effective Communication
The Essence of Successful Staff Selection
The Essence of Marketing
The Essence of Financial Management
The Essence of the Economy
The Essence of Economics
The Essence of International Marketing
The Essence of Taxation
The Essence of Services Marketing
The Essence of Business Process Re-engineering
The Essence of Mathematics for Business
The Essence of International Business
The Essence of Organizational Behaviour
The Essence of Managing People
The Essence of Negotiation
The Essence of Business Ethics
The Essence of Management Creativity
The Essence of Mergers and Acquisitions
The Essence of Women in Management

The Essence of
Statistics for Business

MICHAEL C. FLEMING
Professor of Economics,
Loughborough University

and

JOSEPH G. NELLIS
Professor of International Management Economics,
Cranfield School of Management, Cranfield University

Prentice Hall

New York   London   Toronto   Sydney   Tokyo   Singapore
Madrid   Mexico City   Munich

First edition published in 1991
This edition published in 1996
Both editions published by
Prentice Hall Europe
Campus 400, Maylands Avenue
Hemel Hempstead
Hertfordshire, HP2 7EZ
A division of
Simon & Schuster International Group

Typeset in 10/12pt Palatino
by Keyset Composition, Colchester

Printed and bound in Great Britain by
Hartnolls Limited, Bodmin, Cornwall

Library of Congress Cataloging-in-Publication Data

Fleming, M. C.
 The essence of statistics for business / Michael C. Fleming
and Joseph G. Nellis.
  p.   cm. – (The Essence of management series)
 Includes bibliographical references and index.
 ISBN 0-13-398777-9
 1. Commercial statistics. 2. Economic – Statistical methods.
 3. Statistical decision. I. Nellis, J. G. II. Title.
 III. Series.
 HF1017.F56 1996
 519.5 – dc20   95-46128
                                                          CIP

British Library Cataloguing in Publication Data

A catalogue record for this book is available from
the British Library

ISBN 0-13-398777-9

---

1 2   3   4   5   00   99   98   97   96

To Ruth, Anne, Stephen and Rachel
Helen, Gareth, Daniel and Kathleen

Contents

Preface to the first edition

A knowledge of statistics is essential for effective decision making in business. It is not necessary, however, for managers to have the same depth of technical knowledge as the professional statistician. What is needed for practical purposes is a broad understanding of the underlying principles of statistical analysis, an appreciation of the situations in which statistical analyses may be helpful, an ability to communicate with professional statisticians and an ability to interpret statistical findings.

The aim of this book, therefore, is two-fold. Firstly, it is intended to bridge the communication gap that often arises between professional managers and professional statisticians. Consequently, we present the essence of statistics with the emphasis on practical applications in the context of business. Theoretical issues are not considered here and technical jargon is kept to a minimum. Secondly, our aim is to develop the confidence and competence of managers in the use of basic statistical techniques.

In recent years, the use of computers and statistical software packages in business has mushroomed. This development has considerably widened the application of statistical techniques, facilitating the analysis and solution of complex problems, and made the subject more accessible to managers and other users. In this book, we include some illustrations of the use of one of the more popular general purpose statistical packages – MINITAB – in problem solving and graphical presentation of business-related data. At the same time, there is an inherent danger that the untutored non-specialist may approach the subject matter rather slavishly, without a clear understanding of the mechanics of the 'statistical black box', oblivious of the pitfalls in using and misusing statistical techniques. The development of this understanding has been at the forefront of our minds in writing this book.

To help managers unravel the complexities of statistics, we steer a course

xi

in this book between what may be described as a simple 'primer' on statistics, which glosses over technical details, and the 'heavy' approach of an advanced specialist textbook. In order to convey, therefore, the essence of statistical judgement we focus our attention on the central concepts of most relevance in business management.

The book is designed to meet the needs of a wide general audience. It will be particularly attractive to managers working towards professional management qualifications such as the Master of Business Administration (MBA) and the Diploma in Management Studies (DMS) as well as for managers attending the large range of continuing education and professional development courses of varying design and duration. We have also had in mind the needs of others preparing for a range of other professional qualifications, especially those in the business and commercial fields of accounting, marketing, banking, financial services, etc. Finally, the book may also usefully serve as a foundation text for students who require an overview of the essential elements of statistics as part of any of a wide range of courses in colleges of further and higher education, polytechnics and universities.

It is a pleasure at this stage to acknowledge the help and support received from others. We are particularly indebted to Ruth Fleming for the many hours she spent in meticulously scrutinizing the manuscript and making many suggestions for improvement. We are also indebted to Su Spencer for typing several drafts of the manuscript with her customary speed, accuracy and good humour. As always, any remaining errors are the sole responsibility of the authors. A special word of thanks is due to our friends M. and Mme Ferrière for their kindness during the writing of the book while we were in 'solitary confinement' in Rue de la Prison, Vieil Hesdin, France.

Not unusually, the authors' families have borne the brunt of authorship as much as the authors themselves, and we are deeply grateful for their support and understanding, and indeed for their forgiveness for many hours and days of absence.

MICHAEL C. FLEMING
Loughborough

JOSEPH G. NELLIS
Cranfield

1991

Preface to the second edition

For this second edition we have introduced a number of changes throughout the text to improve the overall style and usefulness of the book. In particular we have incorporated a new chapter on multiple regression and correlation analysis. We feel that this is an important addition given the widespread use of this technique in business and many other fields and the ready availability nowadays of personal computers and user-friendly software packages. We have also included at the end of each chapter a set of key learning points in order to condense the material into a convenient ready-reference guide. These will also naturally serve as useful revision guides. On this occasion we are indebted to Chris Williams for preparing the revised material.

MICHAEL C. FLEMING
Loughborough

JOSEPH G. NELLIS
Cranfield

1995

1

The essence of statistics for business

The use of statistics

The word *statistics* has two meanings. At the simplest level, it refers to numerical data such as weekly production figures, employment totals, average earnings, profitability, etc. Such statistics merely provide descriptive information. The word is also used to refer to techniques and procedures for collecting, describing, analyzing and interpreting numerical data. In this sense, statistics may be referred to as a science.

The application of statistics is evident in almost all areas of everyday life. At the individual level, decisions are made, albeit in a rough and ready fashion, by using whatever numerical information is available. These may concern expectations about the future based on what has happened in the past, involving matters such as house buying and selling, living standards, life expectancy, etc. At government level, the science of statistics is applied in virtually every department and laboratory for purposes of analysis and forecasting as well as in the collection and presentation of economic, financial, social and demographic data. Similarly, academics and research workers use statistical techniques in their enquiries, again across many fields of interest, including the economic, social and physical sciences as well as in 'non-quantitative' subjects in which statistics have been used, for example, to judge the authorship of anonymous works.

In business, the science of statistics has a great number of applications. Decision making by managers requires them to summarize and analyze the various data available to them. This requires the application of a range of statistical techniques. Examples of the areas in business where these techniques are to be most frequently encountered are:

□ *Financial analysis*
Managerial accounts and shareholder reports require a statistical analysis of business performance based on costs and revenues.

□ *Product planning*
Forward planning in product development requires the statistical analyses of economic and business trends, detailed sales budgeting, inventory control systems, etc.

□ *Forecasting*
In conjunction with product planning, this involves the forecasting of sales, determination of employment requirements, productivity trends, etc.

□ *Market research*
This involves the collection and analysis of information about consumer preferences and trends.

□ *Process and quality controls*
Statistical analysis aids the maintenance of standards and the enhancement of productivity.

□ *Employee records*
Business monitoring, particularly in larger companies, is also likely to involve the use of statistical procedures to analyze such matters as turnover of staff, absenteeism, staff appraisal, etc.

Basic terms and concepts

In this book in the *Essence* series, we do not intend to use technical jargon for its own sake but, as with any other specialist subject, certain terms are commonly used in statistics for the sake of precision and clarity. We describe the main ones here.

□ *Descriptive statistics*
Tabular, graphical and numerical methods used to summarize data sets. These can be used for data sets which relate to entire populations or samples (see below).

□ *Inferential statistics*
Techniques employed in making estimates and drawing conclusions about the characteristics of a statistical 'population' using results from a sample data set.

☐ *Population*
The set of *all* items (such as products, individuals, customers, firms, employees, prices, etc.) which are of interest in a particular study (also sometimes referred to as a *universe*). Normally information is collected from a sample set drawn from the population.

☐ *Sample*
A portion of the population, selected so as to represent the whole population.

☐ *Census*
The collection of information about every member of a statistical population.

☐ *Parameter*
A numerical value, such as an average, used as a summary measure for an entire population.

☐ *Statistic*
A numerical value, such as an average, used as a summary measure for a sample (e.g. the sample average).

☐ *Variable*
A characteristic or phenomenon which takes on different values for different members of the population or sample data sets (e.g. weight, monthly sales, sex of employee, wages, etc.).

☐ *Discrete variable*
A numerical variable whose values can vary only in steps, often associated with counts (e.g. number of employees, products, firms, etc.).

☐ *Continuous variable*
A numerical variable which, in contrast to a discrete variable, is measured on a continuous scale and, hence, is not restricted to specific, discrete values (e.g. weights, ages, heights, etc., of objects or people).

Statistics for managers

Just as firms employ specialized staff to carry out certain specialized functions (e.g. accountants, lawyers, corporate treasurers, etc.), so too many large firms today will employ professional statisticians. The task of these statisticians is to assist management in performing its wide range of functions. The aim of this book, however, is not to serve the needs of professional statisticians. Instead the book is specifically designed to serve the needs of general managers. It is important for general managers to understand the relevance of statistical methods, to be able to interpret statistical results and, where necessary, to be able to communicate with professional statisticians. Hence we present in this book only the 'essence' of statistics for managers, concentrating on their use and interpretation in business situations. Unnecessary theoretical proofs and derivations of statistical formulae are avoided, although selected references for further reading which may be found helpful are attached at the end.

Schematic overview of the book

The study of statistics covers a wide range of techniques for describing and analyzing sets of data. In this book we cover the fundamental topics of relevance to business managers. These range from simple graphical presentations of data to a range of tests of statistical significance. A schematic overview of the whole book, showing its structure and the interrelationships between the various topics, is presented in Figure 1.1. It will be seen that, starting with a set of data, the book subdivides into two main branches:

☐ Descriptive techniques.
☐ Analytical techniques.

Descriptive techniques

These involve tabular and graphical presentations of data, methods for describing sets of data by single summary measures (of central location and variability), and the derivation of index numbers.

Analytical techniques

These represent the core of statistical theory. There are a large number of techniques but, as indicated above, we confine our attention to those of central importance, indicated in Figure 1.1.

The concepts of probability and probability distributions lie at the heart of statistical analysis and, in particular, statistical inference and decision making. The study of probability involves assessing, in the context of uncertainty, the likelihood that something will occur by chance, e.g. that

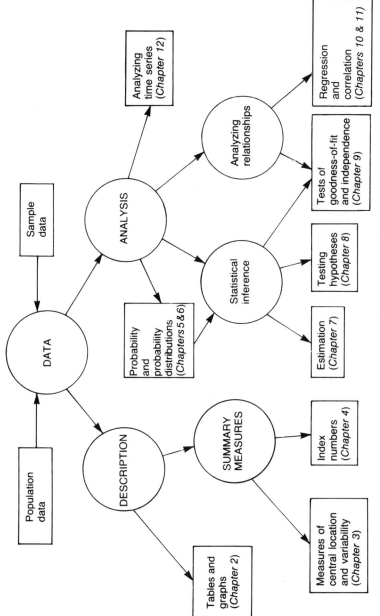

Figure 1.1 Schematic overview of the book.

a machine will break down, goods will be defective, or the wrong decisions will be arrived at. In statistical inference we typically wish to make some decision about population parameters, given information available only from a sample of data drawn from the population. There are two main areas of the subject: estimation of the population parameters and testing hypotheses about them.

Another important aspect of data analysis is the measurement of relationships between variables. This topic involves, on the one hand, statistical tests of association (so-called 'goodness-of-fit' tests) between actual and assumed distributions of data as well as tests of independence of categorized data. On the other hand, we are able to determine the nature of relationships and the degree of association between observations on variables, using regression and correlation analysis.

The final topic of data analysis covered in this book is the study of time series. This involves the measurement of trends as well as seasonal and cyclical variation.

Statistical computer packages

The application of the statistical techniques outlined above can, at first sight, seem like a daunting task, especially when large sets of data are involved. However, in this context, it is worth noting that the application of statistical techniques has been facilitated considerably in recent years by the use of computers. Statistical software packages are readily available which allow a wide range of statistical measures to be calculated very easily and quickly. Some of the principal packages are MINITAB, SAS (Statistical Analysis System) and SPSSX (Statistical Package for the Social Sciences). These are in common use in business applications today. Brief details concerning these are given in Appendix B. Examples of the use of the MINITAB program – one of the most popular packages available for use on personal (as well as mainframe) computers – are given at the end of each chapter wherever appropriate.

2

Summarizing data using tables and graphs

The essence of descriptive tables and graphs in business

We are concerned in this chapter with tabular and graphical methods of arranging and presenting statistical data. The purpose of these methods is, of course, to condense the information from a mass of figures (raw data) into a form which provides an informative summary and readily conveys the essential features of the data. There are many snags waiting to trap the unwary, both those applying these methods and for those who merely see and interpret the results.

Tables and frequency distributions

Tabulation of data is generally the first step in sorting out a mass of raw figures into a form which directly conveys some useful information. Consider, for example, the data shown in Table 2.1. This shows the beer sales in each of the 60 public houses owned by Bitter Beer Brewery for January 1995.

A simple way to condense such data is to draw up a tabular summary in the form of a *frequency distribution*. This is shown in Table 2.2 below in which the variable (beer sales) has been *grouped* in order to reduce it to a manageable form. Note that this table consists of the following:

Table 2.1 Beer sales (number of barrels) for 60 public houses owned by Bitter Beer Brewery in January 1995

48	71	52	53	36	41	69	58	47	60
53	29	41	72	81	37	43	58	68	42
73	62	59	44	51	53	47	66	59	52
34	49	73	29	47	16	39	58	43	29
46	52	38	46	80	58	51	67	54	57
58	63	49	40	54	61	58	66	47	50

Table 2.2 Frequency distribution of beer sales

Number of barrels (a)	Number of public houses (frequency) (b)	Relative frequency (%) (c)
10–19	1	1.7
20–29	3	5.0
30–39	5	8.3
40–49	16	26.7
50–59	20	33.3
60–69	9	15.0
70–79	4	6.7
80–89	2	3.3
	60	100.0

☐ A number of groups (*classes*), each of which covers a range of the number of barrels sold in each public house (a *class interval*) – shown in column (a).

☐ *Class frequencies* (the number of public houses with beer sales falling within each class interval) – shown in column (b).

☐ *Relative frequencies*, in which each absolute frequency is shown as a proportion of the total frequency – shown in column (c).

This has reduced 60 observations to only 8 and is clearly much more informative. It can be seen immediately that the *range* of beer sales is from below 20 to above 80 barrels but that most are clustered in the 40–49 and 50–59 classes. In relative frequency form, of course, it is easy to see the relative importance of different groups. Thus, for example, over half of the public houses are clustered in the 40–59 range of barrel sales.

As the purpose of tabular summaries in the form of a frequency (or relative frequency) distribution is to reveal an overall pattern, it is important that the number of classes should not be too big or too small. As a general rule, it is usual to have around 5 to 15 classes (depending, of course, on

Table 2.3 Number of firms classified by size

Firm size (number of persons employed)	Number of firms
1–24	45
25–99	31
100–199	23
200–499	15
500 and over	6
	120

the nature of the data). A certain amount of trial and error is often necessary within these limits to find a satisfactory distribution. This may even involve the use of classes covering unequal ranges of the variable under investigation (e.g. beer sales) or leaving the top and/or bottom classes *open-ended*.

Naturally it is important in defining the upper and lower limits of each class (the *class limits*) to ensure that they do not overlap, so that it is clear into which class any observation is meant to fall. In interpreting and defining class limits, particular attention needs to be devoted to whether the variable is discrete or continuous. This is best explained by means of examples. Table 2.3 gives an example in which the variable (firm size) is discrete. If we focus attention on the definition of the class limits here, there might appear to be a gap between successive upper and lower limits, i.e. between 24 and 25, 99 and 100, etc. But the variable is discrete – the size of a firm can only vary by one unit (person) at a time (i.e. it can be 24 or 25 persons, for instance, but nothing in between) – and so there is no doubt about the class to which firms employing 24 or 25 persons are classified. All the classes are mutually exclusive (i.e. non-overlapping), so the classification is unambiguous and therefore satisfactory. Ambiguity about the classification would have arisen above if the variable had been continuous rather than discrete, for the classification of values between 24 and 25, 99 and 100, etc., would then have been unclear.

When the variable is continuous, there is somewhat greater scope for ambiguity because the variable will often be rounded to some convenient unit. For example, an income distribution may be presented as follows:

Personal income (£)	Frequency (number of people)
190–199	225
200–249	1439
250–299	1346
300–399	2606

Note that the class limits are defined in discrete units of £1, but income need not be measured in units of £1 because the variable is continuous, at least down to two decimal places (i.e. to the nearest penny). It is clear, therefore, that the data have been rounded to the nearest pound. Thus the implication is that the first class (£190–199) would include all incomes from £189.50 up to and including £199.49. These figures are the *true class limits* (or *class boundaries*) of the first class.

Graphical methods of data presentation

The construction of a frequency distribution is often only the first step in summarizing a collection of data. The next step, commonly, is to present the data in some sort of graphical form. This is particularly useful for conveying information very quickly and succinctly and for comparing one distribution with another. Such visual aids can have a particularly powerful impact – it is often said that 'a picture is worth a thousand words'! At the same time, of course, it should be appreciated that graphical presentations are, in the main, only other ways of describing or revealing the essential features of data sets and are not substitutes for statistical analysis.

The most common graphical methods are the following:

□ Line graphs.
□ Line charts.
□ Bar charts.
□ Histograms.
□ Frequency polygons.
□ Cumulative frequency curves (ogives).
□ Pie charts.
□ Pictograms.
□ Logarithmic graphs.

We briefly describe the essential features of each of these in turn.

Line graphs

An example of a line graph is shown in Figure 2.1(a). The horizontal axis is often time, therefore giving rise to a *time series* line graph. In business, movements over time are often of special interest in that they highlight trends. However, as comparison of Figure 2.1(b) with Figure 2.1(a) shows,

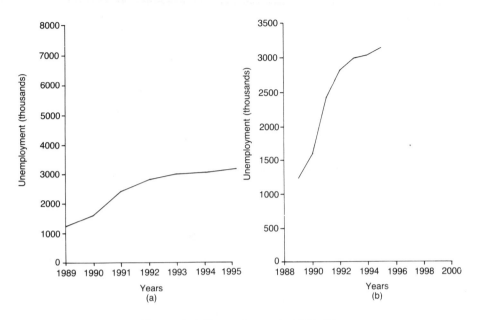

Figure 2.1 Unemployment, 1989–95.

the choice of scale for the vertical and horizontal axes is very important. By stretching or condensing the axes it is possible to convey a very different, and indeed misleading, impression of the same set of data. It will be seen that the rate of increase in unemployment is made to look modest in Figure 2.1(a) but very sharp in Figure 2.1(b). This warning, of course, applies to most of the other types of graphical presentation shown below.

Sometimes the range of data values is such that they can only be suitably graphed by suppressing the origin (zero point). This can also be misleading and where it is done attention should be drawn to it by showing a break in the scale.

Line graphs may also be used to show changes in the components of a series over time. Figure 2.2 shows the change in the composition of imports into a country according to type of goods.

Line charts, bar charts and histograms

Figure 2.3 is an example of a line chart, illustrating the results of surveys by a company of the number of defective goods returned to each of its 60 distributors. Line charts are appropriate where, as in this case, the variable (number of defective goods) is discrete and the data are ungrouped. For

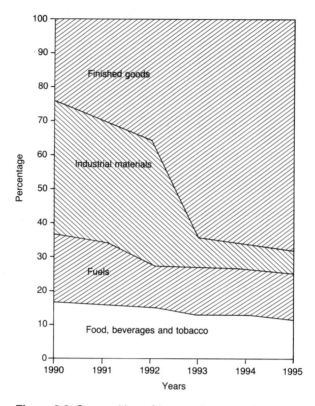

Figure 2.2 Composition of imports by type of goods.

grouped data, bar charts or histograms are appropriate, depending on whether the variable is discrete or continuous respectively.

A bar chart is a simple extension of the idea of a line chart, the essential point being that lines are replaced by bars (or blocks) in the case of discrete data. Bar charts can be drawn horizontally or vertically (as shown in Figure 2.4).

Bar charts are also particularly useful when the variable of interest can be subdivided into a number of components which are to be illustrated at the same time. This gives rise to a *component bar chart* such as Figure 2.5, which shows the breakdown of the labour force for a large company according to sex and marital status.

A histogram is similar to a bar chart except that no gaps are left between the bars. It can be used in cases involving either discrete or continuous data, unlike bar charts which apply only to the former. If we assume, for the sake of example, that the data shown in Table 2.2 for the number of barrels of

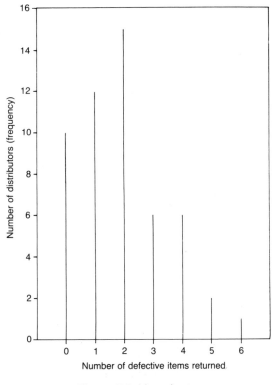

Figure 2.3 Line chart.

beer sold by the 60 public houses were continuous, rather than discrete, then a histogram of these data would appear as in Figure 2.6. A second essential point to note about histograms is that it is the *area* of each column which represents the frequency rather than its height. Thus, if a class interval is twice as wide as the others in a histogram, the height of the column must be taken as half of the frequency for this larger class interval.

Frequency polygons

Frequency polygons provide a useful alternative to the histogram, particularly when one wants to compare two distributions on the same diagram. To try to do this with histograms would mean that some parts would overlap and it would be difficult to distinguish one histogram from

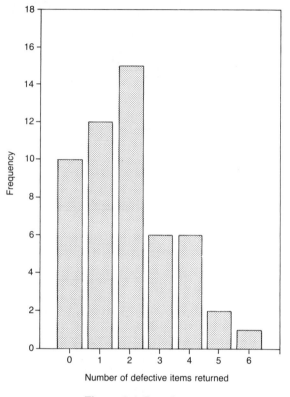

Figure 2.4 Bar chart.

the other. Figure 2.7 shows the comparison of two frequency polygons illustrating the distribution of weights of male and female passengers carried by an aircraft. This information is important, for example, to aircraft manufacturers in determining performance and design specifications for their aircraft.

It should be noted that the frequency polygon is equivalent to joining up the mid-points of the tops of an equivalent histogram, except that the ends of the frequency polygon have to be extended at each end to meet the horizontal axis at the mid-point of what would have been the next class below or above. The necessity of this arises from the fact that like the histogram, the impression of the total frequency is conveyed by the area enclosed.

It will be seen that the frequency polygons in Figure 2.7 allow the distributions of the weights of men and women to be compared easily. It can be seen that there is a considerable degree of overlap but that male

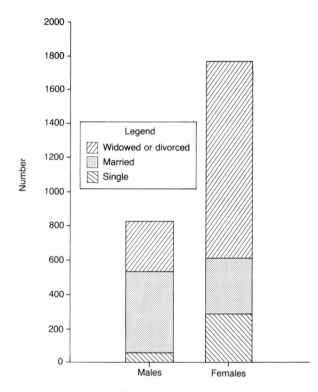

Figure 2.5 Composition of labour force by sex and marital status.

passengers tend to be heavier than female passengers with more women at the lower end of the range and more men at the top end. In addition, it will be seen that there were many more male than female passengers.

Cumulative frequency curves (ogives)

The data shown in Table 2.4, from which part of Figure 2.7 was derived, show the distribution of the weights of male passengers on a *cumulative* basis. The data, presented in this form, are referred to as a *cumulative frequency distribution* and the graphical representation as a *cumulative frequency curve* (or *ogive*). This is shown in Figure 2.8. Notice that this has been drawn up on a 'less than' basis and thus each cumulative frequency refers to the upper class limits (true class limits), i.e. there were no men weighing *less than* 50 kilos but there were 28 men weighing *less than* 60 kilos,

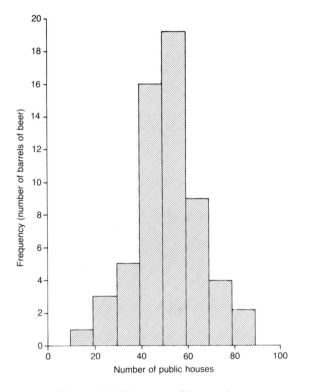

Figure 2.6 Histogram of beer sales.

etc. This point is of crucial importance when plotting a cumulative frequency curve: the cumulative frequency must be plotted against the *limits – not the mid-points* (unlike the construction of frequency polygons).

It is also worth noting that a second cumulative frequency curve may be drawn using frequencies cumulated from the bottom up rather than the top down (as above). These would focus, by contrast, on the *lower* class limits to give a cumulative frequency curve on an 'or more than' basis. Thus we would have 22 male passengers with a weight of 90 kilos *or more*, 84 with 80 kilos *or more*, etc. It is possible, therefore, to plot two cumulative frequency curves: a 'less than' curve and an 'or more' curve – but in practice this is not necessary because one is merely the complement of the other and thus all the information that can be derived from one curve can equally well be derived from the other.

Two kinds of question which the cumulative frequency curve may be used to answer may be illustrated as follows:

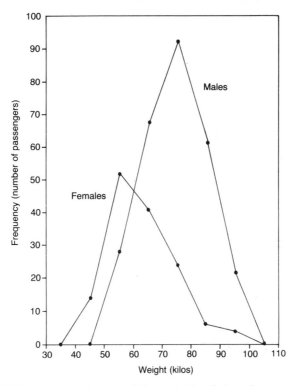

Figure 2.7 Frequency polygons of the weights of aircraft passengers.

Table 2.4 Distribution of weights of male passengers

Weight (kilos)	Cumulative frequency
Less than 50	0
Less than 60	28
Less than 70	96
Less than 80	188
Less than 90	250
Less than 100	272

1. How many male passengers had weights less than 66 kilos? The answer, shown on the graph, is approximately 69 men.
2. What is the top weight of the lightest 150 male passengers? The answer, also shown on the graph, is about 76 kilos (i.e. 150 men had weights of less than 76 kilos).

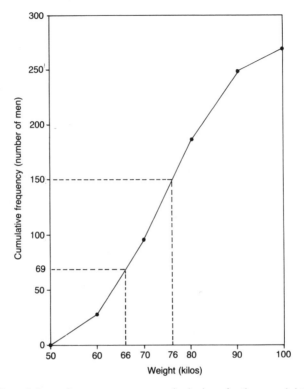

Figure 2.8 Cumulative frequency curve (ogive) of the weights of male passengers.

Pie charts

Examples of pie charts are shown in Figure 2.9. These are derived from the same data set used to illustrate component bar charts in Figure 2.5 above. Pie charts are useful where the variable represents categories of data. Sectors of the 'pie' indicate the relative importance of the different categories.

Pictograms

Pictograms provide another means of visual representation of data which are very popular in non-specialist publications and on television. As the name implies, they employ pictures in place of diagrams to convey the message. For example, pictures of people may be used for labour force data, factories for industrial data, cars for car production, etc. The possibilities are almost limitless, constrained only by the inventiveness of the artist or

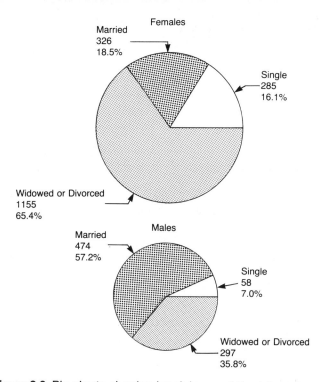

Figure 2.9 Pie charts showing breakdowns of the labour force.

draughtsman. We deal with the subject here only for the sake of completeness and to draw attention to a common pitfall in using this method. Our treatment is therefore brief. An example of a pictogram is given in Figure 2.10, which shows the number of dwellings completed in selected regions of England in 1983. Such methods make a direct impression very easily but they necessarily lack precision. In this case, it will be seen that the number of dwellings built was about 60,000 in the South East, 20,000 in the South West and just over 10,000 in East Anglia. Where more accuracy is required then one of the other graphical or tabular methods of presentation needs to be employed.

   A major snare in the use of pictograms is the ease with which it is possible to give a misleading impression. This often arises, particularly when three-dimensional pictograms are used. The essential point is that the area in two-dimensional diagrams and the volume in three-dimensional pictograms must be made proportional to the data values being illustrated, but it is not always easy to adjust the area or volume of pictograms accurately.

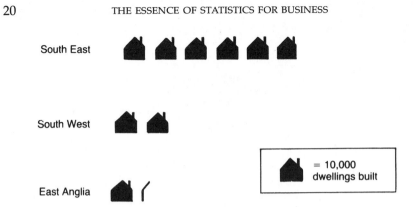

Figure 2.10 Pictogram showing the number of dwellings built in 1983 in certain regions of England.

It is normally better, therefore, to use a series of pictures of the same size (as in Figure 2.10).

Logarithmic graphs: proportionate rates of change

So far we have been concerned only with graphing absolute (or relative) values of a variable. However, one is often interested in illustrating the rate of change in a variable rather than changes in its absolute value as such. This is easily accomplished by plotting logarithms of the variable (log values) instead of its absolute values: such graphs show proportionate changes directly. This may be illustrated very easily. Consider the following figures:

Time period	Absolute value (a)	Logarithm value to base 10 (b)
1	2	0.3
2	4	0.6
3	8	0.9
4	16	1.2

The absolute values are growing at a constant rate – by a factor of 2 each time. It will be seen that the logarithm of these values (using logarithms to the base 10) changes by a constant absolute amount (from 0.3 to 0.6, from 0.6 to 0.9, etc.). Thus on a graph the logarithm of values showing a constant rate of change comes out as a straight line. This is shown in Figure 2.11 which illustrates the two sets of data (a) and (b) respectively. By plotting logarithms, therefore, it is possible to observe whether the variable is

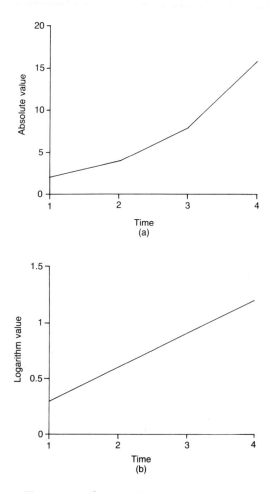

Figure 2.11 Comparative rates of change.

changing at a constant rate or by more than or less than a constant rate. It is also possible – and this makes the use of logarithm scales a particularly useful device – to compare the rates of change of two variables where the magnitude of their absolute values may differ very considerably, because the slopes of the curve are directly comparable, and equal slopes represent equal rates of change.

Consider the data shown in Table 2.5, which show the total costs and the labour costs of a company. Figures 2.12 and 2.13 show graphs of the absolute values and logarithm values of these data respectively. These two series change by the same absolute amount each year and, as a consequence,

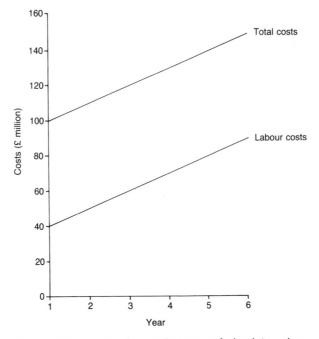

Figure 2.12 Graphs of costs in terms of absolute values.

Table 2.5   Total costs and labour costs

Year	Total costs (£m)	Labour costs (£m)
1	100	40
2	110	50
3	120	60
4	130	70
5	140	80
6	150	90

the two graphs are parallel to each other when the absolute values are plotted (Figure 2.12). The unwary might therefore conclude that labour costs constitute the same proportion of total costs throughout the period. In fact, however, they constitute 40 per cent at the beginning but 60 per cent at the end, because annual increases in labour costs (identical in amount to those for total costs) represent a greater proportionate increase. This comes out very clearly in Figure 2.13, which plots the logarithms of the values. The higher rate of increase in labour costs over total costs is indicated by a much steeper curve.

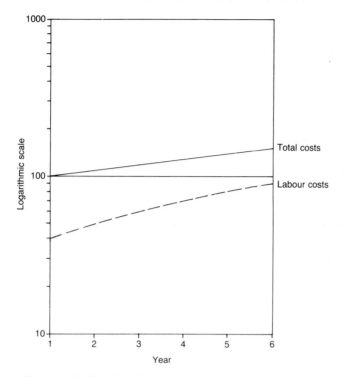

Figure 2.13 Graphs of costs using a logarithmic scale.

It is tedious, of course, to have to take logarithms of a set of data values. In practice, the preparation of such graphs is facilitated by the use of graph paper in which one of the axes is already scaled in ratio (logarithmic) terms. This is called *semi-logarithmic* graph paper ('semi-log' paper), so-called because one axis only is in ratio form. The absolute values of the variable may be plotted directly on such paper, thereby eliminating the need to substitute logarithm values in place of the absolute values.

A final point to note about the use of logarithms in graphs is that although they possess the advantages described above, they also have certain limitations. These are that it is impossible to show zero and negative values of the variable because such values have no logarithm.

Use of MINITAB

Two illustrations of the use of the MINITAB statistics package for preparing graphical presentations, based on data used above, are shown in Computer illustrations 2.1 and 2.2. They show histograms (using the data on beer sales in Table 2.1) and a cumulative frequency curve (using the data on airline passengers from Table 2.4).

Computer illustration 2.1   MINITAB and histograms
(data from Table 2.1)

```
MTB > NAME C1 'Sales'
MTB > SET C1
DATA> 48 71 52 53 36 41 69 58 47 60
DATA> 53 29 41 72 81 37 43 58 68 42
DATA> 73 62 59 44 51 53 47 66 59 52
DATA> 34 49 73 29 47 16 39 58 43 29
DATA> 46 52 38 46 80 58 51 67 54 57
DATA> 58 63 49 40 54 61 58 66 47 50
DATA> END
MTB > HISTogram of data in C1;  (Basic command)
SUBC> STARt at 15;              (Specifies mid-point of first
                                 class — optional sub-command.)
SUBC> INCRement = 10.           (Specifies class interval —
                                 optional sub-command.)
         (These commands and sub-commands give the following output.
          Graphical output may also be obtained — as shown below.)

Histogram of C1 N = 60

Midpoint  Count
    15.0      1  *
    25.0      3  ***
    35.0      5  *****
    45.0     16  ****************
    55.0     20  ********************
    65.0      9  *********
    75.0      4  ****
    85.0      2  **

MTB > GHISTogram of data in C1;   (Command for graphical output.)
SUBC> STARt at 15;
SUBC> INCRement = 10.

Histogram of C1  N = 60
```

```
Midpoint  Count
    15.0      1
    25.0      3
    35.0      5
    45.0     16
    55.0     20
    65.0      9
    75.0      4
    85.0      2
```

Computer illustration 2.2 MINITAB and a cumulative frequency curve
(data from Table 2.4)

```
MTB > NAME C1 'ClassLmt' C2 'Freq'
MTB > SET C1
DATA> 50 60 70 80 90 100       (Puts upper class limits into column 1.)
DATA> end
MTB > SET C2
DATA> 0 28 68 92 62 22         (Puts frequencies into column 2.)
DATA> end
MTB > PARSums C2 C3            (Computes cumulative frequencies and
                                  puts results into column 3.)

MTB > NAME C3 'CumFreq'
MTB > PRINt C1-C3             (Prints columns 1-3 as follows.)

  ROW   ClassLmt   Freq   CumFreq
   1        50       0        0
   2        60      28       28
   3        70      68       96
   4        80      92      188
   5        90      62      250
   6       100.     22      272

MTB > GPLOT C3 C1;            (Command to plot cumulative frequencies
                                  in C3 on Y-axis against class limits
                                  in C1 on X-axis.)
SUBC> LINES C3 C1.            (Sub-command to join up the plotted
                                  points.)
```

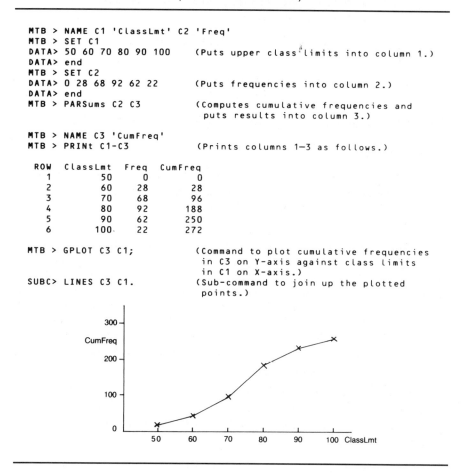

Key learning points

Frequency distribution   A tabular summary of a set of data showing the frequency (or number) of items in each of several non-overlapping classes.

Classes   The groups into which a set of data may be classified.

Class intervals   The range of values which define the width of each class (group).

Class frequencies   The number of observations contained in each class.

Relative frequencies   Each class frequency expressed as a percentage of the total number of observations.

Class limits   The upper and lower limits for the classes of a frequency distribution.

Line graph   Graphical presentation of data often used for showing movements in a variable over time.

Line chart   Graphical presentation for showing the information contained in a frequency distribution where the variable is discrete and the data are ungrouped.

Bar chart   Similar to a line chart but used when discrete data are grouped into classes with each class corresponding to a rectangle, the base of which is the class interval and the height of which is the class frequency.

Histogram   Similar to a bar chart and may be used in the cases of continuous or discrete grouped data but with no gaps left between the bars.

Frequency polygons   A graph formed by plotting class frequencies against the mid-points of the corresponding classes, connecting the points to form a graph and extending it to each end of the distribution to meet the horizontal axis at the mid-point at what would have been the next class below or above, respectively.

Cumulative frequency distribution   A tabular summary of a set of data that shows the total number of data items with values *either* less than or equal to the upper limit of the class *or* greater than or equal to the lower limit of each class.

Cumulative frequency curve (ogive)   A graph of the cumulative frequency distribution.

Pie chart   A pictorial device for presenting categorical data in which a circle is divided into wedges (like slices of a pie), each wedge corresponding to the relative frequency of each class.

Pictogram   A visual representation of categorical data in which pictures are used to summarize data, each picture being scaled in size or repeated a number of times to indicate relative magnitudes.

Logarithmic graph   A graphical presentation in which absolute values of a variable are plotted against a logarithmic scale or the logarithms of the variable (log values) are plotted on a conventional scale.

EXERCISES

1 The data below show the value of orders (£000s) obtained by 50 salesmen during a particular week.

6.0	5.9	3.5	2.9	8.7	7.9	7.1	5.0	5.2	3.9
3.7	6.1	5.8	4.1	5.8	6.4	3.8	4.9	5.7	5.5
6.9	4.0	4.8	5.1	4.3	5.4	6.8	5.9	6.9	5.4
2.4	4.9	7.2	4.2	6.2	5.8	3.8	6.2	5.7	6.8
3.4	5.0	5.2	5.3	3.0	3.6	3.8	5.8	4.9	3.7

(a) Arrange these data as a frequency distribution (about 7 classes will be sufficient).
(b) Present the frequency distribution as:
   (i) a histogram
   (ii) a frequency polygon.
(c) Draw a cumulative frequency curve and use it to answer the following questions:
   (i) How many salesmen achieved orders of £6000 or more?
   (ii) How many salesmen achieved orders of £4000 or less?
   (iii) How accurate are the answers to these, using the cumulative frequency curve, compared with the raw data presented above?

2 The data below show the distribution of the labour force in a company according to occupational categories for 1990 and 1995.

	1990 (%)	1995 (%)
Administrative	10	15
Professional and technical	12	12
Skilled manual	24	24
Unskilled manual	40	24
Clerical	14	25
Total (%)	100	100
(numbers)	(820)	(1200)

(a) Present the data using:
   (i) pie charts
   (ii) bar charts
   (iii) component bar charts.
(b) Comment on the change in size and structure of the labour force between 1990 and 1995.

3 The following information shows an analysis of the sources of a firm's imports of raw materials from overseas.

Source of imported raw materials (percentage breakdown)						
Source	1990	1991	1992	1993	1994	1995
EEC	33.7	37.0	41.9	41.3	44.3	44.5
Rest of Western Europe	14.4	14.0	15.2	14.6	14.7	17.0
North America	14.1	13.8	13.4	15.0	14.2	14.0
Rest of the World	37.8	35.2	29.5	29.1	26.8	24.5
Total (%)	100	100	100	100	100	100

(a) Draw a component line graph to show how the relative importance of the sources has changed.

(b) What other methods could be used to illustrate the changes shown by these data?

4 The following figures are index numbers showing the rise in raw material costs and labour costs for a firm between 1989 and 1995 (taking 1989 as equal to 100).

	Raw material costs	Labour costs
1989	100	100
1990	106	112
1991	108	122
1992	121	127
1993	182	133
1994	244	142
1995	310	146

Draw a graph to show *directly* the *relative* rates of growth of the two cost series over any particular period.

3

Summarizing data numerically

The essence of descriptive summary measures in business

In Chapter 2 we examined various ways of summarizing and presenting data using tabular and graphical methods. It is more helpful in many cases, however, to 'reduce' data to one or more summary numbers, particularly for purposes of comparison. Summary numbers of this sort are called *descriptive statistics*. A statistical set or group of data may be concisely summarized with reference to two particular descriptive statistics:

□ Measures of location or central tendency – commonly referred to as *averages*.
□ Measures of dispersion or variability.

These measures are undoubtedly the most commonly used statistics in the analysis of business data.

Measures of location

There are four measures of location in common use. These are:

□ Arithmetic mean.
□ Median.

□ Mode.
□ Geometric mean.

Arithmetic mean

This is the measure in most common use and is known to most people simply as the *average* or the *mean*. It is obtained, of course, simply by adding the value of all the items in a data set (denoted by $X_1, X_2, \ldots X_n$) and dividing by the number of items (denoted by n). The process for obtaining the arithmetic mean (denoted by $\bar{X}$) can be summarized using algebraic notation. The reason for doing so is that it provides a very convenient shorthand and precise means of expression. Thus:

$$\text{Arithmetic mean} = \bar{X}\text{('X-bar')} = \frac{\Sigma X_i}{n}$$

where 'Σ' (pronounced 'sigma') is a sign of summation and ΣX_i denotes the sum of all values of X (i.e. $X_1 + X_2 + \ldots + X_n$). This definition is appropriate only in the case of unit frequencies in which case X is referred to as a *simple arithmetic mean*.

Often, however, observations on particular X values may occur more than once or, indeed, we may need to attach differential weights to certain values (either to reflect relative frequencies or relative importance). In these situations the mean is referred to as a *weighted arithmetic mean* (*weighted average*). Thus, if f_i denotes the frequencies (or weights) attached to each X_i value, we have:

$$\text{Weighted arithmetic mean} = \bar{X} = \frac{\Sigma f_i X_i}{\Sigma f_i}$$

$$= \frac{f_1 X_1 + f_2 X_2 + \ldots + f_n X_n}{f_1 + f_2 + \ldots + f_n}$$

Example
Bitter Beer Brewery employs 468 workers, of which 56 are management staff, 130 are clerical administrative and technical staff, while the remaining 282 are manual workers. The average weekly wage for each group is £500, £300 and £200 respectively. The financial director wishes to compute the mean wage of the workforce in total.

Method 1: Simple arithmetic mean
This is found by simply taking the average of the three average weekly wage figures:

$$\bar{X} = \frac{\Sigma X_1}{n} = \frac{£500 + £300 + £200}{3}$$

$$= £333.33$$

It will be appreciated that this is not appropriate because it gives an equal weighting to each of the three weekly rates in the calculation.

Method 2: Weighted arithmetic mean
In this case, the weights correspond to the numbers of workers employed in each category. Hence:

$$\bar{X} = \frac{\Sigma f_i X_i}{\Sigma f_i} = \frac{(56 \times £500) + (130 \times £300) + (282 \times £200)}{468}$$

$$= \frac{£123,400}{468}$$

$$= £263.68$$

This example shows that the weighted arithmetic mean is the correct method of calculating the mean when items vary in their importance.

Median

The median of a set of data is, as its name may suggest, the value in the middle of the data set when the observations are arrayed in order from smallest to largest. Consider the following 9 observations:

8, 5, 4, 9, 5, 11, 6, 5, 8

Rearranging these in ascending order gives:

4, 5, 5, 5, 6, 8, 8, 9, 11
           ↑
        Median

The median is 6 because it has an equal number of observations above and below it. In the case of an even number of observations, there is no clearly defined middle observation. The median is then taken as the mean of the *two* central observations.

The use of the median as a measure of central tendency is appropriate when the data set contains *outliers* or extreme values which would produce a mean value that is atypical and could be misleading. For example, say five payments are made as follows:

£9, £10, £10, £11, £60

Then the mean payment is £100/5 = £20. Clearly, this is not a good representative value. However, the median value (£10) would be a good representative value.

Mode

The mode of a set of data is simply the value that occurs the most often. Consider the earlier data:

   8, 5, 4, 9, 5, 11, 6, 5, 8

The mode is 5 because it occurs three times whereas other values occur only once or twice.

A good example of a situation in which the mode is the appropriate average of interest is in the clothing trade where manufacturers, wholesalers and retailers are more interested in the most common sizes rather than mean sizes in order to take decisions about production, stocks, etc.

Note that for some data sets there may be no mode, whereas for others there may be more than one mode (i.e. where more than one data value occurs the same and the largest number of times). In addition, if a mode does exist, it may not necessarily lie near the centre of the data set – it can equally lie at or near the extremes. If a mode clearly exists for a data set, the distribution of values is described as being *unimodal*. A distribution is described as being *bimodal* when two non-adjoining values have relative high frequencies (even though the frequencies are not necessarily equal). These cases are illustrated in Figure 3.1 below. Distributions with several modes (or relative high frequencies) are called *multimodal*.

Relationship between the mean, median and mode

Figure 3.2 illustrates the relationship between the three measures of location discussed so far. It will be seen that the three measures coincide if the distribution of values of the variable in question is perfectly symmetrical. If the distribution is negatively skewed or positively skewed then the mean and the median are pulled to the left or to the right respectively, i.e. in the

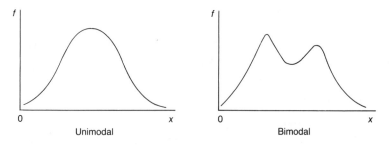

Figure 3.1 Unimodal and bimodal distributions.

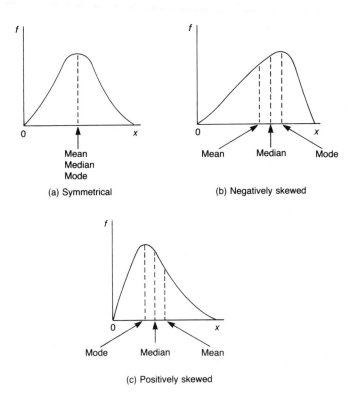

Figure 3.2 Relationships between mean, median and mode in symmetrical and skewed distributions.

direction of the skewness. For a negatively skewed distribution the mean has a lower value than the median or the mode, and the mode has the highest value – the median falls in between. For a positively skewed distribution the position is reversed – the mean will have the greatest value and the mode the smallest value with, again, the median in between.

Mean, median and mode for grouped data

So far in this chapter we have dealt only with raw or ungrouped data. As we saw in Chapter 2, a large set of data may be presented in grouped (or class) form as a frequency distribution. Commonly, this is the only form of data available to the user. For grouped data, the mean, median and mode are calculated as follows.

Mean for grouped data

If n data values have been grouped into classes, and the mid-points of the class intervals are denoted by X_i and the frequencies for each class are denoted by f_i, then

$$\bar{X} = \frac{\Sigma f_i X_i}{n}$$

Median for grouped data

The median for grouped data must be found by interpolation. It is first necessary to identify the class in which the median value falls and then to interpolate within this class as follows:

$$Md = L + \frac{f_c}{f_m} W$$

where L is the lower limit of the median class, f_m is the frequency of the median class, W is the width of the median class and f_c is the number of observations that must be covered in the median class in order to reach the middle of the distribution. Note that the mid-point of the distribution is located by $n/2$ and *not* by $(n + 1)/2$. The latter is not appropriate here because, once the data have been grouped, it is no longer possible to identify a discrete observation (or pair of observations) at the centre of the distribution.

Mode for grouped data

For grouped data with equal class intervals, the modal class is the class with the largest frequency. The mode is then defined as follows:

$$Mo = L + \frac{\Delta_1}{\Delta_1 + \Delta_2} W$$

where L is the lower limit of the modal class, Δ_1 is the difference between the frequency of the modal class and the frequency of the previous class, Δ_2 is the difference between the frequency of the modal class and the frequency of the next class and W is the width of the modal class. The rationale of this formula is illustrated in Figure 3.3.

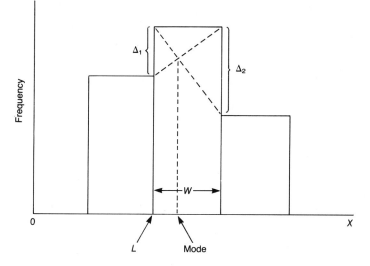

Figure 3.3 Mode for grouped data.

Example

The table below shows a frequency distribution for grouped data. Calculate the mean, median and mode.

Frequency distribution			Worksheet		
Classes	Class frequencies (f_i)		Class mid-points (x_i)	$f_i x_i$	Cumulative frequency
0– <5	2		2.5	5	2
5– <15	6		10.0	60	8
15– <25	20		20.0	400	28
25– <35	15		30.0	450	43
35– <45	8		40.0	320	51
45– <100	4		72.5	290	55
Total	$n = 55$			1525	

Solution

Mean: $\bar{X} = \dfrac{\Sigma f_i X_i}{n} = \dfrac{1525}{55} = 27.7273$

Median: $Md = L + \dfrac{f_c}{f_m} W$

The median class is the class which contains the middle value $n/2 = 55/2 = 27.5$th. From the worksheet above, this is in the class '15 and under 25'. Thus:

$$Md = 15 + \left(\frac{27.5 - 8}{20}\right)10 = 15 + \left(\frac{19.5}{20}\right)10 = 24.75$$

(Recall that since we are dealing with grouped data now we cannot identify the actual median – the $[(n+1)/2]$th value – and so the median, obtained by interpolation, must be taken at the exact centre of the distribution of values, defined as the $(n/2)$th position. Note than $f_c = 27.5 - 8 = 19.5$, where 8 is the sum of the class frequencies below the median class.)

Mode: The modal class is the class with the greatest frequency. This is the '15 and under 25' class. Hence:

$$Mo = L + \left(\frac{\Delta_1}{\Delta_1 + \Delta_2}\right)W$$

$$= 15 + \left\{\frac{(20 - 6)}{(20 - 6) + (20 - 15)}\right\}10$$

$$= 15 + \left(\frac{14}{14 + 5}\right)10$$

$$= 22.37$$

Geometric mean

The geometric mean may be used when it is desired to produce an average of percentage changes. This is particularly relevant in business situations where the manager may be interested in measuring the rate of increase in sales, costs, prices, etc. The geometric mean is simply the nth root of the product of n items. Thus:

Geometric mean $= g = \sqrt[n]{X_1 \times X_2 \times X_3 \times \ldots \times X_n}$

Example
The costs of raw materials used by a firm have increased over the period as follows:

	1992	1993	1994	1995
Costs (£)	200	228	239.4	244.2
Annual change (%)	–	14	5	2

What is the average annual percentage rate of increase of costs?

Solution
The simple arithmetic mean of the figures above is 7 per cent. It can be shown easily that this is not the true average annual percentage increase and that the true answer is 6.88 per cent. This is derived by taking the geometric mean of the price level in each year as a percentage of the preceding year's figure, i.e. taking 1992 as a base of 100 then the cost level in 1993 is 114 per cent of this, in 1994 it is 105 per cent (relative to 1993) and in 1995 it is 102 per cent (relative to 1994). Thus:

$$g = \sqrt[3]{114 \times 105 \times 102} = \sqrt[3]{1,220,940}$$

$$= 106.88$$

This shows that the level of costs of raw materials rose, on average, by 6.88 per cent each year – not by the 7 per cent given by the arithmetic mean.

It will be appreciated that the calculation of the geometric mean, involving as it does the extraction of the nth root, can be carried out easily on pocket calculators with an exponent key facility. Alternatively, the use of statistical computer packages makes life even easier. Details of three popular packages are given in Appendix B.

Compound formula
An alternative method to the geometric mean for calculating average rates of change is to use the *compound formula* which may be better known as the formula for calculating compound interest, expressed as follows:

$$A(1 + r)^n = F$$

where A denotes original amount
**   r denotes rate of increase**
**   n denotes number of periods**
**   F denotes final amount.**

In the example above, we have:

$A = 200$ (i.e. the level of raw material costs in 1992 – the base year)
$n = 3$
$F = 244.2$ (this represents the final price level in 1995 for raw materials)

Thus, we have:

$$200(1 + r)^3 = 244.2$$

Rearranging to isolate r (the average annual compound growth rate),

$$(1 + r)^3 = \frac{244.2}{200}$$

$$1 + r = \sqrt[3]{\frac{244.2}{200}} = 1.0688$$

$$r = 1.0688 - 1$$

$$= 0.0688$$

This is equivalent to 6.88 per cent, as before.

It will be noted that use of the compound formula in order to calculate the average rate of increase (r) requires that the final amount (F) be known. In situations where we have a set of percentage increases – as in the original example above – then it is easier to use the geometric mean to calculate the average annual rate. Naturally, in cases where we know only the original and final amounts, then the average rate can *only* be calculated using the compound formula. Both these methods of calculation, therefore, are useful, depending on the problem in hand.

It will also be appreciated, of course, that the compound formula may be used to calculate any one of the elements in the formula (A, r, n or F), provided that the other three elements are known.

Measures of dispersion

The summary measures discussed above provide extremely useful ways of summarizing a set of data. However, they focus on one feature of a set of data – its location on the scale of possible values – and neglect another very important feature, namely how scattered or dispersed the data values are. It is possible for several data sets to have identical averages but for the data values in each case to differ considerably. Figure 3.4 illustrates this point using (a) line graphs and (b) histograms. Measures of dispersion, therefore, aim to provide a summary measure of this feature. As with averages, there is more than one way of summarizing dispersion. We consider the main measures in turn as follows:

☐ Range.
☐ Modified ranges – interquartile, semi-interquartile, interdecile and interpercentile ranges.

☐ Mean deviation.

☐ Standard deviation.

☐ Variance.

☐ Coefficient of variation.

Of these the most important measures are the standard deviation and variance.

To illustrate all of these dispersion measures we employ a common set of data relating to the number of employees absent from a firm each day owing to illness over a 10-day period. Company records provide the following information:

Day	1	2	3	4	5	6	7	8	9	10
Number of absentees	4	6	2	8	10	3	6	4	7	10

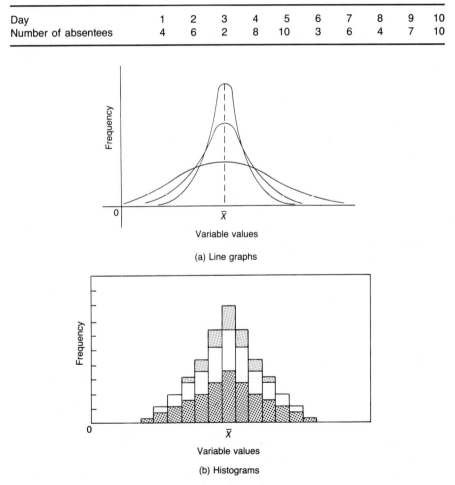

(a) Line graphs

(b) Histograms

Figure 3.4 Dispersion about the same mean.

Range

The simplest measure of dispersion is the *range*. This is simply the difference between the highest and lowest values in the data set. Thus, for absenteeism:

Range $= 10 - 2 = 8$

Clearly the range is easy to calculate (once the data have been arrayed in order), but the amount of information provided by this measure is limited because it focuses only on the two extreme values and ignores all the other observations in between. It is therefore greatly affected by outliers and two very different sets of data may give identical ranges but otherwise differ very considerably. For example, data sets ranging from 0 to 10 and 100 to 110 both have a range of 10. In practice, therefore, it is often useful to quote the upper and lower limits of the range rather than merely the difference. Reports on the stock market, for example, regularly quote ranges by giving the high and low prices of the day, the week, etc. Owing to its limitations, the range is not widely used as a measure of dispersion.

Modified ranges

Because the range is dependent on the two extreme values in a data set, a useful alternative is to quote a modified range covering a central proportion of the observations only, i.e. excluding a certain proportion of the observations at both extremes of the data set. There are a number of possibilities but the most common are those based on *quartiles, deciles* or *percentiles*. As their names suggest, quartiles divide the distribution of a data set into four quarters, deciles divide it into 10 parts and percentiles divide it into 100 parts.

Interquartile and semi-interquartile ranges

The *interquartile range* is the interval which covers the central 50 per cent of the observations. It is simply the difference between the *lower quartile* (i.e. the value below which the lowest 25 per cent of the observations lie) and the *upper quartile* (i.e. the value above which the highest 25 per cent of the values lie). The lower and upper quartiles are the first and third quartiles, denoted Q_1 and Q_3 respectively. The second quartile divides the distribution into equal halves and is, of course, the same as the median considered earlier in this chapter.

Similarly, the *semi-interquartile range* (or *quartile deviation*) is simply defined as the interquartile range divided by 2. Thus:

Semi-interquartile range $= \dfrac{Q_3 - Q_1}{2}$

To compute the interquartile and semi-interquartile ranges for the number of absentees, we first calculate Q_1 and Q_3 by interpolation, having arranged the data in ascending order, as follows:

Q_1 position $= (10 + 1)/4 = 2.75$th	Q_3 position $= 3\,(10 + 1)/4 = 8.25$th
i.e. between 3 and 4	i.e. between 8 and 10
Thus:	Thus:
$Q_1 = 3 + 0.75\,(4 - 3)$	$Q_3 = 8 + 0.25\,(10 - 8)$
$\quad = 3.75$	$\quad = 8.5$

$$2 \quad 3 \quad 4 \quad 4 \quad 6 \quad 6 \quad 7 \quad 8 \quad 10 \quad 10$$

	$\uparrow$	$\uparrow$	$\uparrow$
Quartiles:	Q_1	Median	Q_3
	$= 3.75$		$= 8.5$

Interquartile range: $\qquad Q_3 - Q_1 = 8.5 - 3.75 = 4.75$

Semi-interquartile range: $\qquad \dfrac{Q_3 - Q_1}{2} = \dfrac{4.75}{2} = 2.375$

The interquartile range and the semi-interquartile range would be used in conjunction with the median for describing a set of data. Thus in describing the data above, one would say that the median was 6 with an interquartile range of 4.75 or that the median was 6 with a semi-interquartile range (or quartile deviation) of 2.375.

Deciles and percentiles

Deciles and percentiles may be used in exactly the same way as quartiles, either as single indicators of position (i.e. values above or below which a stated proportion of the observations lie) or as a means of defining a range within which a stated proportion of observations lie. The upper and lower quartiles are of course the same as the 75th and 25th percentiles respectively and the upper and lower deciles are the same as the 90th and 10th percentiles respectively. Calculation of the deciles and percentiles follows the same principles as for quartiles, merely involving the substitution of the appropriate fractions for determining the position of the measure required. Percentiles, deciles and quartiles are collectively known as *quantiles*.

A disadvantage of all these modified ranges is that they concentrate on only two values of the variable in question and hence give no information about the degree of dispersion of the other values in the distribution. For this reason, a measure of dispersion that incorporates all of the items in a data set is generally preferred. For this, we must turn to other measures of dispersion generally referred to as *deviation measures*.

Deviation measures

Deviation measures focus on the extent to which each individual value in a data set deviates from the mean of the set. These measures are the *mean deviation*, the *standard deviation* and the *variance*.

Mean deviation

Consider the data on the number of absentees above. The average (mean) number $(\bar{X})$ is 6. As a measure of dispersion about this mean, consider the deviation of each value of X (the variable 'number of absentees') from its mean (i.e. $X_i - \bar{X}$) and the *absolute* value of each deviation, denoted $|X_i - \bar{X}|$ (where the two vertical lines indicate *absolute* value, i.e. the value ignoring negative signs). The calculations are shown in Table 3.1.

It may be thought that a possible measure of dispersion would be to average the sum of all the deviations from the mean:

$$\frac{\Sigma(X_i - \bar{X})}{n}$$

In this example, this would give: $0/10 = 0$. In fact, for *any* set of data, the value would always be 0 because, by virtue of the definition of the mean, there will always be positive and negative deviations and these will necessarily balance out. One solution to this problem is to ignore the positive and negative signs and to take the average of the *absolute* values of the deviations. This is the *mean deviation*. So we have:

Mean deviation $= \dfrac{\Sigma|X_i - \bar{X}|}{n}$

For the example above, we have:

Mean deviation of the number of absentees $= 22/10 = 2.2$

The information about absenteeism can therefore be described succinctly as having a mean of 6 absentees with a mean deviation of 2.2.

Table 3.1 Deviation measures for absenteeism

Number of absentees X_i	Deviation from mean $X_i - \bar{X}$	Absolute deviation from mean $\lvert X_i - \bar{X} \rvert$
4	−2	2
6	0	0
2	−4	4
8	2	2
10	4	4
3	−3	3
6	0	0
4	−2	2
7	1	1
10	4	4
$\bar{X} = 6$	$\Sigma(X_i - \bar{X}) = 0$	$\Sigma\lvert X_i - \bar{X}\rvert = 22$

However, the mean deviation is not widely used. Instead the alternative deviation measures – the standard deviation and the variance – are much more highly favoured, the reason being that they have mathematical properties which are very useful in further statistical applications.

Standard deviation and variance

The mean deviation overcomes the problem that the sum of deviations from the mean, $\Sigma(X_i - \bar{X})$, necessarily equals 0 by taking the absolute values only of these deviations. The standard deviation and variance deal with the problem by *squaring* the deviations, thereby removing all the negative signs. So, using the same data as before, the squared deviations are shown in Table 3.2. It will be seen that the sum of the squared deviations, $\Sigma(X_i - \bar{X})^2 = 70$. The average of these squared deviations $(70/10 = 7)$ gives a measure of dispersion called the *variance*.

Distinction between variance of a sample and of a population

At this point it is important to make a distinction between data representing an entire population and data representing a sample from this population. We will see later that sample data are frequently used to make inferences or estimates about the population. In this particular case, a sample variance is used as an *estimator* of a population variance and it can be shown that a better estimator is obtained by dividing the sum of the squared deviations by $n - 1$ rather than n. We make a distinction, therefore, between the *sample variance*, denoted by s^2, and the *population variance*, denoted by σ^2 (the lower case Greek sigma, read as 'sigma squared'). So in general we have:

Table 3.2　Squared deviations for absenteeism

Number of absentees X_i	Deviations $X_i - \bar{X}$	Squared deviations $(X_i - \bar{X})^2$
4	−2	4
6	0	0
2	−4	16
8	2	4
10	4	16
3	−3	9
6	0	0
4	−2	4
7	1	1
10	4	16
$\bar{X} = 6$	$\Sigma(X_i - \bar{X}) = 0$	$\Sigma(X_i - \bar{X})^2 = 70$

Sample variance:

$$s^2 = \frac{(X_1 - \bar{X})^2 + (X_2 - \bar{X})^2 + \ldots + (X_n - \bar{X})^2}{n - 1}$$

$$= \frac{\Sigma(X_i - \bar{X})^2}{n - 1}$$

where $\bar{X}$ is the mean of the sample, and
n is the size of the sample.

In defining the population variance we now need to make a distinction also between sample and populatin means. The symbol $\bar{X}$ used until now to denote the mean is conventionally used to denote a *sample mean* and the symbol μ (read as 'mu'), which is the Greek letter 'm', is conventionally used to denote a *population mean*. So in general we have:

Population variance:

$$\sigma^2 = \frac{(X_1 - \mu)^2 + (X_2 - \mu)^2 + \ldots + (X_n - \mu)^2}{N}$$

$$= \frac{\Sigma(X_i - \mu)^2}{N}$$

where μ is the mean of the population, and
N is the size of the population.

Thus, for our example above, representing a *sample* of observations on absenteeism, we have:

$$\text{Sample variance} = s^2 = \frac{\Sigma(X_i - \bar{X})^2}{n-1}$$

$$= \frac{70}{10-1}$$

$$= 7.8 \text{ (approximately)}$$

It will be appreciated that a variance of 7.8 is somewhat difficult to interpret in the sense that the units of measurement (number of absentees) are squared! Consequently, the square root of the variance is generally preferred, and this is known as the *standard deviation*, expressed for samples and populations as follows:

Sample standard deviation: $s = \sqrt{\dfrac{\Sigma(X_i - \bar{X})^2}{n-1}}$

Population standard deviation: $\sigma = \sqrt{\dfrac{\Sigma(X_i - \mu)^2}{N}}$

Thus, in the example above, the standard deviation of the number of absentees is:

$$s = \sqrt{7.8} = 2.8 \text{ (approximately)}.$$

It is worth noting, perhaps, that computer software and many electronic calculators include pre-programmed functions to calculate the standard deviation and variance automatically with divisors of both N and $n-1$ as required. In the absence of computer facilities, the above formulae are laborious to use when the data sets are large and the values themselves are large numbers. Fortunately, it is possible to simplify the formulae into equivalent expressions which are quicker and easier to use. These are set out below.

Short methods of calculating the variance and standard deviation

Sample variance – computation formula:

$$s^2 = \frac{\Sigma(X_i^2) - (\Sigma X_i)^2/n}{n-1}$$

Population variance – computation formula:

$$\sigma^2 = \frac{\Sigma(X_i^2) - (\Sigma X_i)^2/N}{N}$$

The corresponding standard deviation formulae are, naturally, simply the square root of each of these expressions as before.

These formulae are much quicker to use because they eliminate the need to calculate deviations, requiring only the computation of X_i^2 and the summation of X_i^2 and X_i.

Example (based on the sample data for absenteeism above)
The figures on the following page give the raw data (X_i) and the corresponding values of X_i^2.

Number of absentees	
(X_i)	(X_i^2)
4	16
6	36
2	4
8	64
10	100
3	9
6	36
4	16
7	49
10	100
$\Sigma X_i = 60$	$\Sigma(X_i^2) = 430$

Sample variance, $s^2 = \dfrac{\Sigma X_i^2 - (\Sigma X_i)^2/n}{n-1}$

$$= \frac{430 - (60)^2/10}{10-1}$$

$= 7.8$ approximately (as before)

Sample standard deviation, $s = \sqrt{7.8} = 2.8$ approximately (as before).

Coefficient of variation: a measure of relative dispersion

In certain circumstances a measure of *relative* dispersion is more appropriate than the absolute measures given by the standard deviation or variance. That is, we may wish to compare variation in two separate data sets where the units of measurement may not be the same or, even if the units of measurement are the same, may vary so much in magnitude that comparison of absolute dispersion measures is misleading. For example, a standard deviation of 5 mm would be considered very large for a batch of pistons used in car engine production whereas the same standard deviation would be considered negligible in the case of large-scale construction works.

To obtain a relative measure of dispersion for comparative purposes we need to consider how big the dispersion of each data set is relative to its mean. The usual solution is to express the standard deviation as a percentage of the mean. This measure is the *coefficient of variation*. In general:

Coefficient of variation $= (s/\bar{X})\,100$

For example, in the case of the absenteeism data above, the coefficient of variation is equal to $(2.8/6)100 = 46.7$ per cent. This indicates that the standard deviation is very large – almost half the value of the mean. This variability could be compared with data, say, on production over the same 10-day period. Suppose that the company records indicate the following:

Day	1	2	3	4	5	6	7	8	9	10
Production (Y_i tonnes)	10	15	25	15	10	25	15	20	15	10

Following the procedures described earlier, we can derive the values for the mean ($\bar{Y}$) and standard deviation (s_Y) of production. These are:

$$\bar{Y} = 16; \; s_Y = 5.68$$

Thus, the coefficient of variation is $5.68/16 = 35.5$ per cent. It will be noted that 35.5 per cent is much less than 46.7 per cent, so we can conclude that the variability in production is much less than that in absenteeism.

Use of MINITAB

The use of the statistical package MINITAB to compute summary measures is illustrated in Computer illustration 3.1 using one of the examples used earlier in this chapter. It will be seen that while specific measures may be obtained using specific commands, it is also possible to obtain a whole range of measures using a single command (DESCRIBE).

Computer illustration 3.1   MINITAB and summary measures
(using the data on absentees on page 39)

```
MTB > NAME C1 'Absentee'
MTB > SET C1
DATA> 4 6 2 8 10 3 6 4 7 10
DATA> END

MTB > MEAN C1
    MEAN     =      6.0000

MTB > MEDIan C1
    MEDIAN   =      6.0000

MTB > STDEv C1
    ST.DEV.  =      2.7889

MTB > MINImum C1
    MINIMUM  =      2.0000
                                Allows calculation of the RANGE.
MTB > MAXImum C1
    MAXIMUM  =      10.000

MTB > DESCribe C1          (Provides a range of descriptive measures.)

                N       MEAN   MEDIAN   TRMEAN   STDEV   SEMEAN
Absentee       10       6.000   6.000    6.000   2.789   0.882

              MIN        MAX      Q1       Q3
Absentee    2.000     10.000    3.750    8.500
```

Lower quartile

Upper quartile

Trimmed mean – i.e. with smallest 5% and largest 5% of values removed

Sample standard deviation

Standard error of the mean – see Chapter 7

Key learning points

Arithmetic mean   A measure of the central location of a data set. It is computed by summing all the values in the data set and dividing by the number of items.

$$\overline{X} = \frac{\Sigma X_i}{n}$$

Weighted arithmetic mean   A measure of the central location of a data set used when observations on particular values may occur more than once or when we need to reflect relative frequencies or the relative importance of certain values.

$$\overline{X} = \frac{\Sigma f_i X_i}{\Sigma f_i}$$

Median A measure of central location of a data set. It is the value which splits the data set into two equal groups – one with values greater than or equal to the median, and one with values less than or equal to the median.

Mode A measure of central location of a data set, defined as the most frequently occurring data value.

Geometric mean A measure of central location of a data set used when it is desired to produce an average of rates of change.

$$g = \sqrt[n]{X_1 \times X_2 \times X_3 \times \ldots \times X_n}$$

Compound formula A formula for calculating compound rates of change or the outcome of compound rates of change.

$$A(1 + r)^n = F$$

Range A measure of dispersion for a data set, defined to be the difference between the highest and lowest values.

Quartiles, deciles and percentiles Measures which divide a data set into 4, 10 and 100 parts respectively, each part containing the same number of observations.

Interquartile range A measure of dispersion which covers the central 50 per cent of the observations in a data set – i.e. the difference between the lower quartile (the value below which the lowest 25 per cent of the observations lie), denoted Q_1, and the upper quartile (the value above which the highest 25 per cent of the observations lie), denoted Q_3.

Semi-interquartile range (or quartile deviation) Simply defined as the interquartile range divided by 2.

Mean deviation A measure of dispersion of a data set expressed as the average of the absolute differences between each observation (X_i) and the arithmetic mean of all observations ($\bar{X}$).

$$\frac{\Sigma |X_i - \bar{X}|}{n}$$

Variance A measure of dispersion for a data set, found by summing the squared deviations of the data values about the mean and then dividing the total by N if the data set is a population or by $n - 1$ if the data set is for a sample.

Population variance: $\sigma^2 = \dfrac{\Sigma(X_i - \mu)^2}{N}$

Sample variance: $s^2 = \dfrac{\Sigma(X_i - \bar{X})^2}{n - 1}$

Standard deviation A measure of dispersion for a data set, found by taking the positive square root of the population or sample variance.

Population standard deviation

$$\sigma = \sqrt{\frac{\Sigma(X_i - \mu)^2}{N}} = \sqrt{\frac{\Sigma(X_i)^2 - \Sigma(X_i)^2/N}{N}}$$

Sample standard deviation

$$s = \sqrt{\frac{\Sigma(X_i - \bar{X})^2}{n - 1}} = \sqrt{\frac{\Sigma(X_i^2) - \Sigma(X_i)^2/n}{n - 1}}$$

Coefficient of variation A measure of relative dispersion for a data set, found by dividing the standard deviation by the mean and multiplying by 100 to express the coefficient as a percentage, i.e. $(s/\bar{X})\,100$.

EXERCISES

1 The weights of 15 loads to a firm's delivery bay, measured in kilograms, are recorded as follows:

64	59	72	69	55
72	60	48	75	72
81	54	61	58	90

Calculate, for these weights:
(a) the arithmetic mean
(b) the median
(c) the mode
(d) the range
(e) the upper and lower quartiles
(f) the interquartile range
(g) the semi-interquartile range (quartile deviation)
(h) the mean deviation
(i) the variance
(j) the standard deviation.

Comment on the best measures to use to describe the data set.

2 The distribution of the value of orders received by a mail order firm during a week is shown below.

Value of order (£)	Number of orders
10 and less than 20	4
20 and less than 30	16
30 and less than 50	27
50 and less than 70	24
70 and less than 100	19
100 and less than 150	15
Total number	105

(a) Calculate for these values:
  (i) the mean (taking the mid-point of each class as the representative value for each class)
  (ii) the median
  (iii) the mode
  (iv) the standard deviation (again, taking class mid-points as representative values for each class, as above)
  (v) the lower and upper quartiles
  (vi) the quartile deviation.
(b) Draw a cumulative frequency curve and use it to estimate the upper and lower quartiles and compare these estimates with those in (a).

3 A firm's labour costs as a percentage of annual turnover for the last five years are shown below, together with the value of turnover.

	Turnover (£m)	Labour costs (as percentage of turnover)
1991	2.2	35
1992	1.8	30
1993	2.1	31
1994	2.5	30
1995	3.4	28

What is the average percentage labour cost?

4 The distribution of average weekly rents for housing association dwellings of different sizes in a town is given below.

	Number	Average rent (£)
1-bedroom dwelling	560	14.50
2-bedroom dwelling	840	15.64
3-bedroom dwelling	1700	17.11
4-bedroom dwelling	84	17.82
Total number	3184	

What is the average weekly rent for all dwellings?

5 Industrial production grows in four successive years as follows:

   1.3%   2.8%   4.1%   2.9%

What is the average annual percentage rate of increase?

6 A finance company charges a rate of interest of 2.5 per cent per month. What is the annual percentage rate (APR)?

7 If a firm expects its sales volume to grow by 5 per cent per year, how long will it take for sales volume to double?

8 In order to assist car manufacturers, a survey of car owners reveals the following information about the heights and weights of male and female drivers.

	Weight (kilos)		Height (cm)	
	Average	Standard deviation	Average	Standard deviation
Male	80	10	175	20
Female	60	12	160	12

(a) Do the heights of male drivers vary more than the heights of female drivers?
(b) Do female drivers vary more in weight than in height?

9 The number of households and the number of persons in each household recorded as part of a large consumer survey conducted by a firm are shown below.

Number of persons in household	Number of households (000s)
1	3.3
2	5.8
3	3.4
4	3.1
5	1.5
6	0.7
7 or more*	0.5
Total	18.3

*For the purpose of calculation, assume that this group is equivalent to 8 persons per household, on average.

(a) Calculate the average household size in this survey.
(b) What is the variance of household size?

4

Index numbers

The essence of index numbers in business

An index number is a statistical measure which is designed to express changes or differences in a variable or, more importantly, a *group* of related variables. Index numbers are widely used in reporting economic data and in business for monitoring trends, measuring performance, etc. Most index numbers measure changes over time, such as the change in prices or the change in quantity produced between one period and another. An index is normally expressed in percentage terms. Thus a price index of 110 indicates that prices have risen by 10 per cent over some base period (taken as 100). Index numbers may also be used to measure differences in a variable or group of variables between different industries, occupations, etc. For the purpose of exposition here, however, we confine most of our attention to the construction of index numbers measuring changes over time.

Perhaps the most well-known example of a *price* index in the United Kingdom is the Retail Prices Index (RPI) which measures inflation. It is generally a prominent news item every month, especially when prices are rising fairly quickly. What the index does is to express in a single summary measure exactly how much prices in general have changed for a broad range of goods and services over some period of time. This is frequently a crucial element in wage bargaining. Another well-known index in the United Kingdom is the index of output of the production industries, which measures the change in the output of the broad range of manufacturing and other industries. This index, in contrast to the RPI, is a *quantity* index and is an important measure of economic growth.

The principles involved in constructing price and quantity indexes are similar. We consider each in turn.

Price index numbers

Consider the data given in Table 4.1 showing the prices paid in 1993 and 1995 by a bakery, and the quantities consumed of its four major 'raw material' inputs in these years.

Table 4.1 Raw material inputs for a bakery: unit prices and quantities

Inputs	Unit	Unit prices (£)		Quantities used	
		1993 (P_{i0})	1995 (P_{it})	1993 (Q_{i0})	1995 (Q_{it})
Flour	Kilo	0.75	0.90	500	700
Eggs	Dozen	1.60	2.00	100	130
Milk	Litre	0.40	0.60	160	200
Sugar	Kilo	1.00	1.40	50	70

It will be seen that each of the individual inputs has increased in price over the period 1993–95 by different percentages. The actual increases in unit prices (P_i) are derived by calculating a *price relative* for each item, i.e. by expressing price in the later period (P_{it}) as a ratio of price in the base period (P_{i0}). Thus price relatives for the four items over the period 1993–95 are as follows:

Inputs	Price relatives, P_{it}/P_{i0} 1995/1993	Price changes for each item 1993–95
Flour	0.90/0.75 = 1.20	+20%
Eggs	2.00/1.60 = 1.25	+25%
Milk	0.60/0.40 = 1.50	+50%
Sugar	1.40/1.00 = 1.40	+40%

By definition, the price relative for an input is computed as the ratio between its prices at two different time periods.

One key issue confronting the manager in monitoring the performance of this bakery and in taking decisions about cost control and pricing policy is the determination of a summary measure of the increase in input costs as a whole. It should be appreciated that it would be inappropriate in this example simply to take an average of the four unit prices for each year and then to take a ratio of these averages. This is because the totals of prices are dependent on the units of measurement used for the inputs (e.g. kilos or tonnes of flour). Alternatively, we could compute the average of the price relatives for each input (as above) since this would not be affected by the units of measurement. However, a potential problem that remains is the fact that equal importance has been attached to price changes for each input.

In other words, a 10 per cent increase in the price of flour is assumed to be of the same importance as a 10 per cent increase in the price of eggs, even though the amounts of flour and eggs used are different. So the simple averaging of price relatives is only satisfactory as a general measure of the change in prices for this group of four commodities if the quantities purchased of each item are the same. This will not normally be so, and it is important, therefore, to allow for the quantities purchased of each item and to construct a *weighted* average of price changes – either a weighted aggregate or a weighted average of price relatives. Both of these are considered below.

Weighted aggregate price index

This is defined as:

$$\frac{\Sigma P_{it} Q_i}{\Sigma P_{i0} Q_i} \times 100$$

where P_{it} = unit price for item i in period t
P_{i0} = unit price for item i in the base period 0
Q_i = quantity purchased of each item
and the summation (Σ) is carried out over all items to be included in the price index.

A choice now arises in arriving at an overall index I_t:

□ *Either* to use quantities for the *base* year (1993), Q_0 – this produces an index known as a *Laspeyres index,*

□ *Or* to use quantities for the *current* year (1995), Q_t – this produces an index known as a *Paasche index*.

Thus we have the following formulae for each type:

Laspeyres weighted aggregate price index:

$$I_t = \frac{\Sigma P_{it} Q_{i0}}{\Sigma P_{i0} Q_{i0}} \times 100$$

Paasche weighted aggregate price index:

$$I_t = \frac{\Sigma P_{it} Q_{it}}{\Sigma P_{i0} Q_{it}} \times 100$$

where Q_{i0} and Q_{it} represent the quantities of each input i bought in the base period (0) and current period (t) respectively.

Table 4.2 Calculation of aggregate price indexes for a bakery (data from Table 4.1)

Input	Base-weighted price aggregates		Current-weighted price aggregates	
	$P_{it}Q_{io}$	$P_{io}Q_{io}$	$P_{it}Q_{it}$	$P_{io}Q_{it}$
Flour	450	375	630	525
Eggs	200	160	260	208
Milk	96	64	120	80
Sugar	70	50	98	70
Summations (Σ)	816	649	1108	883

Price indexes

Base-weighted price index (Laspeyres-type index):

$$\frac{\Sigma P_{it}Q_{io}}{\Sigma P_{io}Q_{io}} \times 100 = \frac{816}{649} \times 100 \approx 125.7$$

Current-weighted price index (Paasche-type index):

$$\frac{\Sigma P_{it}Q_{it}}{\Sigma P_{io}Q_{it}} \times 100 = \frac{1108}{883} \times 100 \approx 125.5$$

Applying these formulae to the bakery data given in Table 4.1 produces index numbers for 1995 with 1993 taken as the base year (i.e. 1993 = 100) as shown in Table 4.2. Thus, the base-weighted (Laspeyres) index shows a rise in the cost of inputs in total of 25.7 per cent between 1993 and 1995, while the current-weighted (Paasche) index comes out at 25.5 per cent.

The fact that the Laspeyres and Paasche methods will generally give different answers may appear unsatisfactory. It should be appreciated, however, that by definition they are measuring somewhat different things: the Laspeyres index measures a change in the cost of buying the same 'basket' of inputs as that purchased in the base year (1993 here) whereas the Paasche index measures the change in cost if the basket of inputs bought in the base year, 1993, had been the same as that bought in the later year, 1995. An appreciation of these differences of principle is therefore important for an understanding of the information that index numbers provide.

Weighted average of price relatives

An alternative method of calculation is to compute weighted averages of price relatives, rather than weighted aggregates of prices as above, using again either base or current weights to produce Laspeyres- or Paasche-type

Table 4.3 Calculation of weighted price relative indexes for a bakery

Input	Price relative (P_{it}/P_{i0}) (a)	Expenditure weights		Weighted relatives	
		1993 $(P_{i0}Q_{i0})$ (b)	1995 $(P_{it}Q_{it})$ (c)	1993 (a) × (b)	1995 (a) × (c)
Flour	1.20	375	630	450.0	756.0
Eggs	1.25	160	260	200.0	325.0
Milk	1.50	64	120	96.0	180.0
Sugar	1.40	50	98	70.0	137.2
Summations (Σ)		649	1108	816.0	1398.2

Price indexes

Base-weighted average of price relatives (Laspeyres-type index):

$$\frac{\Sigma(P_{it}/P_{i0})P_{i0}Q_{i0}}{\Sigma P_{i0}Q_{i0}} \times 100 = \frac{816}{649} \times 100 \approx 125.7$$

Current-weighted average of price relatives (Paasche-type index):

$$\frac{\Sigma(P_{it}/P_{i0})P_{it}Q_{it}}{\Sigma P_{it}Q_{it}} \times 100 = \frac{1398.2}{1108} \times 100 \approx 126.2$$

---

index numbers. Denoting the weights for *each* commodity as W_i, we have:

$$l_t = \frac{\Sigma(P_{it}/P_{i0})\,W_i}{\Sigma W_i} \times 100$$

Note that the weights, W_i, cannot be the same as Q_i used in the weighted aggregate index because each Q used there was measured in different units of measurement – kilos, dozens and litres – which of course cannot be added together to provide the ΣW_i needed in the denominator above. The only common unit of measurement is money; the appropriate weights in this case, therefore, are the *expenditures* on each commodity. Again, we have a choice of weights for use in compiling a weighted average of price relatives: W_i can either be taken as expenditures in the base year, i.e. $P_{i0}Q_{i0}$ (producing a Laspeyres-type index), or as expenditures in the current year, i.e. $P_{it}Q_{it}$ (a Paasche-type index).

Table 4.3 shows the price relatives for the four bakery inputs, the two sets of expenditure weights ($P_{i0}Q_{i0}$ and $P_{it}Q_{it}$) and the calculation of weighted relatives using these two sets of weights.

It should be noted that in the case of the base-weighted (Laspeyres) indexes, the index calculated as a weighted aggregate is the same as that calculated as an average of price relatives (125.7 in each case). This will always be the case because the average price relatives formula reduces to the weighted aggregate formula. However, note that in the case of the Paasche indexes, the formulae are not equivalent. They would only be equivalent if the weights employed represented *current* quantities valued at *base period* prices ($P_{i0}Q_{it}$).

From a practical point of view the Laspeyres method has the advantage of being easier, quicker and cheaper to calculate compared with the Paasche method, simply because the weights remain fixed. By contrast, with Paasche indexes, the new (current) weights have to be regularly determined and, strictly speaking, the whole of the previous series ought to be recalculated using the new current weights each time. In practice, recalculation is not normally done and the index for the current period is simply 'chained' on to the previous series, but the redetermination of weights in each period still involves additional calculation and cost. As a consequence most indexes in practice are derived using base weights, these weights being revised periodically.

Quantity index numbers

The principles of the methodology for computing quantity indexes are the same as those used for computing price indexes. Consequently they can be dealt with very briefly. A quantity index is a composite measure of the change in output, sales, etc., of a group of different commodities. The index of the output of UK production industries is one example of a quantity index which, as its name implies, measures changes in the output of a range of manufacturing and other industries.

As before, there are two methods which may be employed to calculate a quantity index:

☐ The weighted aggregate of quantities method.
☐ The weighted average of quantity relatives method.

Weighted aggregate quantity indexes

Weighted aggregate quantity indexes involve measuring the change in the value of quantities produced (or sold, etc.) over a period of time in terms of unchanged prices. In effect, therefore, weighted aggregates are calculated in which the weights this time are prices. Again, Laspeyres- or Paasche-type indexes can be calculated, depending on whether base period prices or current period prices respectively are chosen as weights. Thus:

Base-weighted (Laspeyres): $\dfrac{\Sigma Q_{it} P_{i0}}{\Sigma Q_{i0} P_{i0}} \times 100$

Current-weighted (Paasche): $\dfrac{\Sigma Q_{it} P_{it}}{\Sigma Q_{i0} P_{it}} \times 100$

The close parallel with the corresponding formulae for aggregate price indexes will be noted: each simply requires the P_S and the Q_S in the formulae to be transposed. As an example we apply these formulae to the bakery data (as before); the relevant summations are already given in Table 4.2. Thus, the calculations of both types of weighted aggregate quantity indexes are as follows:

Base-weighted (Laspeyres) aggregate quantity index:

$$\frac{\Sigma Q_{it} P_{i0}}{\Sigma Q_{i0} P_{i0}} \times 100 = \frac{883}{649} \times 100 = 136.1$$

Current-weighted (Paasche) aggregate quantity index:

$$\frac{\Sigma Q_{it} P_{it}}{\Sigma Q_{i0} P_{it}} \times 100 = \frac{1108}{816} \times 100 = 135.8$$

Again, it will be appreciated that the difference in these two types of index arises because of the use of base period prices to revalue inputs in one period but the use of current prices to revalue inputs in the other. For the same reasons as above in the case of price indexes, the Laspeyres-type index is normally preferred for practical purposes.

Weighted averages of quantity relatives

Just as price indexes may be calculated as weighted averages of price relatives, so quantity indexes may be calculated using weighted averages of quantity relatives. As before, the weights used in these cases must be value weights (i.e. prices × quantities).

Using the data in Table 4.1 again, we first need to compute the *quantity relatives* (in the same way as we previously computed price relatives), as well as the base and current period expenditure weights and the weighted quantity relatives.

Inputs	Quantity relatives, Q_{it}/Q_{i0} 1995/1993	Quantity changes 1993–95
Flour	700/500 = 1.40	+40%
Eggs	130/100 = 1.30	+30%
Milk	200/160 = 1.25	+25%
Sugar	70/50 = 1.40	+40%

The two types of quantity indexes may be expressed generally as:

$$\frac{\Sigma(\text{quantity relative}) \times \text{weight}}{\Sigma \text{ weights}}$$

Thus for base-weighted and current-weighted quantity indexes we have:

Base-weighted (Laspeyres): $\dfrac{\Sigma(Q_{it}/Q_{i0})\,P_{i0}\,Q_{i0}}{\Sigma P_{i0}\,Q_{i0}} \times 100$

Current-weighted (Paasche): $\dfrac{\Sigma(Q_{it}/Q_{i0})\,P_{it}\,Q_{it}}{\Sigma P_{it}\,Q_{it}} \times 100$

The applications of these formulae are shown in Table 4.4.

Table 4.4 Calculation of weighted quantity relative indexes for a bakery

		Expenditure weights		Weighted relatives	
Input	Quantity relative (Q_{it}/Q_{i0}) (a)	1993 $(P_{i0}Q_{i0})$ (b)	1995 $(P_{it}Q_{it})$ (c)	1993 (a) × (b)	1995 (a) × (c)
Flour	1.40	375	630	525	882.0
Eggs	1.30	160	260	208	338.0
Milk	1.25	64	120	80	150.0
Sugar	1.40	50	98	70	137.2
Summations (Σ)		649	1108	883	1507.2

Quantity indexes

Base-weighted average of quantity relatives (Laspeyres-type index):

$$\frac{\Sigma(Q_{it}/Q_{i0})\,P_{i0}\,Q_{i0}}{\Sigma P_{i0}\,Q_{i0}} \times 100 = \frac{883}{649} \times 100 \approx 136.1$$

Current-weighted average of quantity relatives (Paasche-type index):

$$\frac{\Sigma(Q_{it}/Q_{i0})\,P_{it}\,Q_{it}}{\Sigma P_{it}\,Q_{it}} \times 100 = \frac{1507.2}{1108} \times 100 \approx 136.0$$

We conclude this chapter by briefly outlining the construction of the index of output of the UK production industries. This is calculated monthly and, as noted earlier, it is an important indicator of the growth of the economy and thus of economic performance.

The official index of output of the production industries in the United Kingdom

'Production industries' in the United Kingdom are defined as mining and quarrying, manufacturing, electricity, gas and water industries. Agriculture, construction and services industries are excluded. The index is a Laspeyres-type (base-weighted) arithmethic mean of quantity relatives. The weights are based on the value of net output (i.e. output less payments made to other industries for goods and services supplied) contributed by each industry in a base year. This information is obtained in a census of production. Currently the weights are based on the year 1990.

Around 300 indicators are used as measures of the change in output for the various subdivisions and products of the industries. The information ideally required, i.e. about changes in the *volume* of net output, is rarely available, so that proxy indicators have to be used based on either gross output (quantities or values at constant prices) or input data or employment data. Each quantity indicator is used to derive quantity relatives for each of the subdivisions into which the industries are divided and then weighted in the normal way. The 1990 base weights and the indices for 1993 and 1994 are given in Table 4.5 below. It will be seen that the output of the production

Table 4.5 The UK index of output of the production industries: the 1990 base weights and the indexes for 1993 and 1994

	Weights (1990 base)	Indexes (1990 = 100)	
		1993	1994
Total Production Industries	*1000*	*98.1*	*103.2*
Mining and quarrying	77	115.0	136.1
All Manufacturing Industries	844	95.2	99.1
Basic metal and metal products	74	86.1	86.0
Coke, petrol and nuclear fuels	23	112.8	112.4
Chemicals and man-made fibres	86	107.4	113.2
Engineering and allied industries	302	91.6	96.9
Food, drink and tobacco	110	99.6	100.9
Textiles, leather and clothing	47	89.7	90.7
Other manufacturing industries	202	94.9	99.3
Electricity, gas and water	79	111.8	115.1

Note: Indexes are also published for various subdivisions of the industries shown above. Monthly and quarterly series are available in both unadjusted and seasonally adjusted form. Seasonal adjustment methods are considered in Chapter 12.

industries in total decreased by 1.9 per cent over the period from 1990 to 1993 (the index fell from 100.0 in 1990 to 98.1 in 1993) but then rose strongly in 1994 to reach a level 3.2 per cent higher than in 1990. It will also be seen that the growth performance by industry was very mixed, ranging from an increase of 36.1 per cent in the case of the mining and quarrying industry between 1990 and 1994 and a decrease of 14.0 per cent in the case of the basic metal and metal products industry over the same period.

The index is published in several government statistical publications including the *Monthly Digest of Statistics*, the *Annual Abstract of Statistics* and *Economic Trends* (all published by HMSO, London) as well as being reported in the media periodically.

Key learning points

Weighted aggregate price index A composite price index where the prices of the items in the composite are weighted by their relative importance (denoted Q_i).

$$I_t = \frac{\Sigma P_{it} Q_i}{\Sigma P_{i0} Q_i} \times 100$$

Laspeyres weighted aggregate price index A weighted aggregate price index where the weight for each item is its base-period quantity (denoted Q_{i0}).

$$I_t = \frac{\Sigma P_{it} Q_{i0}}{\Sigma P_{i0} Q_{i0}} \times 100$$

Paasche weighted aggregate price index A weighted aggregate price index where the weight for each item is its current-period quantity (denoted Q_{it}).

$$I_t = \frac{\Sigma P_{it} Q_{it}}{\Sigma P_{i0} Q_{it}} \times 100$$

Price relative A simple price index which is computed by dividing a current unit price for a single item by its base-period unit price.

$$I_t = \frac{P_t}{P_0} \times 100$$

Weighted average of price relatives A composite price index computed by taking a weighted average of price relatives, using either base or current weights to produce Laspeyres- or Paasche-type index numbers respectively.

$$I_t = \frac{\Sigma (P_{it}/P_{i0})\, W_i}{\Sigma W_i} \times 100$$

Quantity index   An index that is designed to measure changes in quantities over time.

Weighted aggregate quantity indexes   A composite quantity index where the quantities of the items in the composite index are weighted in terms of unchanged prices: base-period prices or current-period prices may be used to produce Laspeyres- or Paasche-type quantity indexes respectively.

Base-weighted (Laspeyres): $\dfrac{\Sigma Q_{it} P_{i0}}{\Sigma Q_{i0} P_{i0}} \times 100$

Current-weighted (Paasche): $\dfrac{\Sigma Q_{it} P_{it}}{\Sigma Q_{i0} P_{it}} \times 100$

Weighted averages of quantity relatives   A composite quantity index computed by taking a weighted average of quantity relatives, using either base or current weights to produce Laspeyres- or Paasche-type index numbers respectively.

Basic-weighted (Laspeyres): $\dfrac{\Sigma (Q_{it}/Q_{i0})\, P_{i0} Q_{i0}}{\Sigma P_{i0} Q_{i0}} \times 100$

Current-weighted (Paasche): $\dfrac{\Sigma (Q_{it}/Q_{i0})\, P_{it} Q_{it}}{\Sigma P_{it} Q_{it}} \times 100$

EXERCISES

1 A firm uses three materials in its manufacturing processes. The quantities bought in 1990 and 1995 and the prices are as follows:

Material	Units	Prices (£)		Quantities	
		1990	1995	1990	1995
A	Thousands	100	150	10	16
B	Gallons	1	2	100	120
C	Metres	2	5	50	70

Calculate Laspeyres and Paasche price indexes for 1995, with 1990 = 100, using:
(a) the aggregative method, and
(b) the average of price relatives method.

2 Expenditure on materials by the firm in Exercise 1 above amounted to £1200 in 1990 and £2990 in 1995.
   (a) Deflate expenditure in 1995 to 1990 price levels, using the Paasche aggregative price index.
   (b) Indicate the percentage increase in purchases of materials in real terms.

3 For the data in Exercise 1, calculate a current-weighted (Paasche) quantity index to measure the change in the total quantity of materials purchased between 1990 and 1995 using:
   (a) the aggregative method, and
   (b) the average of relatives method.

4 The average weekly earnings of manual employees in manufacturing industry increased from £255.10 in April 1990 to £312.70 in April 1994. The RPI increased from 125.1 to 144.2 over this period. What was the percentage increase in earnings in *real terms*?

5 A person retired in 1990 with an index-linked pension of £5000. The index is linked to the increase in the RPI which increased from 126.1 in 1990 to 144.1 in 1994. What would the pension be in 1994?

6 With reference to Exercise 5, given the change in the RPI between 1990 and 1994,
   (a) What was the purchasing power of the pound in 1994 compared with 1990?
   (b) If the pension was not index-linked, how much would it have been worth in 1994?

7 A firm employs 470 workers, broken down into three categories, with hourly wage rates for 1993 and 1995 as shown below.

Category of worker	Number of workers	Hourly wage rates	
		1993	1995
Craftsmen	120	£4.50	£6.00
Labourers	200	£3.20	£3.80
Drivers	80	£3.80	£4.60

(a) Compute the price relatives for each category of worker separately between 1993 and 1995.
(b) Compute an index of labour costs for 1995 for the workforce in general, taking 1993 equal to 100, using the aggregative method.
Comment on the results for (a) and (b).

5

Probability

The essence of probability in business

So far in this book we have been dealing with sample data drawn from a population and then describing the sample information in various ways – tables, graphs, measures of location and dispersion and index numbers. We have thus been dealing with data sets recording actual observations. However, if we wish to *infer* something about populations on the basis of samples, we are dealing with *uncertainty*, i.e. *probabilities*. The concepts of probability form the foundation of all decision making and statistical reasoning.

The concepts of probability are especially relevant in business. Businessmen make decisions in the face of uncertainty day by day. For example:

☐ When a company launches a new product, the sales potential is uncertain but the prospect of a successful launch can be estimated and a probability assigned.

☐ The exact timing of peak demand level for a firm's products is uncertain (in shops, petrol stations, warehouses, etc.), but again probability concepts can be applied in arriving at suitable decisions about capacity, stock-holding, staffing levels, etc.

☐ The likelihood of a new investment project being profitable may be unknown, but again a probability can be assigned.

☐ Suppliers of components to a firm are unlikely to know in advance the exact number of defective items that will occur in any one batch, but sampling permits probabilities to be assigned to various possible outcomes occurring, such as one, two or three defects being discovered in the whole batch.

In this chapter we introduce the fundamental concepts of probability and begin to illustrate their application as decision-making tools in business. In subsequent chapters this analysis is extended and we show the important role that probability plays in drawing inferences in the business world. The chapter is structured as follows:

☐ Assigning probabilities.
☐ Rules of probability.
☐ Expectations.
☐ Decision trees.
☐ Permutations and combinations.

Probability theory is a branch of mathematics, but the non-mathematically minded managers should not panic! The essential ideas can be readily conveyed with little mathematical or statistical jargon.

Assigning probabilities

Probability is a numerical measure of the likelihood of an event occurring. It is measured on a scale from 0 to 1, with zero indicating the impossibility of the event taking place and unity representing certainty. By definition, the nearness to certainty increases up this scale with 0.5 indicating that the event has a 50:50 chance of occurring. In business, given that firms generally operate in an uncertain environment, values of zero and unity are rarely encountered – outcomes are uncertain to a greater or lesser degree. As indicated earlier, managerial decision making therefore has to be based on some assessment of the probability of possible outcomes occurring.

Notation

It is conventional to use shorthand notation when assigning probabilities. For example, the question 'What is the probability of 5 defective parts being discovered in a batch sample?' may be expressed simply as:

$P(X = 5)?$

where X (or any other symbol) is used to represent the number of defective components. Similarly, the probability of a successful marketing launch (however defined) may be denoted as:

$P(S)$

where 'S' signifies 'success'. If this is estimated to be 0.6 then, by definition, the probability of failure (F) may be denoted as:

$P(F) = 1 - 0.6 = 0.4$

$P(F)$ is referred to as the *complement* of $P(S)$ – no other outcome being possible.

The first question to consider is how probability values can be determined. The ways in which probability values can be assigned may be classified in three ways:

☐ Classical (theoretical) approach.

☐ Relative frequency (empirical) approach.

☐ Subjective approach.

Classical (theoretical) approach

This approach applies only in situations in which a particular outcome can be assigned a probability on *a priori* grounds. Some examples will illustrate this:

☐ In tossing a 'fair' coin only two outcomes are possible: head (H) or tail (T). Thus:

$P(H) = P(T) = 0.5$

☐ In throwing a 'fair' die,

$P(6) = P(5) = \ldots = P(1) = 1/6$

☐ In drawing an ace from a pack of 52 playing-cards,

$P(Ace) = 4/52$

The classical method largely stems from the analysis of gambling problems, in which the assumption of equally likely outcomes is often a reasonable one. However, in the context of business, this assumption often does not apply. Hence other methods of assigning probabilities are required.

Relative frequency (empirical) approach

This approach assigns probabilities on the basis of empirical evidence obtained from surveys or a firm's historical records. The following example illustrates the essence of this approach.

Example
The data shown in Table 5.1 give the expected lifetimes of 100 torchlight batteries made and tested by a firm. Using these data, *relative frequencies* can be readily calculated (shown in the last column). Thus, for example, out of the 100 batteries, 20 have been found to last less than 10 hours: this gives a relative frequency of 20/100 = 0.20. If batteries are selected at random from a batch of 100, assuming that these data are representative of all batches, then we can assign probabilities for expected lifetimes using relative frequencies. Thus:

P(less than 10) = 0.20

P(10 and less than 15) = 0.42, etc.

In general, if f_i denotes the frequency with which an event (E_i) occurs (such as a battery lasting less than 10 hours), then using the relative frequency approach,

$$P(E_i) = \frac{f_i}{\Sigma f_i} = \frac{f_i}{N}$$

where N = total number of events.

Since a battery, selected at random, must fall within only *one* of the four categories in Table 5.1, these categories are said to be *mutually exclusive*, i.e.

Table 5.1 Frequency distribution of battery lives

Lifetime of batteries (hours)	Number of batteries	Relative frequency
less than 10	20	20/100 = 0.20
10 and less than 15	42	42/100 = 0.42
15 and less than 20	28	28/100 = 0.28
20 or more	10	10/100 = 0.10
	100	Sum = 1.00

events are mutually exclusive if they *cannot* occur simultaneously. (For example, head and tail are mutually exclusive events in coin tossing.) It will be seen from the above that the sum of the relative frequencies of mutually exclusive events is 1, i.e.

P(less than 10) + P(10 and less than 15) + P(15 and less than 20)

$$+ P(20 \text{ or more}) = 1$$

In general, for mutually exclusive events,

$\Sigma P(E_i) = 1$, i.e. $P(E_1) + P(E_2) + P(E_3) + \ldots + P(E_n) = 1$

Theoretical considerations (the classical approach) would not, of course, have offered any help in assigning probabilities in this case. Empirical evidence was essential. This example can also be used to illustrate any practical application of probability in a business context. For instance, if the above firm decides to guarantee a refund if any battery fails to last at least 10 hours, then what is the probability that refunds will arise? The answer is 0.20 or 20 per cent. (Clearly in this example the problem of verification of battery usage would be subject to question!)

Subjective approach

This approach to assigning probabilities is based on a measure of an individual's degree of belief or strength of conviction that an event will occur, i.e. a subjective assessment. Inevitably, this must be employed in situations in which the other two approaches cannot be applied. For example, electoral outcomes, the results of football matches, etc., and in a business context the likelihood of a successful product launch, or investment outcomes, or many other events in the future for which past records are of no help. In such business situations it is often essential to obtain a consensus view of probabilities rather than rely on any one individual and to obtain expert advice. For example, a mining company is unlikely to rely on the view of only one engineer in determining the probability of profitable exploitations of different sites.

The rules of probability

Up to this point we have discussed only the probabilities of *single* events occurring. The applications of probability, however, are often concerned with a number of *related* events. For example, for two events A and B, one may be interested in knowing whether *both* A *and* B will occur or, alternatively, whether *at least one* of them will occur. The analysis outlined so far can readily be extended to deal with these and even more complicated problems. But to facilitate this extension we must first introduce two fundamental rules which the assigned probabilities must follow. These rules (or 'laws') are commonly referred to as:

☐ *The addition rule of probability.*
☐ *The multiplication rule of probability.*

The addition rule of probability

The addition rule of probability applies when we are considering two (or more) events and wish to determine the probability that *at least one* of the events will take place. There are two variations of the addition rule, however, depending on whether events are *mutually exclusive* or not.

Addition rule for mutually exclusive events:

If A and B are two mutually exclusive events, then the probability of obtaining *either* A *or* B is equal to the probability of obtaining A *plus* the probability of obtaining B, i.e.

$P(A \text{ or } B) = P(A) + P(B)$

Addition rule for non-mutually exclusive events:

If A and B are not mutually exclusive events then 'A or B' means that A occurs *or* B occurs, or *both* A *and* B occur simultaneously. In this case, we must subtract the probability of the *joint occurrence* of A and B from the sum of their probabilities to avoid double counting, i.e.

$P(A \text{ or } B) = P(A) + P(B) - P(A \text{ and } B)$

Note that if A and B are mutually exclusive, then $P(A$ and $B)$ equals zero.

These rules can be readily appreciated with reference to Figures 5.1 and 5.2. If we let a circle represent a particular event, then clearly mutually exclusive events can be shown as non-overlapping circles (Figure 5.1), while if these are not mutually exclusive, then the circles overlap (Figure 5.2) and the intersection represents the *joint* occurrence of A and B. Such diagrams are referred to by statisticians as *Venn diagrams*.

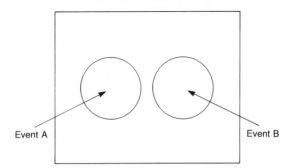

Figure 5.1 Mutually exclusive events.

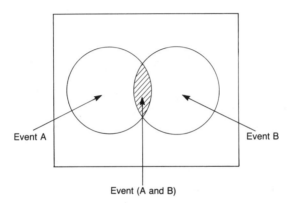

Figure 5.2 Non-mutually exclusive events.

Example
To illustrate the application of the addition rule, consider a firm which employs 100 people who work on an assembly line. Each employee is required to complete a certain task in a given time and the work has to pass a quality inspection. From time to time, some workers fall behind and some work is produced which is sub-standard. At the end of a work study period, the records show that 9 workers had failed to complete work on time, 12 workers had produced sub-standard work and, of these 21 workers, 4 had produced work which was both late *and* sub-standard. If we let L denote late work and S sub-standard work, we can define the following probabilities:

$$P(L) = \frac{9}{100} = 0.09$$

$$P(S) = \frac{12}{100} = 0.12$$

$$P(L \text{ and } S) = \frac{4}{100} = 0.04$$

Suppose that any worker who fails to meet the time and/or quality standards is not entitled to a bonus payment. What is the probability that any single worker, randomly selected, will fall into this category? The events L and S are clearly not mutually exclusive since some workers produce both late and sub-standard work. Thus, the probability follows directly from the appropriate addition rule above, i.e.

$$P(L \text{ or } S) = P(L) + P(S) - P(L \text{ and } S)$$
$$= 0.09 + 0.12 - 0.04$$
$$= 0.17$$

This tells us that there is a 17 per cent probability of a worker, selected at random, not qualifying for a bonus.

The two variations of the addition rule shown above can, of course, be generalized to more than two events as follows:

Generalization of addition rules

Mutually exclusive events:

$P(A \text{ or } B \text{ or } C \text{ or } \ldots) = P(A) + P(B) + P(C) + \ldots$, etc.

Non-mutually exclusive events:

$P(A \text{ or } B \text{ or } C) = P(A) + P(B) + P(C)$
$\quad\quad\quad\quad - P(A \text{ and } B) - P(A \text{ and } C) - P(B \text{ and } C)$
$\quad\quad\quad\quad + P(A \text{ and } B \text{ and } C)$ **and so on for more than three events.**

It is helpful to use Venn diagrams to clarify these extensions – see Figure 5.3(a) and (b). In the case of (b), it should be noted that $P(A \text{ and } B \text{ and } C)$, i.e. the shaded area in Figure 5.3(b), is first *included* three times through the summation of $P(A)$, $P(B)$ and $P(C)$, and then *subtracted* three times through the subtraction of $P(A \text{ and } B)$, $P(A \text{ and } C)$ and $P(B \text{ and } C)$, and so it must be added back again at the end of the expression.

The multiplication rule of probability

The analysis above using the addition rule illustrates how we can assign the probability of any single event occurring out of a number of possible

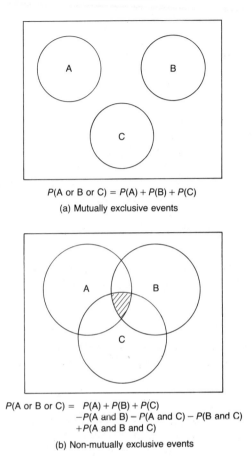

$$P(A \text{ or } B \text{ or } C) = P(A) + P(B) + P(C)$$

(a) Mutually exclusive events

$$P(A \text{ or } B \text{ or } C) = \begin{aligned} &P(A) + P(B) + P(C) \\ &-P(A \text{ and } B) - P(A \text{ and } C) - P(B \text{ and } C) \\ &+P(A \text{ and } B \text{ and } C) \end{aligned}$$

(b) Non-mutually exclusive events

Figure 5.3 Generalization of the addition rule.

events, e.g. $P(A \text{ or } B \text{ or } C)$. However, we may be interested in other, more complex situations in which we wish to ascertain the probability of the joint or successive occurrence of two or more events, e.g. $P(A \text{ and } B)$. The answer to this problem is given by the *multiplication rule* of probability, whereby the separate probabilities of each event are multiplied together if A, B, etc., are *independent* events.

Definition of independent events:

Two events are *independent* when the occurrence (or non-occurrence) of one event has no effect on the probability of occurrence of the other event.

Hence, for independent events, we have:

Multiplication rule for independent events:

$P(A \text{ and } B) = P(A) \times P(B)$

Example
An oil exploration company assesses that the probability of a successful 'strike' in the North Sea is 0.6 (i.e. 6 out of every 10 test drillings strike oil) while in the Irish Sea the probability is only 0.4. If the oil company drills two bore holes, one in each sea, simultaneously, what is the probability that it will strike oil in both cases? Clearly, the probability of success in one sea is quite independent of success in the other. Therefore the required probability is $0.6 \times 0.4 = 0.24$.

By contrast, if events are *dependent*, rather than independent, then the multiplication rule above needs to be modified.

Definition of dependent events:

Two events are *dependent* when the occurrence (or non-occurrence) of one event affects the probability of occurrence of the other event.

Example
If 20 employees, two of whom are women, have applied for a management training programme, what is the probability that the first two selected are women? As there are only two women applicants, the chance of the first candidate selected being a woman is 2/20; the chance of the second candidate being a woman, given that the first one was a woman, is 1/19. This demonstrates the concept of dependence and introduces the further concept of *conditional probability*.

   In general, if two events A and B are dependent such that the probability of B taking place depends upon the probability of A having already occurred, then the multiplication rule for $P(A \text{ and } B)$ modifies to the unconditional probability of A multiplied by the *conditional* probability of B, i.e.

Multiplication rule for dependent events:

$P(A \text{ and } B) = P(A) \times P(B|A)$

where $P(B|A)$ denotes the probability of B occurring given that A has already occurred (note that the vertical line in this expression is read as 'given').

Table 5.2 Analysis of 100 assembly line workers by performance criteria

	Late (L)	Not late (NL)	Totals
Sub-standard (S)	4	8	12
Not Sub-standard (NS)	5	83	88
Totals	9	91	100

Naturally, conditional probability expressions such as $P(B|A)$, are not required for independent events because, by definition, there is no relationship between the occurrence of such events. Hence $P(B|A)$ reduces to $P(B)$. The application of this rule for dependent events can readily be demonstrated with reference to our previous data on the performance of assembly line workers by expressing the information in the form of a two-way *contingency table* (Table 5.2).

From the table the following probabilities can be calculated:

$P(L) = 9/100; \; P(S) = 12/100; \; P(L \text{ and } S) = 4/100$

as before when we discussed the addition rule. Conditional probability can be illustrated by considering the chance that a worker who has been selected at random and found to fail the time limit for his task, will also have produced sub-standard work – i.e. $P(S|L)$. This is found from Table 5.2 as follows:

$$P(S|L) = \frac{P(L \text{ and } S)}{P(L)}$$

$$= \frac{4/100}{9/100}$$

$$= 4/9$$

Bayes' rule for conditional probabilities

A particularly useful extension of conditional probability in the context of a number of sequential events gives rise to so-called *Bayes' rule*. This provides a general method for revising *prior* probabilities (such as the probability of event A occurring) in the light of new information (such as the fact that certain other events B, C, etc., have already occurred) to provide what is referred to as *posterior* probability. In a two-event case, A and B,

Bayes' rule is, of course, the same as the conditional probability statement above, i.e.

Bayes' rule – two events:

$$P(A|B) = \frac{P(A \text{ and } B)}{P(B)}$$

This rule can be extended to the case where there are, say, n mutually exclusive events, $A_1, A_2, A_3, \ldots, A_n$ and where one of the n events must occur. In such a case Bayes' rule for the calculation of any posterior probability $P(A_i|B)$ is as follows:

Bayes' rule – general form:

$$P(A_i|B) = \frac{P(A_i)\,P(B|A_i)}{P(A_1)\,P(B|A_1) + P(A_2)\,P(B|A_2) + \ldots + P(A_n)\,P(B|A_n)}$$

$$= \frac{P(A_i)\,P(B|A_i)}{\Sigma P(A_i)\,P(B|A_i)}$$

An example of the application of Bayes' rule in general form is as follows:

Example
A car repair firm employs three paint-sprayers, Tom, Dick and Harry. Owing to the different speeds of their respective production lines, Tom is responsible for painting 25 per cent of all the cars produced, Dick for 35 per cent and Harry for the remaining 40 per cent. On the basis of frequent quality inspections it is discovered that, on average, 5 per cent of the cars sprayed by Tom fall below the minimum acceptable standard (as regards the quality of painting), while the corresponding figure for Dick is 8 per cent and for Harry 10 per cent. If a car is selected at random from the firm's throughput of cars and its paint finish is judged to be sub-standard, what is the probability that it was sprayed by Harry?

Solution
Let S = event that the car is sub-standard
    T = event that a car is sprayed by Tom
    D = event that a car is sprayed by Dick
    H = event that a car is sprayed by Harry

Thus, the problem is to find $P(H|S)$.
    From the above information, we know that

$P(T) = 0.25$, and $P(S|T) = 0.05$

(i.e. Tom sprays 25 per cent of the cars and of these 5 per cent are sub-standard, on average). Similarly, for Dick and Harry:

$P(D) = 0.35$, and $P(S|D) = 0.08$.

$P(H) = 0.40$, and $P(S|H) = 0.10$.

Applying Bayes' rule, the probability that a randomly selected car, found to be sub-standard, was sprayed by Harry, is:

$$P(H|S) = \frac{P(H)P(S|H)}{P(T)P(S|T) + P(D)P(S|D) + P(H)P(S|H)}$$

$$= \frac{(0.40)(0.10)}{(0.25)(0.05) + (0.35)(0.08) + (0.40)(0.10)}$$

$$= \frac{0.04}{0.0805}$$

$$= 0.5 \text{ approximately}$$

Tree diagrams

The above kinds of problem can also be solved very simply using what are known as *tree diagrams*. These are often a useful way of clarifying the problem at hand. The following example illustrates this.

Example
Batches of microchips with 50 in each batch are known to contain, on average, 4 defective components, i.e. 8 per cent. A batch is to be sold to a dealer specializing in microchips. The dealer decides to test a sample of the microchips for reliability. Each one tested is subsequently put to one side, i.e. sampling is *without replacement*. What is the probability that the first three microchips to be tested are all defective?

Solution
When sampling is carried out *without replacement* from a finite population such as that given here, the probability values associated with various events are *dependent* on what events (sampled microchips) have already occurred. On the other hand, when sampling is *with replacement*, all events are, by definition, *independent*. A tree diagram for this problem is shown in Figure 5.4 with defective microchips denoted by 'D' and good ones by 'G'. The probability of three defective microchips being selected one after the other, without replacement, may be denoted by:

$P(D_1 \text{ and } D_2 \text{ and } D_3)$

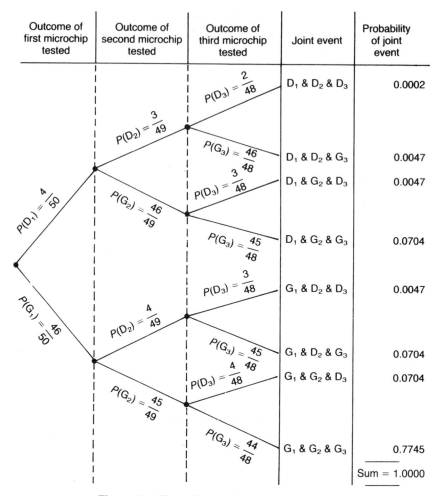

Figure 5.4 Tree diagram for microchip problem.

where the subscripts 1, 2 and 3 denote each successive test. From the diagram, it will be seen that the probability of the joint event (D_1 and D_2 and D_3) is 0.0002. This could also have been found using the multiplication rule for conditional events, i.e.

$$P(D_1 \text{ and } D_2 \text{ and } D_3) = P(D_1) \times P(D_2|D_1) \times P(D_3|D_1 \text{ and } D_2)$$

$$= \frac{4}{50} \times \frac{3}{49} \times \frac{2}{48}$$

$$= 0.0002 \text{ approximately}$$

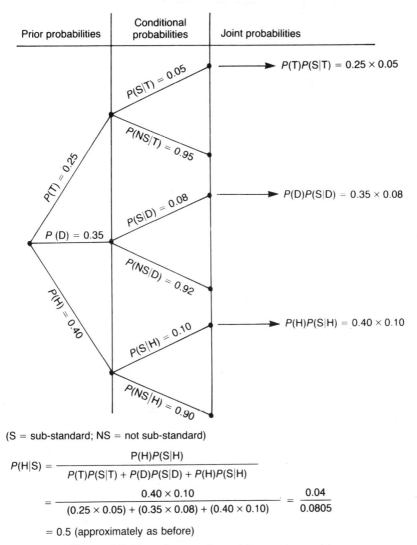

(S = sub-standard; NS = not sub-standard)

$$P(H|S) = \frac{P(H)P(S|H)}{P(T)P(S|T) + P(D)P(S|D) + P(H)P(S|H)}$$

$$= \frac{0.40 \times 0.10}{(0.25 \times 0.05) + (0.35 \times 0.08) + (0.40 \times 0.10)} = \frac{0.04}{0.0805}$$

= 0.5 (approximately as before)

Figure 5.5 Tree diagram for paint sprayers problem.

By extension, the following probabilities can be readily determined from Figure 5.4:

P(only 1 defect from 3 sampled) = 3(0.0704) = 0.2112

P(only 2 defects from 3 sampled) = 3(0.0047) = 0.0141

The earlier example concerning the car sprayers Tom, Dick and Harry, in the context of Bayes' rule, could also have been quickly solved using a tree diagram. The solution is shown in Figure 5.5.

Expectations

The analysis above can also be readily extended to many other business problems such as those involving profit maximization or loss minimization. This introduces the concept of *expectation*. Consider two marketing strategies open to a company, each with different pay-offs attached but with different probabilities of ensuring a successful launch of a new product. These two strategies involve either a national television advertising campaign or widespread newspaper coverage. The probability of success associated with a TV campaign costing £300,000 is 0.75 with a potential pay-off of £2 million profits per year. On the other hand, if this campaign fails, the company stands to lose £300,000. With regard to newspaper coverage, the probabilities of success or failure are equal, i.e. there is a 50:50 chance with potential pay-offs of £1 million for success and a loss of £100,000 for failure. If we assume that the objective of the company is to maximize expected returns, which marketing strategy should it opt for?

The problem can be neatly set out by means of a tree diagram, though, in such situations, it is more commonly referred to as a *decision tree* (Figure 5.6). Note that the decision tree, like the tree diagram introduced above, shows the logical or natural progression in the management decision-making process. In the diagram, expected pay-off values for each outcome are the product of each pay-off and its associated probability of success or failure. Thus, the expected *total* pay-off from each marketing strategy is given by the sum of their expected pay-offs for success or failure. In this example, given that the objective facing the company is to maximize returns, the analysis leads to the recommendation of the adoption of a television campaign – hardly surprising given the associated high probability of success and pay-off anticipated!

Permutations and combinations

By definition, the probability of an event A is equal to the number of outcomes relating to A divided by the total number of possible outcomes. Finding these numbers has been relatively easy in all the examples discussed so far in this chapter. When the problems are simple, the number of outcomes can easily be counted. However, for other problems which may involve a very large number of possible outcomes, it may not be so easy to count them. We conclude this chapter, therefore, by introducing mathematical techniques involving *permutations* and *combinations* which are at our disposal to determine the total number of possible outcomes. Most counting problems fall into one or other of these types. The application of

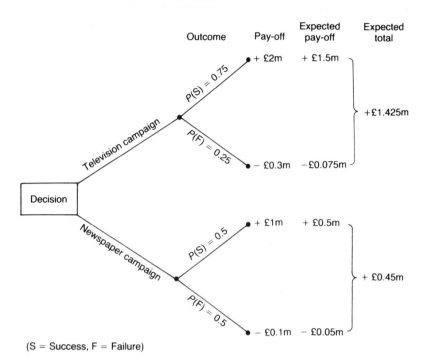

Figure 5.6 Decision tree for choice of marketing strategy.

the mathematical techniques is very easy – the testing aspect of any problem is in deciding which method is appropriate (permutations or combinations).

Permutations

Permutations refer to the number of ways in which a set of objects can be arranged *in order* (the order being crucial). For example, a committee of 5 people (denoted by A, B, C, D, E) has to select two persons to fill the posts of committee treasurer and chairperson. How many different ways can these two posts be filled given that the situation in which A and B (in that order) fill the treasurer and chairperson posts respectively is *not* the same situation as B and A (in that order) filling them? Clearly there are 5 ways of filling the treasurer post, since there are 5 members available for election. Once this post has been filled, there remain only 4 possible candidates to choose from to fill the chairperson post. Intuitively, therefore, there are $5 \times 4 = 20$

ways – i.e. permutations – of selecting a pair of committee members for these two posts. These permutations are set out as follows:

AB   AC   AD   AE
BA   BC   BD   BE
CA   CB   CD   CE
DA   DB   DC   DE
EA   EB   EC   ED

It is assumed here of course that the same person cannot fill both posts, i.e. AA, BB, etc., are impossible outcomes. This problem can be expressed in a general, mathematical form as:

$$P^n_r = \frac{n!}{(n-r)!}$$

where P^n_r denotes the number of permutations of r objects out of a total of n objects; $n!$ (pronounced 'n factorial') denotes $n(n-1)\,(n-2)\,(n-3)$ ... (2) (1). Note that the factorial sequence stops at 1. Zero factorial is defined as equal to 1, i.e. $0! = 1$.

Thus, in our example, where $n = 5$ and $r = 2$, the total number of permutations is:

$$P^n_r = P^5_2 = \frac{5!}{(5-2)!} = \frac{5!}{3!} = \frac{5 \times 4 \times 3 \times 2 \times 1}{3 \times 2 \times 1} = 20$$

The above formula is very simple to apply since all we need to know are the values of n and r.

Combinations

In the cast of permutations, the *order* in which the objects are arranged is important. However, if one is interested only in what particular objects are selected when r objects are chosen from n objects, *without regard to their arrangement*, then the unordered selection is called a *combination*. In these situations, the number of combinations is given by the formula:

$$C^n_r = \frac{n!}{r!(n-r)!}$$

where C^n_r denotes the number of combinations possible in selecting r objects from n different objects.

For instance, if we take the same example as above, but assume now that the order of selection does not matter, then we have a combination, rather than a permutation, problem; i.e. we are then only interested in the number of ways of selecting any two people, regardless of which post they fill. The number of combinations is thus less than the number of permutations since, for example, AB is equivalent to BA (in other words, A and B can fill either of the two posts of treasurer and chairperson). There are only 10 combinations possible as follows:

AB AC AD AE
BC BD BE
CD CE
DE

Using the formula for combinations, we have

$$C^n_r = C^5_2 = \frac{5!}{2!(5-2)!} = \frac{5 \times 4 \times 3 \times 2 \times 1}{(2 \times 1)(3 \times 2 \times 1)} = 10$$

The calculation of factorial expressions for large numbers is not as daunting as it might appear at first sight since, in the cases of both permutations and combinations, a large part of the numerator and denominator can be cancelled out. In any case many electronic calculators and computer software programs have pre-programmed factorial functions to make life even easier.

Key learning points

Probability   A numerical measure of the likelihood that an event will occur.

Classical approach   A method of assigning probabilities which assumes equally likely outcomes.

Relative frequency (empirical) approach   A method of assigning probabilities based on experimental or historical data.

$$P(E_i) = \frac{f_i}{\Sigma f_i} = \frac{f_i}{N}$$

Subjective approach   A method of assigning probabilities based on judgement.

Mutually exclusive events   Events which cannot occur simultaneously.

Addition rule for mutually exclusive events   If A and B are two mutually exclusive events, then the probability of obtaining *either* A *or* B is equal to the probability of obtaining A *plus* the probability of obtaining B.

$$P(A \text{ or } B) = P(A) + P(B)$$

Addition rule for non-mutually exclusive events　If A and B are not mutually exclusive events, then we must subtract the probability of the joint occurrence of A and B from the sum of their probabilities.

$$P(A \text{ or } B) = P(A) + P(B) - P(A \text{ and } B)$$

Generalization of addition rules

Mutually exclusive events:

$$P(A \text{ or } B \text{ or } C \text{ or } \ldots) = P(A) + P(B) + P(C) + \ldots \text{ etc.}$$

Non-mutually exclusive events:

$$P(A \text{ or } B \text{ or } C) = P(A) + P(B) + P(C)$$
$$- P(A \text{ and } B) - P(A \text{ and } C) - P(B \text{ and } C)$$
$$+ P(A \text{ and } B \text{ and } C) \text{ and so on for more than}$$
$$\text{three events.}$$

Independent events　Two events are independent when the occurrence (or non-occurrence) of one event has no effect on the probability of occurrence of the other event.

Dependent events　Two events are dependent when the occurrence (or non-occurrence) of one event affects the probability of occurrence of the other event.

Multiplication rule for independent events

$$P(A \text{ and } B) = P(A) \times P(B)$$

Conditional probability　The probability of one event (say B) occurring given that another event (say A) has already occurred, denoted $P(B|A)$.

Multiplication rules for dependent events

$$P(A \text{ and } B) = P(A) \times P(B|A)$$

Bayes' rule for conditional probabilities　A general method for revising prior probabilities in the light of new information to provide posterior probabilities.

Two events:　　$$P(A|B) = \frac{P(A \text{ and } B)}{P(B)}$$

General form:　$$P(A|B) = \frac{P(A_i)\,P(B|A_i)}{\Sigma P(A_i)\,P(B|A_i)}$$

Tree diagram　A graphical device helpful in defining sample points of an experiment involving multiple steps.

Permutations   These refer to the number of ways in which a set of objects can be arranged in order (the order being crucial).

$$P^n_r = \frac{n!}{(n-r)!}$$

Combinations   These refer to the number of ways in which a set of objects can be arranged without regard to the order of their selection.

$$C^n_r = \frac{n!}{r!(n-r)!}$$

EXERCISES

1 A market research company is employed to conduct a survey to find out where people shop for DIY goods. Out of a group of 110 randomly selected shoppers, 30 stated that they use only specialist town centre shops, 70 said they use only DIY superstores, while 10 said they use both specialist shops and superstores.
   (a) What is the probability that a person, selected at random, shops in both the specialist and superstore shops?
   (b) What proportion of DIY shoppers, who use superstores, also use the specialist shops?
   (c) What is the probability that a person uses specialist shops but not superstores?
   (d) Illustrate the answers to (a), (b) and (c) using Venn diagrams.

2 An employer categorizes job applicants according to whether they have a university degree and whether they have had relevant work experience. In a large group of applicants 70 per cent have a degree with or without any work experience, and 60 per cent have work experience with or without a degree. Fifty per cent of the applicants have both a degree and relevant work experience.
   (a) Draw a Venn diagram to show the probability associated with sampling one applicant from this group.
   (b) Determine the probability that a randomly selected job applicant has *either* a degree *or* relevant work experience.
   (c) What is the probability that the applicant has *neither* a degree *nor* work experience?

3 The customer service department knows from past experience that the chances of a customer returning goods are 1 in 10. In addition, it is known that of all returned goods, 70 per cent are credit sales, while half of all goods which are not returned are cash sales. Using Bayes' rule and tree diagrams, answer the following questions:
   (a) What is the probability that a credit sale will be returned?

(b) What is the probability that a cash sale will not be returned?
(c) Suppose that 60 per cent of all returned goods cost £20 or more and are credit sales and that 45 per cent of all goods purchased are for £20 or more and are credit sales. Find the probability that if an item costs £20 or more and is a credit sale, it will be returned.

4 There are four defective components in a batch of ten. If two components are selected randomly, one after another, what is the probability of each of the following:
(a) One defective and one good component are selected?
(b) Two defective components are selected?
(c) At least one defective component is selected?
(d) Three good components are selected?

5 A machine is composed of five parts, which can be assembled in any order. A test is conducted to determine the length of time taken to assemble the machine, for each possible order of assembly. If each order is tested once, how many tests must be carried out?

6 A consultancy firm submits three proposals for consideration by three different clients. It considers that the chances of the proposals being accepted are one half, one third and one quarter, respectively. What is the probability that:
(a) one and only one proposal is accepted?
(b) no proposal is accepted?
(c) all three proposals are accepted?

7 A machine tool has three key components. Each component has a probability of failing as follows: 0.10, 0.05 and 0.20 respectively. The machine tool is designed so that it will still work even if only one of the key components is functioning. What is the chance that at a given point in time:
(a) the machine tool will not work at all?
(b) the machine tool will have only one component operational?
(c) *at least one* component will be operational?

8 A multinational company recruits a large number of university graduates each year and operates a training programme covering a period of one year. Of these graduates 30 per cent are given time off each week to attend a diploma course in management principles, 10 per cent are sent on a full-time MBA course, while the remainder follow in-company training programmes only.
   Records show that of those who attend MBA courses, 60 per cent reach a senior management position within ten years, of those attending diploma courses the corresponding figure is 20 per cent and of the in-company-trained employees only 5 per cent achieve such positions within the same period.
   Using a tree diagram, state the probability that:
(a) a graduate recruit, selected at random, will be a senior manager within ten years.
(b) a senior manager, who has worked with the company for ten years, has an MBA as a result of the training programme.

6

Probability distributions

The essence of probability distributions in business

The previous chapter dealt with the probability of fairly simple events. However, many other problems may be complex in that they cannot be readily solved in the same way as those involving repetitive 'experiments' such as the inspection of components coming off an assembly line, tossing a coin, etc. For example, in trying to calculate the probability of a person having an accident while travelling by car, plane, boat, etc., it is not feasible to employ individuals to travel continually by these modes of transport in order to record how many of them are killed or injured as a result of an accident. Repetition of the experiment in the laboratory sense is clearly not feasible in this situation.

Fortunately, determining probabilities associated with complex events can be greatly simplified if we can construct a general, mathematical model which accurately describes the situation associated with a particular event in which we are interested. Such a model, used to obtain the probabilities of certain events occurring, is called a *probability distribution* (or probability function).

Probability distributions have defined mathematical properties and are widely used in drawing statistical inferences in business and other fields. Probability distributions, particularly those associated with complex events (such as the probability of being killed in a plane crash), can often be calculated on the basis of sample data drawn from populations (such as the *actual* records of plane crashes). Alternatively, it may be possible to calculate distributions *theoretically*: for example, it is easy to recognize that the model for the probability of obtaining n heads in n consecutive tosses of a coin is $(\frac{1}{2})^n$ (assuming of course that the coin is 'fair'). By their very nature, probability distributions are closely related to frequency distributions (discussed in Chapter 2). However, unlike frequency distributions in which the frequencies are simply the observed number of times an event *occurred*, in a probability distribution the frequency is derived from the probability of the event *occurring*.

Conveniently, in practice many different situations have been shown to have the same underlying structure and can thus be represented by the same probability distribution. This fact will be evident in our discussion of specific distributions and their applications. There are three well-known probability distributions that are suitable for a wide range of business applications. These are:

☐ The binomial distribution.
☐ The Poisson distribution.
☐ The normal distribution.

The first two of these are examples of *discrete* probability distributions while the last one is a *continuous* distribution. For a discrete variable (e.g. X) we can compute the probability of it taking on particular *discrete* values, e.g. $P(X = 5)$. Discrete variables are, as noted in Chapter 1, usually associated with the counting of events. A continuous variable, on the other hand, can take on any value within a range of values along a continuous scale. Continuous variables are usually associated with measurements. Since there are, in theory, an infinite number of values along any continuous scale, it is no longer possible to think in terms of the probability of the variable having a specific value; instead, it is necessary to think in terms of the probability that it lies within a specific range, e.g. $P(X$ falls within the range 12.50–13.30 mm). In these cases, X may be referred to as a discrete or continuous *random variable* respectively. A random variable simply provides a means of assigning numerical values to the possible values (or range of values) that X may take.

The binomial distribution

Many business situations give rise to the compilation of simple 'yes' or 'no'-type answers to particular questions. There are many obvious examples:

☐ In sampling the output of a production line, we could record, for each item coming off the line, whether it is or is not defective.

☐ A salesman may or may not succeed in obtaining an order.

☐ Consumer surveys may indicate whether or not people are likely to buy a product, etc.

In each case only *two* outcomes are possible. Statistical analyses of these types of situation may be referred to as *binomial experiments*, and the distributions of the results follow that of the *binomial distribution*. It is common practice to label the two possible outcomes in such situations as 'Success' (S) and 'Failure' (F), with the probability of obtaining the outcome 'Success' denoted by p and the outcome 'Failure' denoted by q. Thus, since the two outcomes are, by definition, mutually exclusive we have:

$$p + q = 1 \quad \text{or} \quad q = 1 - p$$

In a binomial experiment, we are interested in the *number of successes* (or failures) occurring in n independent trials (such as n items inspected on a production line, n people questioned in a consumer survey, etc.). Independent trials exist when the probability of a specific outcome on any trial is unaffected by the outcome of any other trial. If we let X represent the random variable of the number of successes occurring in n such trials, then X can take on any of the discrete values 0, 1, 2, . . ., n. The probabilities associated with each of the possible outcomes that X may take (i.e. $X = 1$, $X = 2$, . . . or $X = n$) will have a special frequency distribution, namely the binomial probability distribution.

For example, a quality inspector selects 5 components ($n = 5$) at random from a production line in order to test whether the machinery is functioning normally. It is known that when it is functioning normally, the probability of a component, selected at random, being defective is 0.05, i.e. $P(F) = q = 0.05$, and thus $P(S) = p = 0.95$. These probabilities are assumed to remain constant over all trials. A sample of 5 is equivalent to 5 trials in a binomial experiment because each trial results in success or failure. The inspector discovers that in his sample there are two defective components, i.e. S S S F F were recorded. Given this result, is the probability of it happening so unlikely that, since it has occurred, the company may need to consider some remedial action? The probability of this specific result occurring is given by:

$$P(S) \times P(S) \times P(S) \times P(F) \times P(F)$$
$$\downarrow \quad \downarrow \quad \downarrow \quad \downarrow \quad \downarrow$$
$$p \times p \times p \times q \times q$$

$$= p^3 q^2 = (0.95)^3 (0.05)^2$$

$$= 0.00214$$

Note that this follows directly from the multiplication rule of probability when events are independent, i.e. $P(S)$ is independent of $P(F)$. It should also be noted that, in notation form, $p^3 q^2$ is equivalent to $p^X q^{n-X}$. It will be appreciated, however, that this result is only *one* of *ten* possible sets of results containing two defective components. The ten possible sets are:

S	S	S	F	F
S	S	F	S	F
S	F	S	S	F
F	S	S	S	F
S	S	F	F	S
S	F	S	F	S
F	S	S	F	S
S	F	F	S	S
F	S	F	S	S
F	F	S	S	S

Note that we could readily have determined this number using the combination formula from Chapter 5, i.e.

$$C_X^n = \frac{n!}{X!(n-X)!} = \frac{5 \times 4 \times 3 \times 2 \times 1}{(3 \times 2 \times 1)(2 \times 1)} = 10$$

Hence, the total probability of obtaining 2 defective (and thus 3 acceptable) components is given by:

$$10 \times p^3 \times q^2 = 10 \times 0.00214$$

$$= 0.0214$$

In other words, our analysis indicates that there is roughly a 2 per cent chance of obtaining 2 defective components in a random sample of 5. Despite such a small probability, 2 defectives were nevertheless observed and hence the firm should stop the production line and carry out an investigation.

The above can be generalized to any such binomial-type situation. Given n trials and the probabilities of success and failure at each trial, p and q, the probability of obtaining X successes (or, equivalently, $n - X$ failures) is given by this binomial distribution formula:

$P(X \text{ successes}) = C_X^n (p^X)(q^{n-X})$

where $C_X^n = \dfrac{n!}{X!(n-X)!}$

In order to avoid the sometimes tedious task of calculating $P(X)$, especially when n is large, tables of binomial probabilities are available. For various values of n, X and p we can read off from such tables the values of $P(X)$ directly – see Appendix A1. For example, with 5 trials ($n = 5$) and $p = 0.35$, the probability of two successes is:

$$P(X = 2) = C_2^5 (0.35)^2 (0.65)^3$$

This can be read off directly from the tables as 0.3364 – without the need for tedious calculations!

Properties of the binomial distribution

Just as with frequency distributions, we can derive summary measures for probability distributions, namely the mean and variance. For the binomial distribution, calculating the values of these properties is very straightforward. They are given by the following expressions:

Mean $= np$

Variance $= npq$

The mean is defined here as the average number of successes (i.e. the mean of X) we can expect in a long sequence of repetitions of a binomial experiment. Likewise, the variance refers to the dispersion of X around its mean (see Chapter 3).

Example
A daily bus arrives late at a stop with a probability of 0.2 (i.e. $p = 0.2$). If X is the random variable denoting the number of late arrivals at the bus in any given 5-day working week, what is the mean and variance of X during any week?

Solution

Mean $= np = 5 \times 0.2 = 1$

Variance $= npq = 5 \times 0.2 \times 0.8 = 0.8$

Thus, in the long run, we can expect the bus to arrive late, on average, one day a week.

It should be appreciated that once we know the values of n and p, we can set up a frequency distribution table corresponding to the values of $P(X)$

for all possible values of X. This table can be drawn in the form of a histogram. Histograms corresponding to three different binomial distributions are shown in Figure 6.1. Note that since $p = 0.5$ in the case of (b) and (c), the distributions are symmetrical, unlike that in (a) which is skewed to the right.

The cumulative binomial distribution

Up to this point we have stressed that the binomial distribution is used to determine the probability of obtaining *precisely* X successes in n independent trials of an experiment. However, it may often arise that we need to calculate the probability that the number of successes is *less than or equal to* (or even *greater than or equal to*) some value, say k; that is, we may wish to determine

$P(X \leq k)$ or $P(X \, \varepsilon \, k)$

The solutions to such problems merely involve summing the binomial probabilities given in the binomial tables over the appropriate range of the values of X. For example, using the same data as above with $n = 5$, $p = 0.35$, the probability of X being less than or equal to 2, i.e. $P(X \leq 2)$, is given by:

$$P(X = 2) + P(X = 1) + P(X = 0) = 0.3364 + 0.3124 + 0.1160$$

$$= 0.7648$$

Alternatively, tables of *cumulative* binomial probabilities are available and, in addition, many statistical software packages also include appropriate routines (see the use of the MINITAB package later in this chapter).

The Poisson distribution

The *Poisson distribution* is another discrete probability distribution that was originally derived as a *limiting* form of the binomial distribution, in the sense that it acts as a good approximation for calculating binomial probabilities when the number of trials, n, is very large (and tends towards infinity) and when the probability of success at each trial, p, is very small (and tends towards zero). Calculation of probabilities in such situations using the binomial formula is extremely tedious. The use of the Poisson distribution, however, greatly facilitates computation as we shall see below.

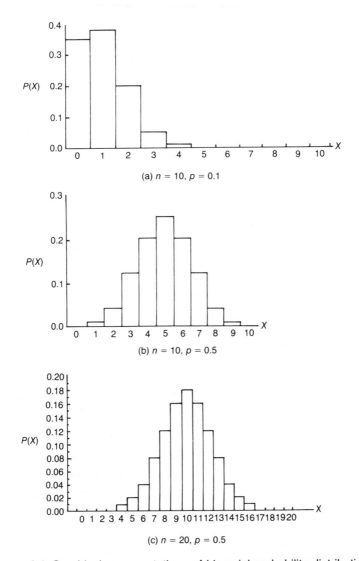

(a) $n = 10$, $p = 0.1$

(b) $n = 10$, $p = 0.5$

(c) $n = 20$, $p = 0.5$

Figure 6.1 Graphical representations of binomial probability distributions.

The Poisson distribution may also be regarded as an important distribution in its own right, with many practical applications in the business world and indeed, along with the normal and binomial, it is one of the most widely used distributions. For example, it is used in quality control analysis to assess the number of defective items, the number of machine breakdowns, etc., in a given interval of time. Likewise it is applicable to many situations relating to waiting time or queuing problems, such as the number of fax messages arriving through a fax machine in any single hour, the number of cars using a car wash in any hour, the number of delivery vans arriving at a depot for unloading, the number of customers passing through a check-out, etc. It is also widely applicable in situations involving the analysis of 'rare' events such as plane crashes, storm damage, etc., and consequently finds a special use in the insurance industry for calculating claim liability, etc.

As noted above, many Poisson-type problems come under the heading of 'waiting time' or 'queuing theory' problems. The attention is focused on the occurrence of relatively rare events because in most business situations in which the distribution applies it is easier (from a practical viewpoint) to observe the number of times such events occur than it is to observe the number of times such events *do not* occur. For example, a 'rare' event may be the discovery of a defective machine component coming off the end of a production run. It is obviously crucial to the firm to be able to assess the rate at which such rare events occur, and clearly it is easier to record the existence of a relatively small number of defective components than it is to record the existence of all non-defective components. In this situation, we can use the Poisson distribution to calculate, for example, the probability of 2 (or any specified number) of defective components being produced in any particular interval of space or time.

In general, if X is the random variable representing the number of rare events under investigation, then the probability of these X events occurring in some specified interval of time or space is given by the Poisson probability distribution, defined by the Poisson distribution formula:

$$P(X) = \frac{(e^{-\mu})\,\mu^X}{X!}$$

where μ is assumed to be constant and is the average number of occurrences of event X for the specified interval. The letter 'e' represents a mathematical constant and has the value of 2.7183 (to four decimal places).

For relatively small values of μ and X this expression can be quickly evaluated on a pocket calculator or computer, as in the first example below. For larger values, the problem of calculation becomes tedious. Consequently, sets of Poisson probability distribution tables are available which give the probability of X occurrences for a Poisson process with a given value of μ – see Appendix A2. The second example below illustrates the use of these tables.

Example
A building society branch manager notices that over a long period of time the number of people using an automated cash point on a Saturday morning

is, on average, 30 people per hour. What is the probability that in say a 10-minute period:

(a) nobody uses the machine?
(b) three people use the machine?

Solution
In order to apply the Poisson distribution formula, shown above, we first need to calculate the value of μ (the number of cash point users, on average, in any 10-minute period). Since we know 30 people on average use the machine in one hour, then μ (for a 10-minute period) = 30/6 = 5.

(a) $P(X = 0) = \dfrac{(e^{-5})5^0}{0!} = e^{-5} = 2.7183^{-5} = 0.0067$

(since 5^0 and $0!$ are both equal to 1).

(b) $P(X = 3) = \dfrac{(e^{-5})5^3}{3!} = 0.1404$

Example
In a production process an item is produced in large quantities and it is known that the proportion of defective items is 1 per cent (i.e. $p = 0.01$). A random sample of 1000 items is inspected. What is the probability that there are 15 defective items in this sample?

Solution
This is a good example of the use of the Poisson distribution as a limiting form of the binomial. As a binomial problem we would need to solve the following expression:

$P(X = 15) = C_X^n p^X q^{n-X}$

$$= \frac{1000!}{15!(1000 - 15)!}(0.01)^{15}(0.99)^{1000-15}$$

Clearly the calculation of this expression would be tedious in the extreme. But since n is relatively large and p is relatively small, the Poisson formula is appropriate:

$P(X) = \dfrac{(e^{-\mu})\mu^X}{X!}$

where $\mu = np = 1000 \times 0.01 = 10$

Thus $P(X = 15) = \dfrac{(2.7183^{-10})10^{15}}{15!}$

This expression is more readily solved than that using the binomial formula. Using a pocket calculator, the answer is 0.0347. Alternatively, the solution is given directly from the Poisson tables which give probabilities corresponding to given combinations of μ and X values. In this example, with $\mu = 10$ and $X = 15$, the tables (Appendix A2) show that $P(X = 15) = 0.0347$ as before.

Properties of the Poisson distribution

As with the binomial distribution, we can define the values of the summary measures, mean and variance, for the Poisson distribution. In this case, however, both of these summary measures are equal to μ. Thus:

Mean $= \mu$

Variance $= \mu$

Thus, once we know the value of μ, the Poisson distribution of X for values of X equal to or greater than 0 can be demonstrated in the form of a histogram (as we did earlier for the binomial). Three examples are shown in Figure 6.2 overleaf. Note that, as shown in this figure, the Poisson distribution is always skewed to the right, but the degree of skewness decreases as μ increases.

Cumulative Poisson distribution

It should be noted that, just as we can derive a cumulative binomial probability distribution, so too we can derive the *cumulative Poisson distribution* for calculating the probability that a random variable X is less than or equal to some value k. For example:

$$P(X \leq 3) = P(X = 3) + P(X = 2) + P(X = 1) + P(X = 0)$$

Each of the separate probabilities on the right-hand side can be computed separately as shown above using the Poisson formula or read directly from the Poisson probability tables noted above (Appendix A2). These probabilities can then be summed to give $P(X \leq 3)$. Tables are also readily available which give such cumulative Poisson probabilities.

With regard to the example above involving the number of customers using a cash point machine, we showed that with $\mu = 5$ the probability of *exactly* three people, on average, using the machine in any 10-minute period

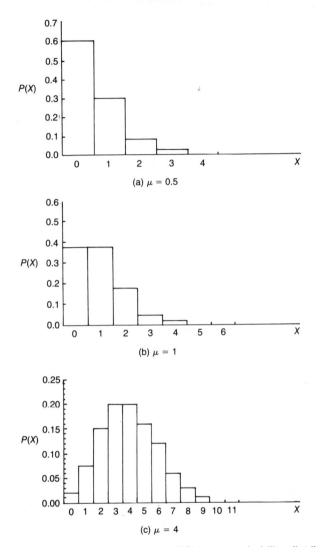

Figure 6.2 Graphical representations of Poisson probability distributions.

was 0.1404. By extension, the probability that *at most* three people will use it is given from the Poisson distribution tables as follows:

$$P(X \le 3) = P(X = 3) + P(X = 2) + P(X = 1) + P(X = 0)$$

$$\downarrow \qquad \downarrow \qquad \downarrow \qquad \downarrow$$

$$= \quad 0.1404 \ + \ 0.0842 \ + \ 0.0337 \ + \ 0.0067$$

$$= \quad 0.2650$$

Cumulative probability distribution tables would, of course, have given this answer directly without the need for computation.

The normal distribution

We turn now to the most important continuous probability distribution, which is without doubt the cornerstone of statistical inference and data analysis, namely the *normal* distribution. Its importance derives from the fact that it has been discovered that many kinds of data tend to follow a normal distribution. Examples are the frequency distributions of heights, weights, readings of instruments, deviations around established norms, etc. In addition, especially important is the fact that statisticians have been able to demonstrate that several important *sample* statistics (such as the mean) tend towards a normal distribution as the sample size increases. This remains so even if the population from which samples have been drawn is *not* normal. Even in the case of the discrete binomial distribution, as we allow the number of trials, n, to increase indefinitely, the distribution will tend towards a normal distribution. Because some distributions, including the binomial, are tedious to calculate even for moderately small values of n, this property of the normal distribution is commonly employed in business and in many other practical applications.

Properties of the normal distribution

The form, or shape, of a normal probability distribution is a symmetrical, bell-shaped curve as shown in Figure 6.3. The most important point, however, about the normal distribution is that it has precise mathematical properties and that these are the same for *all* normal distributions. More specifically, the properties are such that the proportion of all the observations of a normally distributed variable that fall within a range of n standard deviations on both sides of the mean is the same for *any* normal distribution. Thus, as shown in Figure 6.3:

☐ Approximately 68 per cent of all observations fall within the range of 1 standard deviation on both sides of the mean.

☐ Approximately 95 per cent of observations fall within the range of 2 standard deviations on both sides of the mean.

☐ Approximately 99.7 per cent of observations fall within the range of 3 standard deviations on both sides of the mean.

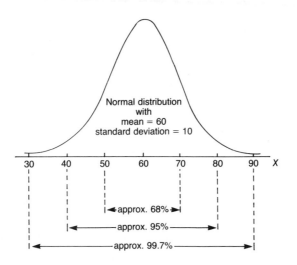

Figure 6.3 Properties of the normal distribution.

Hence, for a random variable X, from a population which is normally distributed with a mean, μ, of 60 and standard deviation, σ, of 10, the probability of any individual value, selected at random, falling within any range can be readily determined. With reference to Figure 6.3, for example:

$$P[(\mu - 1\sigma) \leq X \leq (\mu + 1\sigma)] = 0.68 \text{ (approximately)}$$

$$P[(\mu - 2\sigma) \leq X \leq (\mu + 2\sigma)] = 0.95 \text{ (approximately)}$$

$$P[(\mu - 3\sigma) \leq X \leq (\mu + 3\sigma)] = 0.997 \text{ (approximately)}$$

It will be noted that the range of $(\mu + 3\sigma)$ encompasses virtually all possible values of X, i.e. 99.7 per cent of all observations.

It should be appreciated that there are an infinite number of normal distributions differing according to the value of the mean, μ, and the standard deviation, σ. Some examples are shown in Figure 6.4(a) and (b). In (a) three distributions are given, each having the same standard deviation, but with different means. In (b) we have three distributions, each with the same mean, but different standard deviations.

Unlike the discrete binomial and Poisson distributions considered above, which in certain situations require the application of formulae to determine probabilities, the application of the normal distribution can be carried out without even any need for recourse to its underlying mathematical formula (thankfully, since the formula for the normal distribution is rather complex!).

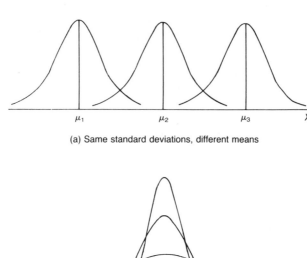

(a) Same standard deviations, different means

(b) Same means, different standard deviations

Figure 6.4 Normal curves for various values of μ and σ.

Instead, all probability calculations can be readily solved using a single table of probabilities for the *standard normal distribution*.

The standard normal distribution

Suppose we have a particular normal distribution for a random variable X with given μ and σ values and we wish to calculate the probability of X falling within the range X_1 to X_2. This is equivalent to finding the *area* under the corresponding normal curve between the values X_1 and X_2. We can read this area off directly from the *standard normal tables*. Before showing how to use these tables, however, we must first discuss their derivation.

The standard normal tables stem from the fact that any normal distribution can be transformed into one *standard* form. To do this, the variable X is expressed as a deviation from its mean μ and then divided by its standard deviation, i.e.:

$$\frac{X - \mu}{\sigma}$$

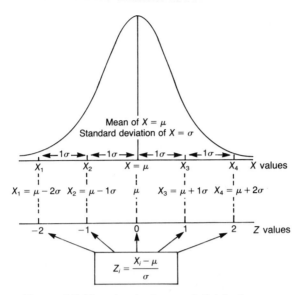

Figure 6.5 The standard normal distribution.

This transforms X into what is referred to as a *standard normal variable* denoted by the letter Z, that is:

$$Z = \frac{X - \mu}{\sigma}$$

where X is an observation
μ is the population mean
σ is the population standard deviation.

If further follows that Z must have a normal distribution with a mean of $0 (\mu = 0)$ and standard deviation of $1 (\sigma = 1)$, i.e. a *standard normal distribution*. These properties are illustrated in Figure 6.5 in which X values are tranformed into Z (standard normal) values. Since the distribution of Z is unique (in having a precise mean and standard deviation of 0 and 1 respectively), and virtually the entire distribution is encompassed within the range $\mu \pm 3\sigma$, a table corresponding to areas under the standard normal curve takes up only one page. This table is given in Appendix A3. Entries in the table are the areas which correspond to the probability of Z lying between 0 (the mean of Z) and Z_1; i.e. $P(0 \leq Z \leq Z_1)$, as shown in Figure 6.6. The total area under a standard normal curve is equal to 1.0.

From the above, we know that $P(0 \leq Z \leq Z_1)$ is equivalent to:

$$P\left(0 \leq \frac{X - \mu}{\sigma} \leq \frac{X_1 - \mu}{\sigma}\right)$$

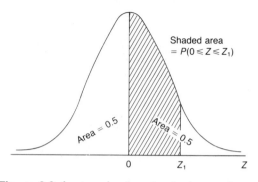

Figure 6.6 Area under the standard normal curve.

so that the shaded area in Figure 6.6 represents the probability that X will be within Z_1 standard deviations of its mean, or, given its standard deviation, σ, that X will be between X_1 and its mean, μ. If, for example, Z is 1.96, the appropriate area found from the table is 0.475, i.e. 47.5 per cent of the total area of 1.0. This means that the probability of a randomly selected X value falling within the range $(\mu + 1.96\sigma)$ is 0.475 (or 47.5 per cent). Note that the table only gives values for half of the distribution (since it is perfectly symmetrical around the mean). Thus, it is the case that the probability of X falling within the range $(\mu - 1.96\sigma)$ is also 0.475. Hence we can state that:

$$P[(\mu - 1.96\sigma) \leq X \leq (\mu + 1.96\sigma)] = 0.475 + 0.475 = 0.95$$

or, equivalently:

$$P[-1.96 \leq Z \leq +1.96] = 0.475 + 0.475 = 0.95$$

Naturally the tables give precise probabilities and hence we can now see that a probability of 95 per cent corresponds only approximately to $\mu \pm 2\sigma$ (as stated above). In addition, it follows that:

$$P(X > \mu + 1.96\sigma) = 0.025 = P(X < \mu - 1.96\sigma)$$

This is equivalent to:

$$P(Z > 1.96) = 0.025 = P(Z < -1.96)$$

These probabilities and associated areas are shown in Figure 6.7.

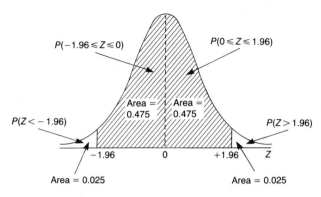

Figure 6.7 Area under the standard normal curve for $Z = \pm 1.96$.

Applications of the normal distribution

Applications of the normal distribution in business are numerous. Three examples are given below.

Example
The times taken for customers to pass through a supermarket check-out have been found to be normally distributed with a mean, μ, of 6 minutes and a standard deviation, σ, of 4 minutes. What is the probability that a customer (randomly surveyed) will require:

(a) between 6 and 10 minutes?
(b) more than 10 minutes?
(c) less than 5 minutes?
(d) between 5 and 10 minutes?

Solution
Figure 6.8 illustrates the problem showing the required probabilities in the form of the corresponding areas (a), (b), (c) and (d). From the standard normal table these probabilities are as follows:

(a) $P(6 \leq X \leq 10) = P\left(\dfrac{6-\mu}{\sigma} \leq Z \leq \dfrac{10-\mu}{\sigma}\right)$

$\qquad = P\left(\dfrac{6-6}{4} \leq Z \leq \dfrac{10-6}{4}\right)$

$\qquad = P(0 \leq Z \leq 1)$

$\qquad = 0.3413$

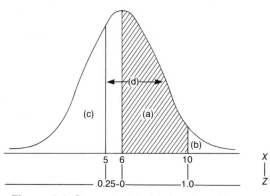

Figure 6.8 Supermarket check-out problem.

(b) $P(X > 10) = P\left(Z > \dfrac{10 - \mu}{\sigma}\right)$

$= P\left(Z > \dfrac{10 - 6}{4}\right)$

$= P(Z > 1)$

$= 0.5 - 0.3413$

$= 0.1587$

(c) $P(X < 5) = P\left(Z < \dfrac{5 - \mu}{\sigma}\right)$

$= P\left(Z < \dfrac{5 - 6}{4}\right)$

$= P(Z < -0.25)$

$= 0.5 - 0.0987$

$= 0.4013$

(d) $P(5 \le X \le 10) = P\left(\dfrac{5 - \mu}{\sigma} \le Z \le \dfrac{10 - \mu}{\sigma}\right)$

$= P\left(\dfrac{5 - 6}{4} \le Z \le \dfrac{10 - 6}{4}\right)$

$= P(-0.25 \le Z \le 1.0)$

$= 1 - (\text{area (b)} + \text{area (c)})$

$= 1 - (0.1587 + 0.4013)$

$= 0.44$

Example
Tests have indicated that the length of lives of television tubes is normally distributed with a mean life of 5.8 years and a standard deviation of 2.3 years. Suppose that a television manufacturer guarantees his tubes for 2 years, what proportion can he expect to replace before the guarantee expires?

Solution
If X denotes the guaranteed life (2 years), the problem is one of estimating $P(X<2)$. Transforming this into the standard normal variable, Z, we have:

$$P\left(Z<\frac{2-\mu}{\sigma}\right) = P\left(Z<\frac{2-5.8}{2.3}\right) = P(Z<-1.65)$$

From the standard normal table, this probability is $0.5-0.4505 = 0.0495$. That is, roughly 5 televisions out of every 100 sold will have to be returned. Figure 6.9 demonstrates this solution.

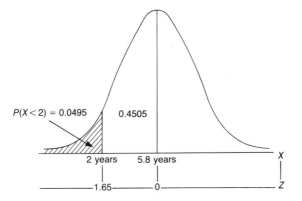

Figure 6.9 Television tube problem.

Example
A machine fills containers with a particular product. The standard deviation of filling weights is known from past data to be 0.6 kilos. If only 2 per cent of the containers hold less than 18 kilos, what is the mean filling weight for the machine, assuming that the filling weights are normally distributed?

Solution
Figure 6.10 sets out the problem diagrammatically. The solution is given

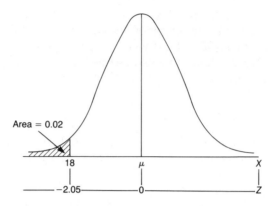

Figure 6.10 Filling of container problem.

from the expression for the value of Z that gives a probability of 0.02 in the left-hand tail of the figure, i.e.:

$$\text{for } X = 18, \ Z = \frac{18 - \mu}{\sigma} = \frac{18 - \mu}{0.6}$$

From the tables, the appropriate value of Z is -2.05. Therefore:

$$-2.05 = \frac{18 - \mu}{0.6}$$

i.e. $\mu = 18 + 2.05 \times 0.6 = 19.23$ kilos

Use of MINITAB

Three examples are included (Computer illustrations 6.1, 6.2 and 6.3) to illustrate the use of MINITAB to compute probabilities involving the three probability distributions considered in this chapter: the binomial, Poisson and normal distributions.

Computer illustration 6.1 MINITAB and the binomial probability distribution

```
MTB > PDF;   (Command to obtain individual, as opposed to cumulative,
             probabilities. The sub-command which follows defines the
             probability distribution, the sample size — number of
             trials — n, and the probability of a success, p).

SUBC> BINomial n=5 p=0.35.

   BINOMIAL WITH N =   5   P = 0.350000
      K              P( X = K)
      0                 0.1160
      1                 0.3124
      2                 0.3364
      3                 0.1811
      4                 0.0488
      5                 0.0053

MTB > CDF;   (Command to obtain cumulative probabilities.)
SUBC> BINomial n=5 p=0.35.

   BINOMIAL WITH N =   5   P = 0.350000
      K   P( X LESS OR = K)
      0                 0.1160
      1                 0.4284
      2                 0.7648
      3                 0.9460
      4                 0.9947
      5                 1.0000
```

Authors' note: Compare these results with those calculated earlier — pages 93 and 94.

Computer illustration 6.2   MINITAB and Poisson probability distribution

```
MTB > PDF;   (Command for individual probabilities — as before.)
SUBC> POISson 5.   (Specification of the distribution and the mean, μ.)

      POISSON WITH MEAN =    5.000
          K              P( X = K)
          0                0.0067  ◄───────  P(X = 0)
          1                0.0337
          2                0.0842
          3                0.1404  ◄───────  P(X = 3)
          4                0.1755
          5                0.1755
          6                0.1462
          7                0.1044
          8                0.0653
          9                0.0363
         10                0.0181
         11                0.0082
         12                0.0034
         13                0.0013
         14                0.0005
         15                0.0002
         16                0.0000
```

Note that this produces the distribution with $\mu = 5$ — compare with the distribution in Appendix A2.
Compare the results for $P(X = 0)$ and $P(X = 3)$ obtained earlier — page 97.

```
MTB > CDF;   (Command to obtain cumulative probabilities — as before.)
SUBC> POISson 5.

      POISSON WITH MEAN =    5.000
          K     P( X LESS OR = K)
          0                0.0067
          1                0.0404
          2                0.1247
          3                0.2650
          4                0.4405
          5                0.6160
          6                0.7622
          7                0.8666
          8                0.9319
          9                0.9682
         10                0.9863
         11                0.9945
         12                0.9980
         13                0.9993
         14                0.9998
         15                0.9999
         16                1.0000
```

Compare the result for $P(X \leqslant 3)$ obtained earlier — page 99.

Computer illustration 6.3 MINITAB and the normal probability distribution

In the example on pages 105–6 we had a normal distribution with a mean (μ) of 6 and standard deviation of 4; and the question involved values of the variable X of 5, 6 and 10. These values are entered into column 1.

```
MTB > NAME C1 'X'
MTB > SET C1
DATA> 5 6 10    (This sets the values of X in which we are interested into
                column 1.)
DATA> end
MTB > CDF for values in C1 put into C2;   (This calculates the probabilities
                                          — areas under the normal curve —
                                          for values of X less than or
                                          equal to those specified in column 1
                                          and puts the results in column 2.)

SUBC> NORMal mean = 6  standard deviation = 4.
MTB > PRINt C1 C2
```

ROW	X	C2
1	5	0.401294
2	6	0.500000
3	10	0.841345

Authors' note: Column 2 gives areas under the whole curve — not just half, as in Appendix A3.
Compare the results here with those obtained on pages 105–6. Using the results here the solutions are obtained as:
(a) 0.841345 - 0.5 $\approx$ 0.3413 (as before)
(b) 1.0 - 0.841345 $\approx$ 0.1587 (as before)
(c) 0.401294 $\approx$ 0.4013 (as before)
(d) 1.0 - (b) - (c) = 1.0 - 0.1587 - 0.4013 = 0.44.

Key learning points

Random variable   A numerical description of the outcome of an experiment (an *event*).

Event   The outcome of an experiment.

Experiment   Any process that generates well-defined outcomes.

Discrete random variable   A random variable that can assume only a finite or infinite sequence of values.

Continuous random variable   A random variable that may assume all values in an interval or collection of intervals.

Probability distribution   A description of how the probabilities are distributed over the values the random variable can take on.

Binomial experiment   A series of identical random trials in which each trial has only two possible mutually exclusive and complementary outcomes and in which all trial outcomes are statistically independent of one another.

Binomial probability distribution   A probability distribution showing the probability of X successes in n trials of a binomial experiment.

$$P(X \text{ successes}) = C_x^n (p^x)(q^{n-x})$$

$$\text{where } C_x^n = \frac{n!}{X!(n-X)!}$$

Properties of the binomial distribution

   Mean = np

   Variance = npq

Poisson probability distribution   A probability distribution showing the probability of X occurrences of an event over a specified interval of time or space.

$$P(X) = \frac{(e^{-\mu})\mu^x}{X!}$$

Properties of the Poisson distribution

   Mean = μ

   Variance = μ

Normal probability distribution   A continuous probability distribution whose form is a symmetrical, bell-shaped curve and is determined by the mean μ and standard deviation σ.

Standard normal distribution   The random variable Z following a normal distribution with a mean of 0 and a standard deviation of 1, where:

$$Z = \frac{X - \mu}{\sigma}$$

EXERCISES

Binomial distribution

1 The four engines of a commercial aircraft are designed so that they each operate independently. Tests, carried out over a long period of time, show that there is a one-in-a-hundred chance of in-flight failure of a single engine. What is the probability that on a given flight:
(a) no failures occur?

(b) no more than one failure occurs?

(c) no more than two failures occur?

2 Suppose a salesman is successful in obtaining an order in one out of every five calls he makes. In a normal working week he contacts 25 firms.

(a) What is the expected number of sales for the week?

(b) What is the variance of the number of sales for the week?

3 Using the table of binomial probabilities, determine:

(a) $P(X = 5)$ given that $n = 12$, $p = 0.30$.

(b) $P(X \leq 3)$ given that $n = 8$, $p = 0.40$.

(c) $P(X > 4)$ given that $n = 6$, $p = 0.50$.

(d) $P(X \geq 1)$ given that $n = 5$, $p = 0.50$.

4 Large consignments of components are inspected for defectives by means of a sampling system. Ten components are examined and the lot is to be rejected if two or more are found to be defective. If a consignment contains exactly 5 per cent defectives, what is the probability that the consignment is:

(a) accepted?

(b) rejected?

Poisson distribution

5 In a study of business activity at a restaurant, it is found that the average number of customers arriving between 10 p.m. and 11 p.m. on Monday night is 5. Using a Poisson distribution, answer the following:

(a) What is the probability that only 1 or 2 customers will arrive between 10 p.m. and 11 p.m. on any Monday night?

(b) What is the probability that exactly 5 customers will arrive?

(c) What is the probability that more than 8 customers will arrive?

(d) What are the mean and standard deviations of this probability distribution?

6 On the basis of past records for road accidents, a car insurance company estimates that the probability of a student policy-holder having a car accident during a one-year period is 0.03. If 300 student policy-holders are selected at random, calculate the probability that four or fewer had car accidents during the past year. Note that this problem can be solved using the binomial distribution but it would be very tedious; fortunately, the Poisson distribution provides a close approximation when n is large ($n \geq 20$) and when p is relatively small ($p \leq 0.05$).

7 A local authority is concerned about the number of traffic accidents which occur at the intersection of two main roads. Records kept by the authority over a period of several years show that, on average, five accidents occur at the intersection per month. Calculate the probability that in any given month,

(a) three or more accidents occur;

(b) three or fewer accidents occur.

Normal distribution

8 Find the area under the normal curve for each of the following:
  (a) $P(0<Z<1.5)$.
  (b) $P(1<Z<2)$.
  (c) $P(-1<Z<3)$.
  (d) $P(Z>1)$.
  (e) $P(-1<Z<+1)$.
  (f) $P(-1.5<Z<1.5)$.

9 The weekly wages of employees are normally distributed about a mean of £100 with a standard deviation of £10. Find the probability of an employee having a weekly wage lying:
  (a) between £95 and £130.
  (b) over £112.50.
  (c) under £80.
  (d) What is the minimum weekly wage received by the top 20 per cent of earners?

10 Lengths of metal rods produced by a manufacturing process are distributed normally with a mean of 31.6 cm and a standard deviation of 0.45 cm.
  (a) What is the probability that a randomly selected metal rod measures between 31.5 and 32.5 cm long?
  (b) Give the length of a metal rod such that the probability of a rod exceeding this length is 0.75.

11 The time required to assemble a particular machine is normally distributed, with a mean of 80 minutes and a standard deviation of 10 minutes.
  (a) What is the probability of someone assembling a machine in 1 hour or less?
  (b) What is the probability of someone assembling a machine in more than 60 minutes but less than 75 minutes?
  (c) If 60 workers are employed to assemble the machines and are required to do so within a maximum of 90 minutes, how many workers will be unable to complete the assembly in the allotted time?

12 A canned food manufacturer uses a machine to fill cans whose contents are supposed to weigh 16 oz. The standard deviation in weights produced by the machine is 0.3 oz. If the contents of cans weigh less than 15.2 oz, these cans are regarded as underweight and the firm is liable to prosecution. To what should the mean filling weight be set such that there is a maximum of 5 per cent chance of a can weighing less than the legal minimum of 15.2 oz?

7

Using samples to make estimates

The essence of statistical inference and estimation in business

In this chapter we are concerned with the problem of drawing inferences about a population parameter (such as the population mean) on the basis of information about samples drawn from the population (sample statistics). It is frequently too costly, or impracticable, to collect information for the whole population, i.e. to conduct a census. For example, in business, quality control checks may involve destructive testing – every component produced cannot therefore be tested to destruction! Likewise, it would be impractical to measure, for example, the diameter of every single ball-bearing produced to check for precision.

In practice, two kinds of issue need to be addressed:

☐ Estimating values of (unknown) population parameters.
☐ Testing hypotheses about the values of the population parameters.

This chapter is concerned with the concepts and principles which underlie the procedures involved in drawing inferences in these two areas. It also shows how the principles are applied to the estimation of the two most important population parameters, i.e. the population mean and variance (the subject of hypothesis testing is left to the next chapter).

As an example of statistical estimation and inference consider the problem of a bicycle manufacturer who, let us say, buys in ball-bearings from a number of different suppliers. The diameters of the ball-bearings and associated tolerance levels are of critical importance in his own manufacturing process and he wishes to estimate the reliability of different suppliers in meeting his specification. Samples are tested from each supplier to estimate the mean and variation of diameters of all ball-bearings supplied by each. But naturally, samples are, by definition, only part of the total production of each supplier, and consequently sample statistics are only *estimates* of the corresponding *true* population parameters for each supplier. Two questions now arise, therefore:

□ How reliable are these estimates based on sample statistics?

□ Can we assign degrees of confidence to these statistics as reliable estimates of the true population parameters?

To address such questions, we first need to develop the underlying statistical principles. An essential prerequisite is that any sample must be selected in such a way as to be representative of the population from which it has been drawn. Various sampling techniques may be employed but a detailed consideration of these is not necessary to the understanding of the central principles involved in making statistical inferences. The fundamental consideration is that any sample should be a *random* sample, i.e. every 'member' of the population should have an equal chance of being selected.

It should be appreciated, however, that a representative sample does not mean that it is an exact replica, in miniature, of the population from which it is drawn. It is impossible to ensure this, and, as a consequence, sample statistics are unlikely to correspond with the true values of the population parameters. We say, therefore, that the results are subject to *sampling error*. In this situation the next best thing to the unattainable 'ideal' sample is one which allows the size of the sampling error to be predicted. To do this, it is necessary to consider the concept of *sampling distributions*.

The subject of sampling and statistical inference is of the utmost importance to a wide range of business applications, but, as is implied by the discussion of the problems above, it is a complex one! Before launching into the subject, it will be helpful to stand back and gain a bird's eye view of the whole topic and the questions that must be addressed at various stages. This is shown in two schematic diagrams (Figures 7.1 and 7.2). Figure 7.1 gives an overview of the structure of the chapter. The bulk of the chapter – referred to as the 'analytical core' – is concerned with the solution to the central problem of estimating population parameters on the basis of sample information and making probability statements about the reliability of these estimates. Figure 7.2 sets out in more detail the structure of the 'analytical core' and is intended to show how each element fits into the whole.

Based on the schematic diagrams (Figures 7.1 and 7.2), the chapter is structured as follows:

□ The concept of sampling distributions.

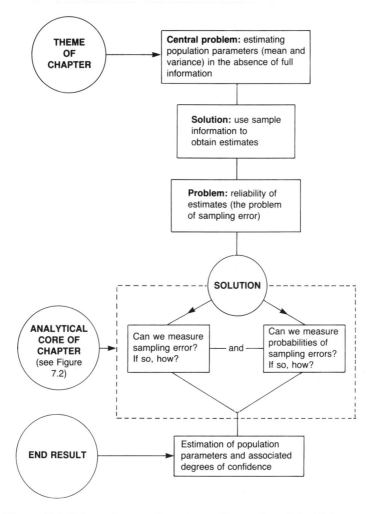

Figure 7.1 Schematic overview of sampling and statistical inference.

☐ The relationship between sample statistics and population parameters.

☐ Point estimation of the population mean.

☐ The size and measurement of the standard error of the mean.

☐ Probability of error.

☐ Determination of confidence limits for the population estimates.

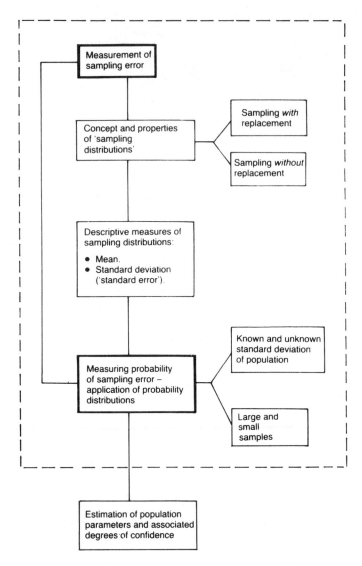

Figure 7.2 Analytical core of the chapter.

Sampling distributions

Consider a population and the samples, each of size n, that may be drawn from this population. There would generally be a large number of such samples and the value of a statistic, such as the arithmetic mean, computed for each sample will vary from one sample to another. The frequency distribution of all such sample statistics is an example of a *sampling distribution*.

To illustrate the concept of a sampling distribution, let us assume that a population (albeit a small one) consists of four elements: X_1, X_2, X_3, X_4 with the following values:

$$X_1 = 1, \ X_2 = 2, \ X_3 = 3, \ X_4 = 4$$

Consider *all* the samples of a given size n (e.g. $n = 2$) that could be drawn from this population. These will depend on whether any one element of the population, once selected, can or cannot be selected again in the same sample, i.e. whether one is sampling with or without replacement. This gives rise to two sampling distributions, as shown in Table 7.1, which are the frequency distributions of all possible sample means in both cases, i.e. sampling distributions of means. It should be noted that sampling with replacement gives rise to 16 possible sample combinations (i.e. each element could be drawn with any one of the other three elements as well as with itself – so the total number of possible samples is 4×4). Without replacement, the total number of samples is 6 – the number of combinations of 2 from 4 (C_2^4).

Relationship between sample statistics and population parameters

Having defined the idea of a sampling distribution above, the next important step is to examine the relationship between the statistics generated by a process of random sampling and the corresponding population parameters. Recall that the purpose of sampling is to draw inferences about a population parameter on the basis of sample information. We concentrate here on the mean, rather than any other statistic, because estimation of the population mean is probably the most frequent objective of sampling.

Now consider how the values of the possible sample means generated in the example above (Table 7.1) compare with the value of the population mean. The population mean is as follows:

$$\mu = \frac{1 + 2 + 3 + 4}{4} = \frac{10}{4} = 2.5$$

Note that the sample means are symmetrically distributed around the value of 2.5 as shown in Table 7.1(c). Thus the probability of obtaining a value

Table 7.1 All possible samples and sample means with sample size $n = 2$ from a population of four values (1, 2, 3, 4)

SAMPLING WITH REPLACEMENT 16 samples				SAMPLING WITHOUT REPLACEMENT 6 samples		

(a) ALL POSSIBLE SAMPLES

1,1	2,1	3,1	4,1	1,2	2,3	3,4
1,2	2,2	3,2	4,2	1,3	2,4	
1,3	2,3	3,3	4,3	1,4		
1,4	2,4	3,4	4,4			

(b) ALL POSSIBLE SAMPLE MEANS

1.0	1.5	2.0	2.5	1.5	2.5	3.5
1.5	2.0	2.5	3.0	2.0	3.0	
2.0	2.5	3.0	3.5	2.5		
2.5	3.0	3.5	4.0			

(c) SUMMARY: THE SAMPLING DISTRIBUTION OF THE MEAN

Sample mean $\bar{X}$	Number of samples f	Probability of occurrence $f/\Sigma f$	Sample mean $\bar{X}$	Number of samples f	Probability of occurrence $f/\Sigma f$
1.0	1	1/16	1.5	1	1/6
1.5	2	2/16	2.0	1	1/6
2.0	3	3/16	2.5	2	2/6
2.5	4	4/16	3.0	1	1/6
3.0	3	3/16	3.5	1	1/6
3.5	2	2/16			
4.0	1	1/16			
Total	16	1.0	Total	6	1.0

(d) MEAN AND VARIANCE OF SAMPLE MEANS $(\mu_{\bar{X}}, \sigma^2_{\bar{X}})$

$\mu_{\bar{X}} = 2.5, \quad \sigma^2_{\bar{X}} = 0.625$ $\mu_{\bar{X}} = 2.5, \quad \sigma^2_{\bar{X}} = 0.417$

for the mean from a sample selected at random that is less than the true population mean is exactly equal to the probability of obtaining a value that is greater than the true population mean. Note also that, given the symmetry of the sampling distributions of the mean around the true population mean, the mean of the sampling distributions of means, i.e. the mean of all the means $(\mu_{\bar{X}})$ in both cases is equal to the population mean, μ. That is:

$$\mu_{\bar{X}} = \mu$$

This is an important property of the sampling distribution of the mean. The other main descriptive statistic, variance (or standard deviation) also needs to be considered in this way but we will return to this later.

We are now in a position to begin to consider one of the main topics in statistical inference, namely estimation in which sample information is used to estimate the population mean, μ.

Point estimation of the population mean

It should be clear from our analysis up to this point that a sample mean derived from a process of random sampling provides a good estimator of the population mean in the sense that it is one that is near to the true population mean. More important, we have shown that the sample means in the sampling distribution of means cluster symmetrically around the true population mean, i.e. $\mu_{\bar{X}} = \mu$. A single sample mean, therefore, may also be regarded as a good estimator in the sense that it provides an unbiased estimate of the population mean. The probability of a sample mean selected at random exceeding μ by certain amounts is *exactly equal to the probability of it being below* μ by the same amounts.

We can say, therefore, that: $\hat{\mu}$ (pronounced 'mu hat') = $\bar{X}$, where the hat (^) on μ indicates that it is an estimate of μ, the unknown population parameter. Thus the sample mean ($\bar{X}$) may be used as an *estimator* – an unbiased estimator – of the population mean, μ.

Since the value of the estimator, $\bar{X}$, computed from a single sample is a single value, we refer to it as a *point estimate* of the unknown population mean because it represents a single point on the scale of possible values.

Example
Suppose we wish to know the average weekly earnings of all part-time workers. It is impracticable to collect information for all such workers and therefore the population mean μ – a fixed parameter – can only be estimated. The mean of a random sample of, say, 300 such workers gives a value $\bar{X}$ of £56. This value gives our best single estimate, i.e. our *point estimate*, of the unknown parameter μ. Thus we may write:

$\hat{\mu}$ = £56.

Obviously, although $\bar{X}$ provides a good estimate of μ, there will often be a discrepancy between $\bar{X}$ and μ. In other words, an *error* may be involved in using $\bar{X}$ to estimate μ. It is naturally useful to know the size of the possible errors and their probability of occurrence, and so it is to this topic that we now turn.

The size and measurement of the standard error of the mean

It is a further important property of sampling distributions of the mean that as sample size is increased, the sample means cluster more and more around the true population mean. Thus the variance and standard deviation of the sampling distribution decline as sample size is increased. This standard deviation is formally referred to as the *standard error* of the mean ($\sigma_{\bar{X}}$). This is defined as:

$$\sigma_{\bar{X}} = \frac{\sigma}{\sqrt{n}}$$

where σ is the population standard deviation and n is the sample size.

Note, therefore, that the standard error declines as the sample size is increased, but not proportionately – it declines according to $\sqrt{n}$, not n. When sampling is *without replacement*, from a *finite* population, this expression should be modified to the following:

$$\sigma_{\bar{X}} = \frac{\sigma}{\sqrt{n}} \sqrt{\frac{N-n}{N-1}}$$

where N is the population size and n the sample size. The expression $\sqrt{N-n)/(N-1)}$ is referred to as the *finite population correction (fpc)* factor. However, in practice, when sampling is carried out without replacement it is often from *large* populations (N) of which the sample size (n) is a small fraction, so that the fpc factor shown is not significantly different from unity, and can thus be ignored. A rule of thumb regarding the use of the fpc factor is that if sample size is less than 5 per cent of the population size, i.e. $n < 0.05\,N$, then it can be ignored.

Recapitulation

We have now reached a point where the relationship between the characteristics of the sampling distribution of means and the population from which this distribution is derived has been made plain. We have shown that:

1. the mean of the sampling distribution of means $\mu_{\bar{X}} = \mu$ and thus $\bar{X}$ provides an unbiased point estimate of μ, and

2. the standard error of the mean, $\sigma_{\bar{X}} = \dfrac{\sigma}{\sqrt{n}}$

These are important results and they mark an important stage in the explanation of the principles of sampling theory, but it is a first stage only. Recall that our objective is not only to estimate a population mean on the basis of information from a single sample, but to say something too about the size of error that may attach to our estimate and its probability of occurrence. At this stage, however, we have made only limited progress towards this objective. Firstly, although we have shown how to obtain a measure of the error due to sampling – the standard error – it has depended on our knowing either the sampling distribution (as opposed to a single sample) or the standard deviation of the population. Normally neither of these will be known. Secondly, the probability of occurrence of these errors has again only been made plain through a knowledge of the sampling distribution obtained by actually generating the whole distribution. To make further progress it is necessary to consider how the probability of error can be measured without generating whole sampling distributions and how the error itself may be measured on the basis of information from a single sample. We consider these two things in the next section. Having done so, we will then be in a position to estimate the population mean on the basis of sample information and to attach to that estimate a probability statement about the likelihood of error.

The probability of error

To consider this question it is instructive to compare the shapes of sampling distributions with those of the populations from which they are drawn. Several examples are shown in Figure 7.3 below. It will be seen that the sampling distribution of means drawn from any population regardless of its shape (i.e. whether it is symmetrical or not) rapidly assumes a symmetrical and increasingly bell-shaped form as the sample size increases. In addition, the size of the standard error, $\sigma_{\bar{X}}$, declines as the sample size is increased.

With regard to measuring the probability of an error of a given size occurring, the important point of the analysis here is that it has been found that as long as relatively large samples are taken, the sampling distribution closely approximates to the normal distribution even if the distribution of the parent population itself is not normal. This property of sampling distributions based on large samples from non-normal distributions is referred to as the *Central Limit Theorem*. Consequently, knowledge of the properties of the normal probability distribution, considered in Chapter 6, may be applied to measuring the probability of error due to sampling. For this reason, the normal distribution is the most important of all probability distributions. Strictly speaking the Central Limit Theorem is only true as

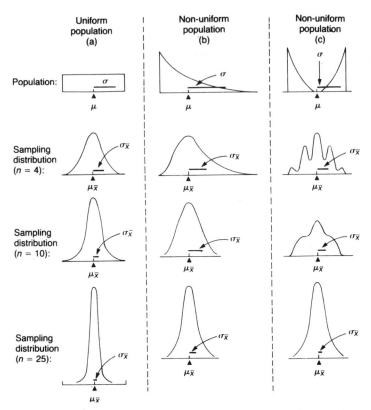

Figure 7.3 Sampling distributions of means drawn from uniform and non-uniform populations (Source: L. J. Tashman and K. R. Lamborn, *The Ways and Means of Statistics*, Harcourt Brace Jovanovich: New York, 1979).

n approaches infinity, but in practice the distribution of $\overline{X}$ approaches a normal distribution very rapidly and becomes very close to it indeed for samples as small as 30. Thus the term 'large sample' is generally taken as being a sample size of 30 or more.

In cases where the parent population is itself normal then the sampling distribution is normal for samples of *any* size. These results of sampling from normal and non-normal populations provide theorems that constitute cornerstones of statistical inference. We therefore restate them formally here.

Sampling from a normal population:

If the population distribution is normal then the distribution of the sample mean is also normal with a mean $\mu_{\overline{x}}$ equal to the population mean μ and a variance of $\sigma_{\overline{X}}^2$ equal to the variance of the population divided by the sample size, i.e. σ^2/n.

Sampling from a non-normal population: Central Limit Theorem:

Where the parent population is not normally distributed, the distribution of the sample mean approaches a normal distribution with a mean of μ and a variance of σ^2/n, as above, as the sample size n becomes large. This is known as the Central Limit Theorem.

Measuring the probability of error: application of the Central Limit Theorem

Example
From past experience it is known that the standard deviation of the numbers of days of absence per worker per year in an industry is 15 days. What is the probability that a random sample of 100 workers will yield a mean value that differs from the true population value by more than 3 days?

Solution
The sample of 100 is well above 30 and can therefore be regarded as large. Consequently the sampling distribution of the sample mean can be regarded as being very close to normal regardless of the distribution of the population by virtue of the Central Limit Theorem. We know that the mean of the sampling distribution will be equal to the population mean μ and that its standard deviation $(\sigma_{\bar{X}})$ is equal to $\sigma/\sqrt{n}$. What we want to measure is the probability of obtaining a sample mean which lies below $\mu - 3$ or above $\mu + 3$. In other words we want to measure the two shaded tail areas in Figure 7.4, which shows the distribution of the sample mean. To do this we first have to convert the two values into standard normal variables (Z) as follows:

$$\frac{(\mu - 3) - \mu}{\sigma_{\bar{X}}} = \frac{-3}{15/\sqrt{100}}$$

$$= \frac{-3}{1.5}$$

$$= -2$$

$$\frac{(\mu + 3) - \mu}{\sigma_{\bar{X}}} = \frac{+3}{15/\sqrt{100}}$$

$$= \frac{+3}{1.5}$$

$$= +2$$

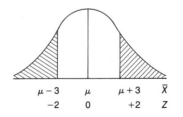

Figure 7.4 Distribution of the sample mean of absenteeism.

The table of areas under the standard normal curve (Appendix A3) shows that the area to the right of $+2$ is $0.5 - 0.4772 = 0.0228$. Correspondingly, because of the symmetry of the normal curve, the area in the other tail, i.e. to the left of -2, is also 0.0228. Thus the total area in the tails is $2(0.0228) = 0.0456$. This measures the required probability – just under 5 per cent.

We are now in a position to consider the second major topic in the estimation of population parameters on the basis of sample information, namely *interval estimation* as opposed to *point estimation* discussed above. This is shown below with regard to the population mean μ.

Interval estimation of the population mean μ

With point estimation the sample mean is taken as an estimate of the unknown population mean. Provided that the sample is obtained at random, we know that the sample mean provides a good estimator, but it is, of course, unlikely that it will be exactly equal to the unknown population parameter. We know that it will be subject to sampling error and thus give an estimate which may be too high or too low. Interval estimation uses the principles we have established in this chapter to define an interval within which we can state, with a given level of probability, that the true mean will lie. The probability that a specified interval contains the unknown population parameter is called *confidence*. The interval itself is called a *confidence interval* or simply an *interval estimate* and takes the following form:

$$\underline{\bar{\mu}} = \bar{X} \pm \text{a sampling error}$$

where the bars above and below μ are used to denote a confidence interval for μ.

The actual allowance for sampling error is computed by taking an appropriate number of standard errors according to how confident we wish to be that our interval estimate will in fact include the true population value μ. It is common to choose a 95 per cent confidence level, that is to say, an interval such that there is a 95 per cent chance that it will contain the population parameter. Given that the sampling distribution of $\bar{X}$ is normally distributed, we may obtain the confidence level of 95 per cent by taking the smallest range of $\bar{X}$ under the normal distribution that just encloses 95 per cent of the area. This we know is that middle section which leaves exactly 2½ per cent of the area excluded in each tail. From the table of areas under the normal curve we know that we need to measure 1.96 standard

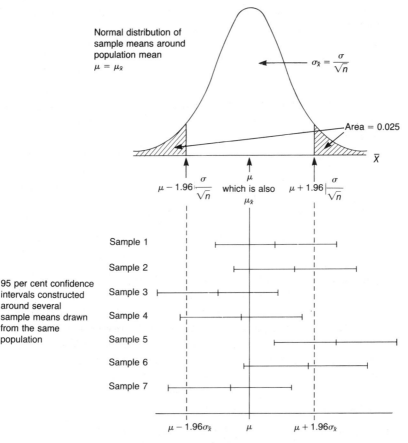

Figure 7.5 Interval estimation of the population mean.

deviations (in this case, standard errors) of $\bar{X}$ on either side of the mean (see Chapter 6).

Thus the following interval:

$$\underline{\bar{\mu}} = \bar{X} \pm a \text{ sampling error}$$

will encompass 95 per cent of all the possible means in the sampling distribution. This is illustrated at the top of Figure 7.5. It follows that a similar interval (i.e. $\pm 1.96\sigma_{\bar{x}}$) constructed around any single sample mean $\bar{X}$ that falls within the range defined by the two vertical broken lines in Figure 7.5, must also enclose the unknown population mean μ. There is only a 5 per cent chance that a sample mean would lie outside this range. Thus a 95 per cent confidence interval for the population mean is defined as:

$$\underline{\mu} = \bar{X} \pm 1.96\sigma_{\bar{X}} \quad \text{i.e. } \bar{X} \pm 1.96\frac{\sigma}{\sqrt{n}}$$

This is illustrated in the bottom half of Figure 7.5. Notice that confidence intervals for the first four and last two samples illustrated do encompass μ but Sample 5 is an example where this is not so. Normally, of course, we would only have one sample and thus only one confidence interval. We repeat, for emphasis, that given large samples, so that the Central Limit Theorem applies, or alternatively, sampling from a population which is itself known to be normal, the probability that a confidence interval constructed as above would fail to include the true population mean is only 5 per cent.

Levels of confidence

Levels of confidence may be set as desired simply by substituting appropriate values of the standard normal variable Z. More generally, the desired level of confidence may be denoted as $100(1 - \alpha)$ per cent, where α is the sum of the two areas in the tails of the normal distribution. Thus, for 95 per cent confidence, $\alpha = 0.05$ and the area in each tail is given by $\alpha/2$ (i.e. 0.025). The general expression for a confidence interval $(\underline{\mu})$ using Z values is:

$$\underline{\mu} = \bar{X} \pm Z_{\alpha/2}\sigma_{\bar{X}}$$

where α denotes the desired level of confidence.
$Z_{\alpha/2}$ denotes the value of Z which cuts off an area of $\alpha/2$ in the top and bottom tails of the distribution.

The most common confidence levels after 95 per cent are 90 per cent and 99 per cent. Obviously the higher the degree of confidence required, the wider the confidence interval. The values of Z that correspond to these levels of confidence are given in Table 7.2.

Table 7.2 Levels of confidence

Required level of confidence	Value of α	Value of $Z_{\alpha/2}$	Area in the interval $\mu \pm Z_{\alpha/2}\sigma_{\bar{X}}$
90 per cent	0.10	1.65	0.90
95 per cent	0.05	1.96	0.95
99 per cent	0.01	2.58	0.99

Example
It is known that the standard deviation, σ, for the days of absence per worker per year in an industry is 11 days. Construct 95 per cent and 99 per cent confidence intervals for the population mean given that a random sample of 100 workers gives a mean of 8 days' absence.

Solution

$$\underline{\mu} = \bar{X} \pm Z_{\alpha/2} \left(\frac{\sigma}{\sqrt{n}} \right)$$

95 per cent confidence interval:

$$\underline{\mu} = 8 \pm 1.96 \left(\frac{11}{\sqrt{100}} \right) = 8 \pm 1.96(1.1)$$

$$= 5.844 \text{ to } 10.156$$

99 per cent confidence interval:

$$\underline{\mu} = 8 \pm 2.58 \left(\frac{11}{\sqrt{100}} \right) = 8 \pm 2.58(1.1)$$

$$= 5.162 \text{ to } 10.838$$

Confidence limits
The two values that together define a confidence interval are known as *confidence limits* – a *lower* confidence limit and an *upper* confidence limit. Thus, in the example above, the lower limit of the 99 per cent interval is 5.162 and the upper limit is 10.838.

The measurement of the standard error of the mean when σ is unknown

The principles we have set out above have been stated on the basis of a known value for σ, the standard deviation of the population. However, this will not usually be known and, consequently, it has to be estimated. The only information normally available comes from the sample. We know that a sample mean $\bar{X}$ is an unbiased estimator of the population mean μ. But the sample standard deviation (denoted s) is an unbiased estimator of the population standard deviation, σ, only when it is calculated with a denominator of $(n-1)$ rather than n, i.e.:

$$s = \sqrt{\frac{\Sigma(X_i - \bar{X})^2}{n-1}} = \textbf{unbiased estimator of } \boldsymbol{\sigma} \textbf{ (denoted } \hat{\sigma})$$

It will be recalled from Chapter 3 that this is how a sample standard deviation was defined.

Measuring the probability of error with σ unknown

Having shown that when σ is unknown it may be estimated by using an adjusted value of s, the final question is whether or not the normal distribution can continue to be used for measuring the probability of error as before. Unfortunately, the answer is no: a different distribution, known as the *t distribution*, has to be used instead. The reason for this, and the form of the t distribution itself, is explained below. It is sufficient to note here that for large sample sizes of around 30 or more the t distribution is very close to normal and that for practical purposes the sampling distribution can be regarded as normal. Thus the procedure for making interval estimates of the population mean, μ, remains the same as before, provided that an unbiased estimate of $\sigma_{\bar{X}}$ is made in the way described above. It will be appreciated, therefore, that the t distribution is particularly important in the case of small samples. This topic is dealt with in the next section.

Sampling and the t distribution

We explained above the circumstances in which the form of the sampling distribution of the mean can be described as normal and how each sampling distribution can be transformed into the standard normal distribution through the transformation:

$$Z = \frac{\bar{X} - \mu}{\sigma_{\bar{X}}}$$

When σ is known, $\sigma_{\bar{X}}$ is measured by $\sigma/\sqrt{n}$ and is constant, therefore, for any one sampling distribution (it will vary only as sample size varies). However,, with σ unknown and, therefore, $\sigma_{\bar{X}}$ having to be replaced by $\sigma_{\bar{X}}$ (*which is estimated by* $s/\sqrt{n}$), the denominator of the expression for Z does not remain constant, but will vary according to each sample standard deviation s. Consequently, the transformation $(\bar{X} - \mu)/\hat{\sigma}_{\bar{X}}$ does not result in the standard normal variable Z. In fact it results in a distribution which is more spread out than the normal distribution because s tends to understate σ. This distribution is known as the *t distribution* or sometimes 'Student's t distribution', where a t statistic is defined, by direct analogy with Z, as follows:

$$t = \frac{\bar{X} - \mu}{\hat{\sigma}_{\bar{X}}}$$

where $\hat{\sigma}_{\bar{X}} = \dfrac{s}{\sqrt{n}}$

Note again that the only difference with Z is in the denominator. Both statistics, Z and t, express deviations of a sample mean from a population mean in terms of the standard error of the mean but in one case the error is known, and in the other case it is estimated.

This deviation can be expressed in terms of probability by reference to the appropriate sampling distribution. For the Z statistic the normal distribution provides the appropriate model; for the t statistic there is not one distribution but a whole family of distributions which vary according to sample size – or, more precisely, the number of so-called *degrees of freedom* *(df)*.

The number of degrees of freedom is given by $(n - 1)$ where n is the sample size. This concept is used in many areas of statistical analysis. Essentially, the number of degrees of freedom indicates the number of values that are free to vary in a random sample of a given size. In general, the number of degrees of freedom lost is equal to the number of population parameters estimated as the basis for a statistical inference procedure. For example, if s (the sample standard deviation) is used to estimate σ (the population standard deviation), because σ is unknown, one degree of freedom is lost. This is because, in calculating s, one population parameter (μ) is estimated using $\bar{X}$ (the sample mean). Thus df is $n - 1$ and

$$s = \sqrt{\dfrac{\Sigma(X_i - \bar{X})^2}{n - 1}}$$

We also explained earlier that in large samples $(n \geq 30)$ the t distribution becomes so similar to the normal distribution that we tend to use the normal distribution for convenience. Consequently, it is only in the context of small samples $(n < 30)$ that use of the t distribution becomes important. For this reason t is sometimes referred to as a *small-sample statistic*.

Finally, we emphasize that t distributions are derived for populations which are *normally* distributed. For other populations the use of t as a measure of probability becomes unreliable, particularly if they depart markedly from normality and the sample size is very small (say, less than 15). So, in the case of small samples drawn from a markedly skewed (non-normal) population, neither the Z nor the t ratios are appropriate descriptive statistics. Some more advanced texts recommend a procedure based on 'Chebyshev's inequality' in these cases but this is beyond the scope of this *Essence* text. An alternative procedure, of course, is to try to increase sample size.

To summarize, when σ is unknown and we replace it by the estimate s, then the appropriate distribution is the t distribution with $n - 1$ degrees of freedom. But for large samples, the t distribution is so close to the normal distribution that use of either t or Z values is acceptable. Thus, the t distribution is important only in the context of small samples (less than 30 observations). Its use here, however, requires that the population from which the samples are drawn does not depart markedly from normality, especially if the sample size is particularly small (less than 15).

We now turn to consider the characteristics of the t distribution and then its application in making interval estimates of the population mean and associated problems.

Characteristics of t distributions

A t distribution resembles the standard normal distribution (Z) in that both are symmetrical about a mean of zero. But t distributions are flatter and more spread out than the normal curve. However, as the sample size n increases, so too the number of degrees of freedom ($n-1$) increases, and the more closely do the t distributions resemble the standard normal curve. In the limit, when the number of degrees of freedom tends to infinity, t distributions become identical to the standard normal curve. Figure 7.6 illustrates t distributions and compares them with the standard normal curve.

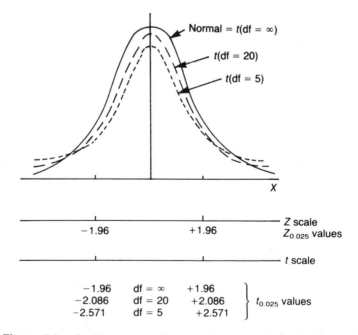

Figure 7.6 t distributions and the standard normal distribution compared.

Tables of t: format and explanation

Tables of areas under the curve of the t distribution, which allow one to make probability statements, are available just as they are for the standard normal curve – see Appendix A4. Note, however, that as the t distribution is not a single distribution but a whole family of distributions the table is laid out differently from the table for the standard normal curve. Whereas the latter gives areas under the curve (i.e. probabilities) for specified values of Z, the t table gives t values corresponding to specified probabilities, each row of the table indicating a separate t distribution according to the number of degrees of freedom. Thus, for example, for 10 degrees of freedom, the value of t which leaves an area of 0.025 in the tail of the distribution (i.e. $t_{0.025}$) is 2.228 from the t tables.

Interval estimation using the t distribution

Interval estimation using the t distribution follows the same principles as those for using the normal distribution in terms of Z set out above. Using Z, a confidence interval for the population mean (μ) may be defined as:

$$\underline{\mu} = \bar{X} \pm Z_{\alpha/2} \sigma_{\bar{X}}$$

where the level of confidence is 100 $(1 - \alpha)$ per cent as defined earlier. Correspondingly, where the t distribution applies, a 100 $(1 - \alpha)$ per cent confidence interval is defined as:

$$\underline{\mu} = \bar{X} \pm t_{\alpha/2}, \text{ where } t \text{ has } n - 1 \text{ degrees of freedom, } \hat{\sigma}_{\bar{X}}$$

Example

The amounts spent (in pounds) by customers in a shop are normally distributed. A random sample of 16 customers gave these values:

19 21 35 29 13 35 7 18 21 14 29 20 12 24 32 23

with a mean of £22 and a standard deviation of £8.33. Estimate a 95 per cent confidence interval for the population mean.

Solution

$$\underline{\mu} = \bar{X} \pm t_{\alpha/2}, \text{ where } t \text{ has } n - 1 \text{ degrees of freedom, } \hat{\sigma}_{\bar{X}}$$

For 95 per cent confidence, $t_{\alpha/2} = t_{0.05/2} = t_{0.025} = 2.131$ from the tables, with $16 - 1$ degrees of freedom.

$$\hat{\sigma}_{\bar{x}} = \frac{s}{\sqrt{n}} = \frac{8.33}{\sqrt{16}} = 2.0825$$

Therefore:

$$\underline{\bar{\mu}} = \pounds22 \pm (2.131 \times 2.0825)$$
$$= \pounds22 \pm 4.44$$
$$= \pounds17.56 \text{ to } \pounds26.44$$

Use of MINITAB

The use of the statistical package MINITAB to compute a confidence interval using the t distribution is illustrated in Computer illustration 7.1 for the same data as in the example on page 133. MINITAB will also compute confidence intervals using the Z statistic (normal distribution) but, as explained earlier, this is only appropriate when the population standard deviation (σ) is known. Since it is rare to know σ, confidence intervals are normally constructed using the t distribution.

Computer illustration 7.1   MINITAB and confidence intervals using the t distribution (compare with the example on page 133)

```
MTB > NAME C1 'Amounts'
MTB > SET C1
DATA> 19 21 35 29 13 35 7 18 21 14 29 20 12 24 32 23
DATA> END
MTB > TINTerval 95% C1   (This command produces the results
                          shown below. Note that it gives a
                          95 per cent confidence interval using the t
                          distribution as well as the other
                          measures shown.)

                N       MEAN     STDEV    SE MEAN    95.0 PERCENT C.I.
Amounts        16       22.00     8.33      2.08   (   17.56,    26.44)
```

Authors' note: Confidence intervals using the Z statistic are obtained using the command ZINTerval instead of TINTerval and by specifying the value of the population standard deviation (σ) on the command line.

Key learning points

Sampling distribution   A probability distribution of all possible values of a sample statistic.

Point estimate   A single numerical value used as an estimate of a population parameter.

Standard error of the mean   The standard deviation of the point estimate of the population mean.

$$\sigma_{\bar{X}} = \frac{\sigma}{\sqrt{n}}$$

Standard error of the mean when σ is unknown

$$\hat{\sigma}_{\bar{X}}(\text{or } s_{\bar{X}}) = \frac{s}{\sqrt{n}}$$

$$\text{where } s = \sqrt{\frac{\Sigma(X_i - \bar{X})^2}{n-1}}$$

Finite population correction factor (fpc)   Used to modify the expressions for $\sigma_{\bar{X}}$ when sampling without replacement from a finite population.

$$\text{fpc} = \sqrt{\frac{N-n}{N-1}}$$

$$\text{so that } \sigma_{\bar{X}} = \frac{\sigma}{\sqrt{n}} \sqrt{\frac{N-n}{N-1}}$$

Central limit theorem   A theorem that allows us to use the normal distribution to approximate the sampling distribution whenever the sample is large, even if the distribution of the parent population is not normal.

Interval estimate   An estimate of a population parameter that provides an interval of values believed to contain the value of the parameter being estimated. The interval estimate is also referred to as a *confidence interval*.

Interval estimate of a population mean

$$\bar{\mu} = \bar{X} \pm Z_{\alpha/2} \sigma_{\bar{X}}$$

Confidence limits   The upper and lower limits that together define an interval estimate.

t distribution A family of probability distributions which can be used to develop interval estimates of a population mean and test statistical hypotheses whenever the population standard deviation is unknown and the population has a normal or near-normal probability distribution.

t statistic: $\quad t = \dfrac{\bar{X} - \mu}{\hat{\sigma}_{\bar{X}}}$ where $\hat{\sigma}_{\bar{X}} = \dfrac{s}{\sqrt{n}}$

Interval estimation using the t distribution

$$\underline{\mu} = \bar{X} \pm t_{\alpha/2}\hat{\sigma}_{\bar{X}}, \text{ where } t \text{ has } n-1 \text{ degrees of freedom}$$

EXERCISES

Standard error, sampling with and without replacement

1 Calculate the standard error of the mean ($\sigma_{\bar{x}}$) in each of the following cases, where N is population size and n is sample size.
(a) $N = 100$, $\sigma = 12$, $n = 9$, sampling with replacement.
(b) $N = 100$, $\sigma = 12$, $n = 9$, sampling without replacement.
(c) N is large, $\sigma = 12$, $n = 36$.

Problems involving the normal distribution

2 A large firm has 240 managers who have an average annual salary of £21,000. The standard deviation of annual salaries is £5000.
(a) In a random sample of 100 managers, what is the probability that the average salary will exceed £21,500?
(b) What is the probability that the sample mean found in (a) will be less than £22,000?

3 The weights of persons using a lift are normally distributed with a mean of 70 kg and a standard deviation of 9 kg. The lift has a maximum permissible load of 300 kg.
(a) Four persons arising at random from this population are in the lift. What is the probability that the maximum load is exceeded?
(b) If one person arising at random is in the lift but accompanied by luggage weighing three times his own weight, what is the probability that the maximum load is exceeded?

4 A finance manager takes a sample of sales of size $n = 36$ from a population of $N = 1000$. The standard deviation (σ) is unknown but the sample standard deviation (s) equals £43. If the true mean value of sales for the population is $\mu = £260$, what is the probability that the same mean will be less than or equal to £250?

5 A company employs 2000 salesmen and wishes to estimate the average mileage they travel by car every year. From past experience it is known that the standard deviation of mileage travelled per salesman is normally 5000 miles. A random sample of 25 cars gives a mean of 14,000 miles.
(a) State the required estimate of the population mean, μ.
(b) Determine a 95 per cent confidence interval for the population mean, μ.
(c) The managers of the company decide to regard the mean as lying within the limits 13,000 to 15,000 miles. What degree of confidence could be placed on this estimate?
(d) If it was desired to have 95 per cent confidence in the estimate in (c), what would be the required sample size?

6 The prices at which a certain type of instant coffee was being sold on a given day were collected from a random sample of 45 shops around the country. The mean price was £1.95 with a standard deviation of 27p. Compute a 99 per cent confidence interval for the population mean.

Problems involving the t distribution

7 Confirm from the t tables in Appendix A4 that, with 11 degrees of freedom:
(a) the t value leaving 5 per cent of the distribution in the right-hand tail is 1.796.
(b) the t value leaving 5 per cent of the distribution in the right- and left-hand tails combined is 2.201.
What is the value of t that leaves 10 per cent of the distribution in the left-hand tail?

8 With 15 degrees of freedom, use the t tables to find the probability that t:
(a) exceeds 2.131.
(b) is less than -2.131.
(c) $-1.753 < t < 1.341$.
(d) $-1.753 > t$ or $t > 1.341$.

9 A company producing contact lenses introduces a new type which it claims has a longer life than the old version. Six people were asked to test the new lens and this gave a mean life of 4.6 years with a standard deviation of 0.49 years. Construct a 90 per cent confidence interval for the mean life of the new type of lens.

10 The operating life of rechargeable cordless screwdrivers produced by a firm is assumed to be approximately normally distributed. A sample of 15 screwdrivers is tested and the mean life is found to be 8900 hours, with a sample standard deviation of 500 hours.
(a) Construct a 95 per cent confidence interval estimate for the population mean.
(b) Construct a 90 per cent confidence interval estimate for the population mean.

8

Tests of statistical hypotheses

The essence of statistical inference and testing hypotheses in business

The testing of statistical hypotheses represents the second main application of the principles of statistical inference (estimation being the first) described in Chapter 7. We now consider their application in the context of hypotheses about population means. The topic is of central importance in statistics because hypothesis tests are very widely used as the basis for making decisions in industry and government and in research more generally. Some examples of the kinds of decisions to which the principles of hypothesis testing may be applied are as follows:

□ Has absence from work in a firm or industry due to sickness increased significantly over its level during a previous period?

□ Is a manufacturing process running 'under control' in the sense that it performs its operation within pre-specified limits (e.g. machining a component to given size limits or filling containers with predetermined amounts of material) or has the machine drifted out of control and thus requires adjustment or repair?

□ Does a new fertilizer increase the yield of a particular crop significantly?

In each of these examples we start with some predetermined standard or knowledge of the previous value of a population parameter (e.g. the population mean) and wish to decide whether the new information drawn from a sample, is or is not consistent with having been drawn from a population with, in this case, the same population mean.

The principles and procedures involved in hypothesis tests of these kinds are set out in this chapter as follows:

☐ The basic principles of hypothesis testing.
☐ Conducting hypothesis tests.
☐ Errors in hypothesis testing.
☐ Extensions of hypothesis testing.

The aim here is to convey the essence of the principles in such a way that their application across a wider range of business problems can be appreciated. Consequently, we focus attention in this chapter mainly on the application of the principles to the most important area, namely hypothesis testing of means.

The basic principles of hypothesis testing

The basic idea behind hypothesis testing, then, is that we begin with an assumption (a hypothesis) about the value of a population parameter, such as the population mean, and then use sample information to test the hypothesis. The test consists of comparing the appropriate sample statistic (in our example here, a sample mean) with the corresponding hypothesized parameter value. If there is no difference between the two values, the hypothesis may be accepted. However, it is more likely, of course, to find some difference either as a result of chance (sampling error – see Chapter 7), the hypothesis itself being true, or because it is in fact untrue. Thus the procedure involved in hypothesis testing is to reject the hypothesis only when the difference is so large that the probability of it occurring by chance is very small.

The rationale for the procedure is best understood by comparing it with that for making interval estimates of the population mean (as described in the last chapter) because there is a direct parallel between the two. In making interval estimates of population means, upper and lower confidence limits are determined with reference to a desired level of confidence or probability. We can have no certainty that the true population mean does not fall outside these confidence limits but, as we saw, the probability of it doing so can be made very small by choosing appropriate values of Z or t in calculating these limits and/or increasing the sample size. Likewise in hypothesis testing a hypothesis may be accepted or rejected not with certainty but with confidence that the likelihood of error in making the decision is small.

In hypothesis testing if the hypothesized mean, denoted by μ_0, is regarded as the true mean lying at the centre of a sampling distribution of $\bar{X}$, shown in Figure 8.1(a), then, as we saw in Chapter 7, there is a 5 per cent probability of any single sample mean falling outside the limits defined by:

$\mu_0 \pm 1.96$ (standard error)

As in the last chapter, the level of probability, in this case 5 per cent, is denoted by the symbol α. If the 5 per cent probability of error is acceptable, then we regard only sample means coming within this range as acceptable evidence that the sample has been drawn from a population with a mean that is *no different* from the hypothesized value (μ_0). Thus the region within the limits becomes an *acceptance region* for the hypothesis and the regions outside the limits are then *rejection regions* for the hypothesis – see Figure 8.1(a). The probability itself is known in this context as the *significance level* of the test. Note, therefore, that a 95 per cent confidence interval corresponds to a 5 per cent level of significance. Similarly a 99 per cent confidence interval corresponds to a 1 per cent significance level.

As will have been seen from Figure 8.1(a), the rejection regions consist of *two* 'tails'. The test for 'no difference' is therefore known as a *two-tailed test*. Consequently, the 5 per cent rejection region is split into two equal halves with 2½ per cent in each tail, i.e. $\alpha/2$. In contrast, so-called *one-tailed* tests deal with the situation in which we are interested in testing hypotheses that the population mean is specifically *greater than* or *less than* some hypothesized value – see Figures 8.1(b) and (c). In such cases there is only *one* rejection region, in only one tail or the other, the whole area of which equals α (and no $\alpha/2$ as above).

Difference between hypothesis testing and confidence interval estimation

It may well be asked what the difference is between the setting of confidence intervals and the testing of hypotheses. The essential difference between the two lies in the objectives. With interval estimation we start with no assumption about the value of the population parameter before sample data are collected: the parameter value is unknown and the statistical objective is to estimate it with a given level of confidence. In hypothesis testing, on the other hand, we *do* start with an assumption about the value of the population parameter and then collect sample data to test the hypothesis. In an interval estimate, therefore, the sample mean $\bar{X}$ is placed at the centre of the interval, whereas in the directly comparable hypothesis test (as outlined here) it is the hypothesized mean (μ_0) that is placed at the centre.

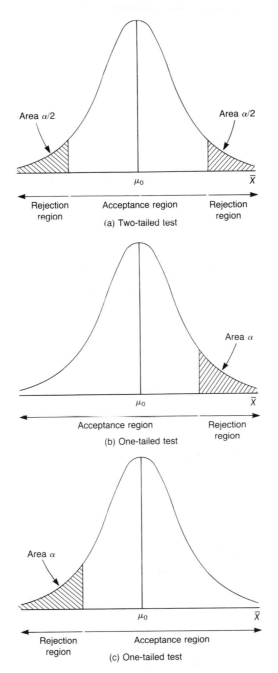

Figure 8.1 Acceptance and rejection regions in hypothesis testing for two-tailed and one-tailed tests.

Conducting hypothesis tests

In this section we set out the procedures for conducting hypothesis tests for two-tailed tests and one-tailed tests.

Null and alternative hypotheses

In any test, *two* hypotheses have to be specified: a *null hypothesis*, designated as H_0, and an *alternative hypothesis*, designated as H_1. The null hypothesis, H_0, specifies the value of the parameter to be tested, e.g. that the population mean μ (unknown) is equal to some hypothesized value, μ_0.

Thus, for two-tailed tests the null hypothesis is expressed as:

Null hypothesis H_0: $\mu = \mu_0$

If this hypothesis is rejected then the alternative hypothesis (H_1) is accepted; that is:

Alternative hypothesis H_1: $\mu \neq \mu_0$

On the other hand, in the case of one-tailed tests, we wish to test the null hypothesis against the alternative hypothesis that the parameter is not simply different (as above) but specifically *bigger* or *smaller* than the hypothesized value (μ_0). In this case we have:

either (a) H_0: $\mu = \mu_0$; H_1: $\mu > \mu_0$

or   (b) H_0: $\mu = \mu_0$; H_1: $\mu < \mu_0$

Having formulated the hypotheses to be tested and thus consequently determined whether a two-tailed or a one-tailed test is required, the next step is to fix the dividing line between the regions of acceptance and rejection. This simply depends upon the level of significance (α) at which it is decided to conduct the test and whether the sampling distribution of the statistic ($\bar{X}$) can be regarded as normal or whether the t distribution needs to be employed. For the present we assume that the sampling distribution of $\bar{X}$ is normal. The circumstances in which the t distribution needs to be used are considered later (again there is a direct parallel with the use of t for confidence interval estimation purposes).

It is most common to work with 5 per cent or 1 per cent significance levels but any level may be chosen. Having chosen a significance level, the dividing line between the acceptance and rejection regions is then determined. The point of division between the two regions marks the critical value of the test statistic. It is a critical value in the sense that it is the value against which the actual sample value is compared. For a two-tailed test there are, of course, two critical values and for a one-tailed test, one critical value. These are shown in Figure 8.1 above. Following this terminology, rejection regions are themselves sometimes called 'critical regions'.

The test statistic

There are two ways of stating the test statistic and thus of carrying out the test. One way is to calculate a critical value of the statistic itself ($\bar{X}$). The other is to work in terms of the standardized normal variable Z (or where appropriate the t value). These two ways are of course equivalent. In practice, statisticians generally prefer to use Z values (rather than $\bar{X}$ values) because they allow the level of significance of any test to be readily identified. However, in the first example below we illustrate the use of both test statistics for completeness. Thus the critical values in each case for testing a hypothesized mean μ_0 are as follows:

Type of test	Hypotheses		Critical values using	
	H_0	H_1	$\bar{X}$	Z
Two-tailed	$\mu = \mu_0$	$\mu \neq \mu_0$	$\mu_0 \pm Z_{\alpha/2}\sigma_{\bar{X}}$	$\pm Z_{\alpha/2}$
One-tailed	$\mu = \mu_0$	$\mu > \mu_0$	$\mu_0 + Z_\alpha \sigma_{\bar{X}}$	$+ Z_\alpha$
One-tailed	$\mu = \mu_0$	$\mu < \mu_0$	$\mu_0 - Z_\alpha \sigma_{\bar{X}}$	$- Z_\alpha$

The equivalence of these tests using $\bar{X}$ or Z as alternative test statistics will be demonstrated in an example below (using a two-tailed test situation, although the same result could, of course, be shown in one-tailed situations). Before doing this, however, we must set up a decision rule for our hypothesis testing.

Decision rule in hypothesis testing

Once the critical values have been determined (using either $\bar{X}$ or Z), then we are in a position to decide whether to accept or reject the null hypothesis in the two-tailed and one-tailed situations. Note that we focus upon acceptance or rejection of the *null* hypothesis – rejection of H_0 implies acceptance of H_1. The decision rule in each case is as follows:

Decision rule: two-tailed test

□ **Using $\bar{X}$ as the test statistic:**
  Accept H_0: if the actual value of the sample mean $\bar{X}$ falls between the
  two critical values of $\bar{X}$.
  Reject H_0: otherwise.

□ **Alternatively, using Z as the test statistic:**
  Accept H_0: if the actual value of Z corresponding to $\bar{X}$, given by
  $(\bar{X} - \mu_0)/\sigma_{\bar{X}}$, falls between the two critical values of Z.
  Reject H_0: otherwise.

Decision rule: one-tailed test

□ **Using $\bar{X}$ as the test statistic:**
  Accept H_0: if the actual value of $\bar{X}$ falls above or below the critical
  value of $\bar{X}$ depending on whether the lower or upper tail
  is the appropriate rejection region.
  Reject H_0: otherwise.

□ **Alternatively, using Z as the test statistic:**
  Accept H_0: if the actual value of Z corresponding to $\bar{X}$ falls above or
  below the critical value of Z depending on whether the
  lower or upper tail is appropriate.
  Reject H_0: otherwise.

All of these cases are shown in Figure 8.1 on page 141.

Example of a two-tailed test
Assume that a manager in a firm wishes to test whether the average number
of days of absence per worker through sickness has changed this year
compared with the average value in the past which was 8 days, with a
standard deviation (σ) of 14 days. A random sample of 49 workers is taken
giving a mean of 10.6 days of absence per worker this year. It is decided
to conduct the test at the 5 per cent level of significance, i.e. $\alpha = 0.05$.

Solution
Note that the *normal* distribution may be used here because the value of
σ is known from past experience.

Given: $\mu = 8$; $\sigma = 14$; $n = 49$

Formulation of hypotheses: H_0: $\mu_0 = 8$
H_1: $\mu_0 \neq 8$ (i.e. two-tailed test)

Level of significance: $\alpha = 0.05$, hence $Z_{\alpha/2} = Z_{0.025} = \pm 1.96$

Standard error of the mean: $\sigma_{\bar{X}} = \sigma/\sqrt{n} = 14/\sqrt{49} = 2$

Critical values: using $\bar{X}$: $\mu_0 \pm Z_{\alpha/2}\sigma_{\bar{X}} = 8 \pm 1.96(2) = 4.08$ and 11.92
or Z: $\pm Z_{\alpha/2} = -1.96$ and $+1.96$

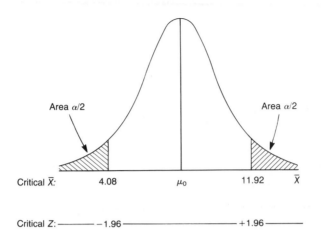

Figure 8.2 Critical values for two-tailed significance tests on absenteeism.

Figure 8.2 illustrates the equivalence of these alternative ways of defining critical values.

Test: (a) Using critical $\bar{X}$ values:
           actual $\bar{X}$ (=10.6) falls between the critical values
           i.e. $4.08 < 10.6 < 11.92$
     (b) Using critical Z values:

$$\text{actual } Z = \frac{\bar{X} - \mu_0}{\sigma_{\bar{X}}} = \frac{10.6 - 8}{14\sqrt{49}}$$

$$= 1.3$$

           which falls between the critical values, as above i.e.
           $-1.96 < 1.3 < +1.96$

Conclusion: The manager must *accept* the null hypothesis, i.e. conclude that, according to the evidence, the absenteeism per worker this year, on average, is not significantly different from past experience, at the 5 per cent level of significance.

Example of a one-tailed test
Using the same information for absenteeism above, we now give an example of the conduct of a one-tailed test in which the manager is interested in ascertaining whether the absenteeism this year is significantly *higher* than it has been in the past, i.e. whether 10.6 days is *significantly greater* than the historical value of 8 days. The steps are as follows:

Solution

Given: $\mu_0 = 8$; $\bar{X} = 10.6$; $n = 49$; $\sigma = 14$ (as in the example above).

1. *Hypotheses:* H_0: $\mu_0 = 8$
   $\quad\quad\quad\quad\quad H_1$: $\mu_0 > 8$

2. *Significance level for test:* $\alpha = 0.05$

3. *Test statistic:* Critical
   $Z = +Z_\alpha = +1.645$

4. *Actual $Z = 1.3$ (as in the example above).*

5. *Comparison of actual and critical test statistics and conclusion:*
   Using Z: $1.3 < 1.645$.

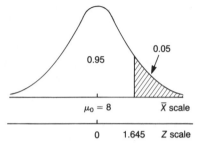
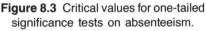

Figure 8.3 Critical values for one-tailed significance tests on absenteeism.

Hence, we *cannot* conclude that the average number of days of absenteeism is significantly greater this year than in the past, at the 5 per cent level of significance.

Choice of t statistic rather than Z statistic in hypothesis testing

In the examples above we assumed that the sampling distribution of the mean was normal and that the value of σ was known. Thus the standard normal variable Z could be used. In cases where the t distribution rather than the normal distribution applies then, of course, a t value must be substituted for Z. The circumstances in which a Z or a t value applies depend on sample size and whether or not σ is known, as was explained in the context of confidence intervals in Chapter 7. As was explained there, for practical purposes the use of t is generally confined to small samples only. However, recall that its use is unreliable if the population from which the sample is drawn is itself not normal – consequently it is desirable in such cases to draw samples of at least 30 so that the Central Limit Theorem may be invoked.

Summary of procedural steps in hypothesis testing:

1. **Formulate the null (H_0) and alternative (H_1) hypotheses (thus determining whether a two-tailed or a one-tailed test is required).**
2. **Specify the level of significance (α) to be used.**
3. **Select the test statistic (either $\bar{X}$ or the corresponding Z or t value) and determine its critical value.**
4. **Determine the actual value of the test statistic.**

5. **Compare the actual value of the test statistic against its critical value and arrive at a conclusion, i.e. accept or reject H_0 and state the conclusion clearly.**

Exercises involving hypothesis tests of population means are given at the end of this chapter. Solutions to these are provided at the end of the book.

Errors in hypothesis testing: Type I and Type II errors

It is important to appreciate that a hypothesis test does not *prove* the truth or falsity of a hypothesis. Proof implies certainty. But since we are dealing with sampling data subject to sampling error we are dealing in probabilities, not certainties. The terms 'acceptance' and 'rejection' should not, therefore, be misconstrued. We repeat, for emphasis, that acceptance of the null hypothesis indicates only that the sample evidence is simply *insufficient to reject* it at the chosen level of significance, *not* that it is necessarily true. It will be understood, therefore, that the conclusions of hypothesis tests are subject to error. We discuss this subject only briefly here – it is not important to the conduct of hypothesis testing as such. It is important, however, from the viewpoint of designing experiments, for it is possible to *control*, to some extent, such errors through sample design.

Focusing attention on the null hypothesis, two types of error can be committed. First, a null hypothesis may be rejected when it is in fact true: such an error is called a *Type I error*. The probability of committing such an error can be controlled by specifying α, i.e. the significance level chosen specifies the *risk* we are willing to take of rejecting a true null hypothesis. The second type of error is acceptance of the null hypothesis when it is in fact false. This is called a *Type II error*.

The possible decisions in hypothesis testing and the associated possible errors can be summarized as follows:

Decision	Situation in the population	
	H_0 true	H_0 false
Accept H_0:	Correct decision	Type II error
Reject H_0:	Type I error	Correct decision

Importance of Type I and Type II errors in business

The balance between these two types of error can be important in many business decision-making situations. Consider the example of a pharmaceutical company testing a new drug. If the company has a null hypothesis that the drug is no better than another one and, after testing, concludes this to be the case, then a Type II error arises if, in fact, the drug is better than the other. This means that the drug will not be applied and that people may suffer or die unnecessarily. Conversely, the conclusion that it is better, *when in fact it is not* (a Type I error) will mean that the drug is applied even though it is, at best, no better than a cheaper alternative and, more seriously, it could even be a dangerous drug!

As noted above, Type I error can be controlled. Type II error cannot be controlled simultaneously, although it is possible to compute it because the two types of error are interdependent. However, it is more usual to control Type I error. The only way to reduce both types of error simultaneously is to increase the sample size, though, of course, this may not be practicable. The techniques required to control Type I and Type II errors are beyond the scope of this book: they involve the development of *operating characteristic curves* or corresponding *power curves* which allow one to judge how well a test performs in minimizing Type II error in various possible test situations.

Operating characteristic (OC) curves and power curves are especially useful in industry in, for example, acceptance sampling. In this context the management will have in mind some values of the probability of making Type I and Type II errors, which it is willing to tolerate, and also some deviation from the hypothesized value of the parameter which it considers of practical importance and wishes to detect. Further consideration of these topics in this context will be found in more specialized texts concerned with the application of statistical principles in business and industry.

Extensions of hypothesis testing

The principles developed above may be applied to a variety of related problems in business and many other fields. A detailed discussion of these is beyond the scope of this book but we deal briefly here with the three major areas of further applications. These are:

□ Hypothesis testing of the difference between two sample means.
□ Hypothesis testing of population proportions.
□ Hypothesis testing applied to quality control.

Hypothesis testing of the difference between two sample means

So far in this chapter we have dealt with hypothesis testing in situations in which we had information about a single sample mean, $\bar{X}$, and we were concerned to test whether or not it was significantly different from a known population mean, μ, or a hypothesized population mean, μ_0. In practice, however, we are frequently faced with the results of more than one sample: samples of different groups of people or objects, samples taken at different places, at different times, etc. For example, we may have sample information showing differences between the accident rates of workers in different industries, or in the lengths of life of different brands of car tyre, or in the heights of male children at age 10, say in 1900 and in 1990. In each case, the problem is to decide whether the difference between the means of the samples ($\bar{X}_1$ and $\bar{X}_2$) is statistically significant or not. Put another way, the problem is to decide whether or not the difference between the sample means is such that one must conclude (with a specified degree of confidence) that the samples could have come from populations with the same mean (i.e. $\mu_1 = \mu_2$, and thus $\mu_1 - \mu_2 = 0$) or different means ($\mu_1 \neq \mu_2$ and thus $\mu_1 - \mu_2 \neq 0$).

The test is set up in exactly the same way as before, with:

H_0: $\mu_1 = \mu_2$

H_1: $\mu_1 \neq \mu_2$

A problem, however, in such situations will be obvious. Because μ_1 and μ_2 are unknown, there is no way of deciding whether the sampling distributions of $\bar{X}_1$ and $\bar{X}_2$ are close together or far apart.

Perfect evidence to support a hypothesis that two samples are drawn from identical populations would be that there was no difference between the two sample means. But we know from the previous discussion of the sampling distribution of means (Chapter 7) that differences in sample means occur, even when the samples are drawn from the same population, as a result of sampling error. The question, therefore, is to determine how large a difference between two sample means would still be acceptable to conclude that they are likely to have come from identical populations or, conversely, how large a difference is necessary for us to conclude that they have probably come from different populations and therefore that the difference between the sample means is 'statistically significant'. Clearly, to determine this question we need to have information about how the possible differences between the sample means could be distributed, i.e. the sampling distribution of the difference between all possible pairs of sample means.

Fortunately, it is possible to construct a sampling distribution of the statistic $(\bar{X}_1 - \bar{X}_2)$, for all possible pairs of sample means. This provides a set of differences between two means, i.e. the sampling distribution of the difference between two means. Provided that the sample sizes are both large (i.e. $n_1 \geq 30$ and $n_2 \geq 30$), the sampling distribution of $(\bar{X}_1 - \bar{X}_2)$ can be approximated by a normal probability distribution. In addition, the mean of this distribution $(\mu_{\bar{X}_1 - \bar{X}_2})$ is *zero* when the samples are drawn under the null hypothesis assumption that $\mu_1 = \mu_2$.

In order to conduct significance tests on the hypothesis that $\mu_1 = \mu_2$, we now need to establish the standard error of this sampling distribution. It can be shown that this is equal to:

Standard error of the difference between two means:

$$\sigma_{\bar{X}_1 - \bar{X}_2} = \sqrt{\frac{\sigma_1^2}{n_1} + \frac{\sigma_2^2}{n_2}}$$

where σ_1 = **standard deviation of population 1**
σ_2 = **standard deviation of population 2**
n_1 = **size of sample from population 1**
n_2 = **size of sample from population 2.**

When σ_1 and σ_2 are unknown, we must use the values of the *sample* standard deviations, i.e. s_1 and s_2. In such situations, provided that the sample sizes are sufficiently large (30 or more), an estimate for $\sigma_{\bar{X}_1 - \bar{X}_2}$ is:

$$s_{\bar{X}_1 - \bar{X}_2} = \sqrt{\frac{s_1^2}{n_1} + \frac{s_2^2}{n_2}}$$

Example
A large food-retailing company is considering installing new electronic checkout systems in its supermarkets throughout the country. Two different systems are available and the company decides to conduct tests to ascertain whether or not one system is preferable to the other in terms of speeding up customer throughput. The two systems are installed and the following sampling information for each is recorded.

System A	System B
$n_1 = 120$	$n_2 = 100$
$X_1 = 4.1$ minutes	$X_2 = 3.3$ minutes
$s_1 = 2.2$ minutes	$s_2 = 1.5$ minutes

Solution

1. *Hypotheses:* H_0: $\mu_1 = \mu_2$ (i.e. $\mu_1 - \mu_2 = 0$)

   H_1: $\mu_1 \neq \mu_2$ (i.e. $\mu_1 - \mu_2 \neq 0$)

2. *Significance level for test:* $\alpha = 0.05$

3. *Test statistic:* Critical $Z_{\alpha/2} = \pm 1.96$

4. *Actual Z:* $Z = \dfrac{(\bar{X}_1 - \bar{X}_2) - (\mu_1 - \mu_2)}{\sqrt{\dfrac{s_1^2}{n_1} + \dfrac{s_2^2}{n_2}}}$

$$= \frac{(4.1 - 3.3) - (0)}{\sqrt{\dfrac{(2.2)^2}{120} + \dfrac{(1.5)^2}{100}}}$$

$$= \frac{0.8}{\sqrt{0.0403 + 0.225}}$$

$$= \frac{0.8}{0.25}$$

$$= 3.2$$

5. *Conclusion:* $Z > Z_{\alpha/2}$;   i.e. $3.2 > 1.96$

Therefore, H_0 is rejected and we can conclude that the two systems are significantly different at the 5 per cent level of significance. System B is to be preferred because of its shorter throughput time on average.

Before leaving the topic of the difference between two sample means, we draw attention to two further aspects. One arises, as before, when the population variances σ_1^2 and σ_2^2 are unknown and sample sizes are small ($n_1 < 30$ and $n_2 < 30$). The test procedure involves the use of the t distribution and, in the special case in which it can be assumed that the two population variances are equal, the 'pooling' of the two sample variances (s_1^2 and s_2^2). For example, it would be reasonable to assume equal population variances when sampling from long-run production processes. This pooling procedure is meant to provide the best estimate of the common population variance (if equal population variances cannot be assumed then this pooling procedure is not appropriate – see below). For example, for two samples of sizes n_1 and n_2 and variances s_1^2 and s_2^2 respectively, the pooled variance of the samples (s_p^2) is computed as the weighted average of the separate variances (using degrees of freedom as the weights), i.e.:

$$s_p^2 = \frac{(n_1 - 1)s_1^2 + (n_2 - 1)s_2^2}{n_1 + n_2 - 2}$$

Hence, the standard error of the difference between two sample means is then estimated as:

$$s_{\bar{X}_1 - \bar{X}_2} = \sqrt{\frac{s_p^2}{n_1} + \frac{s_p^2}{n_2}}$$

In contrast to the above, in situations when it is not reasonable to assume that the population variances are equal, then pooling of the sample variances (s_1^2 and s_2^2) is not appropriate. In such situations, the standard error of the difference between two sample means is as follows:

$$s_{\bar{X}_1 - \bar{X}_2} = \sqrt{\frac{s_1^2}{n_1} + \frac{s_2^2}{n_2}}$$

But note that in this case the degrees of freedom (*df*) are given by the expression:

$$df = \frac{\left(\dfrac{s_1^2}{n_1} + \dfrac{s_2^2}{n_2}\right)^2}{\dfrac{\left(\dfrac{s_1^2}{n_1}\right)^2}{(n_1 - 1)} + \dfrac{\left(\dfrac{s_2^2}{n_2}\right)^2}{(n_2 - 1)}}$$

The second additional aspect is that the sample means may be drawn from *matched* samples; that is, for example, data relating to the performance of a set of workers at one point in time are compared with the performance of the *same* set of workers at another point in time. The importance of this is that such a sample design leads to smaller sampling errors than the use of samples which are independent of each other, i.e. two *separate* groups of workers altogether. Further details of these extensions are to be found in more advanced statistics texts.

Hypothesis testing of population proportions

Consider the problem that the proportion of defects being produced by a particular machine this year has been observed to be 8 per cent. The question arises as to whether this machine is performing less well, on average, than it was last year, or whether it is better or worse than another machine of a different make. It will be recognized that in this type of question we are concerned with population *proportions*, rather than population means. They arise, of course, in situations in which the variable in question is a binomial variable (as discussed in Chapter 6). Proportions are merely the counts of '*x* successes or failures' relative to sample size *n*. The questions posed above demand tests, therefore, of hypotheses about a *single* population proportion or the difference between *two* population proportions. There is a close parallel between testing such hypotheses and the testing of those involving means and the differences between means set out earlier in this chapter. The parallel arises from the fact that it is possible to use the normal distribution as an approximation to the binomial – an approximation which works well provided that $np > 5$ and $nq > 5$, where n is the sample size and p and q are the proportions of successes and failures respectively (see the discussion of the binomial distribution in Chapter 6).

For the purpose of this book, it is not essential to set out in detail the procedural steps to be encountered in problems involving proportions. In practice, analysis of the means discussed earlier in the chapter is of relatively greater importance than proportions. The intention is that the exposition of principles so far developed in the case of means will provide the foundation for understanding their extension to the problem of proportions.

Hypothesis testing applied to quality control

Finally, the principles of hypothesis testing presented in this chapter are also widely used in industry for controlling the quality of production. It is common for variations to occur in the dimensions, tensile strength, finish, etc., of repetitive items of production despite apparently identical conditions of production. The problem is to decide whether observed changes are due to chance fluctuations reflecting the inherent variability of the process or whether they are due to a real change resulting from faults in a machine or materials or to operative error.

Given the required mean value of the item (e.g. mean length, diameter, etc.), the procedure is to take regular samples and to compare their mean values against a range of values indicating acceptable performance: sample means falling within the range indicate that the process is 'under control'; mean values falling outside the range indicate that it is 'out of control' and that remedial action is required. These limits are set by measuring so many standard errors ($\sigma_{\bar{x}}$) on either side of the required mean (μ_0). It is common to set *warning limits* as $\mu_0 \pm 2\sigma_{\bar{x}}$ and *control limits* as $\mu_0 \pm 3\sigma_{\bar{x}}$. These are often drawn on a *control chart* on which the results of repeated sampling are recorded. The following example will make the procedure clear.

Example
A machine is set to produce a metal component to a 'target' mean length μ of 10 cm. The usual variability of the process gives a standard deviation σ of 0.045 cm. From time to time samples of 5 pieces are inspected and the

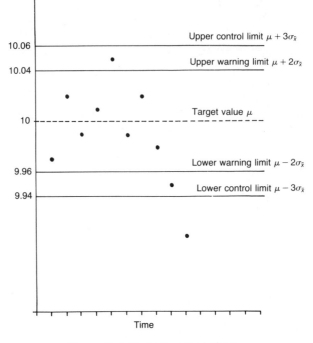

Figure 8.4 Typical control chart.

mean length of each sample is calculated. These sample means are then compared with 'warning limits' of $\mu \pm 2\sigma_{\bar{x}}$ and 'action limits' of $\mu \pm 3\sigma_{\bar{x}}$, to judge whether the process remains under control. If the following ten sample mean results are obtained:

9.97, 10.02, 9.99, 10.01, 10.05, 9.99, 10.02, 9.98, 9.95, 9.91

what action should be taken?

Solution
Standard error of the mean $(\sigma_{\bar{x}}) = \sigma/\sqrt{n} = 0.045/\sqrt{5} = 0.02$

Hence:

Warning limits: $(\mu \pm 2\sigma_{\bar{x}}) = 10 \pm (2 \times 0.02) = 9.96$ to 10.04
Control limits: $(\mu \pm 3\sigma_{\bar{x}}) = 10 \pm (3 \times 0.02) = 9.94$ to 10.06
Action: The fifth sample mean (10.05) falls outside the warning limits but not outside the control limits; this in itself is not serious and no action

is required. But the ninth sample also falls outside the warning limits and the tenth sample falls outside the control limits, suggesting that remedial action is required for this process.

The control chart for this production process is shown in Figure 8.4. The purpose, of course, is to present the values for the successive sample means graphically and thus to indicate very clearly when remedial action is needed. Control charts are also known as *Shewhart charts*.

A similar procedure is operated by firms for controlling the 'quality' of materials bought. Samples of deliveries may be tested to ensure that they comply with requirements before accepting them. This is referred to as *acceptance sampling*.

Use of MINITAB

Illustrations of the use of the statistical package MINITAB to conduct two-tailed and one-tailed significance tests of a sample mean are shown in Computer illustrations 8.1 and 8.2 using the same examples as were given on pages 144–6 (with the full data set, required by MINITAB, reported). The use of MINITAB to produce a quality control chart is also illustrated in Computer illustration 8.3 using the sample given above.

Computer illustration 8.1   MINITAB and significance tests of a sample mean: two-tailed Z test (compare with the example on pages 144–5)

```
MTB > NAME C1 'Absence'
MTB > SET C1
DATA >    16      6     13     16      9     10     14     10      5     16
DATA >     4      7     11      9      6      4     21     22      8     15
DATA >    13     12      5      6      3      7     15      9     10     13
DATA >     3     11     17     10      9      7     10     16      4     19
DATA >    10     24     10      9     13     14      6      8      4
DATA > END
MTB > ZTESt mu = 8 sigma = 14 C1     (This command carries out a two-
                                      tailed test on the sample data
                                      in C1 and gives the results below.)

TEST OF MU =  8.000 VS MU N.E.  8.000
THE ASSUMED SIGMA = 14.0

               N      MEAN     STDEV    SE MEAN       Z    P VALUE
Absence       49    10.592     5.078      2.000    1.30       0.20
```

Authors' note: Because the calculated value of Z (1.30) is less than the critical value of 1.96 (from tables) we arrive at the same conclusion as above (page 145) and accept the null hypothesis.
An alternative way of using these results is to compare the P value of the result (0.20) with the required significance level (0.05).
As 0.20 exceeds 0.05 we accept the null hypothesis, as before.

Computer illustration 8.2 MINITAB and significance tests of a sample mean: one-tailed *Z* test (compare with the example on pages 145–6)

```
MTB > ZTEST mu = 8 sigma = 14 C1;
SUBC > ALTErnative +1.
    (This sub-command specifies that a one-tailed test of the alternative
    hypothesis of 'greater than' is required and gives the results
    below.
    Substitution of −1 in place of +1 specifies a test of the
    alternative test of 'less than'.)

TEST OF MU + 8.000 VS MU G.T. 8.000
THE ASSUMED SIGMA = 14.0
```

	N	MEAN	STDEV	SE MEAN	Z	P VALUE
Absence	49	10.592	5.078	2.000	1.30	0.20

Authors' note: Because the calculated value of Z (1.30) is less than the critical value of 1.645 (from tables) we arrive at the same conclusion as before (page 146) and accept the null hypothesis.
Alternatively, we may compare the P value of the result (0.098) with the required significance level (0.05): as 0.098 > 0.05 we accept the null hypothesis.

Computer illustration 8.3 MINITAB and quality control charts (compare with the example on pages 153–5)

```
MTB > SET C1              (Puts each sample mean into column 1.)
DATA> 9.97 10.02 9.99 10.01 10.05 9.99 10.02 9.98 9.95 9.91
DATA> END
MTB > XBARchart C1 1;     (Basic command to plot each sample mean on a
                          control chart. Together with the sub-commands
                          which follow, it gives the output below.)
SUBC> MU = 10;            (Specifies the target mean.)
SUBC> SIGMA = 0.02;         (Specifies the standard error of the mean.)
SUBC> SLIMITS are 2,3;    (Command for upper and lower warning and
                          control limit lines to be printed.)
SUBC> TEST 1:8.           (Conducts 8 tests to identify problems
                          requiring investigation.)
```

```
                        X-bar Chart for C1

          -
          -   ----------------------------------------------- 3.0S=10.06
     10.050+                            +
    S     -   ----------------------------------------------- 2.0S=10.04
    a     -
    m     -      +                          +
    p     -              +
    l  10.000+  ---------------------------------------------MU=10.00
    e     -          +                 +
          -
    M     -                                        +
    e     -   ----------------------------------------------- -2.0S=9.960
    a   9.950+                                   +
    n     -   ----------------------------------------------- -3.0S=9.940
          -
          -
          -                                         *
     9.900+                                         1
         +---------+---------+---------+---------+---------+--
         0         2         4         6         8        10
                          Sample Number
```

```
TEST 1. One point beyond zone A.
Test Failed at points: 10

TEST 5. Two of 3 points in a row in zone A or beyond (on one side of CL).
Test Failed at points: 10
```

Key learning points

Null hypothesis Specifies the hypothesized value of the parameter to be tested. e.g. $H_0: \mu = \mu_0$

Alternative hypothesis Specifies the hypothesis assumed true if the null hypothesis is rejected. e.g. $H_1: \mu \neq \mu_0$ or $\mu > \mu_0$ or $\mu < \mu_0$

One-tailed test A hypothesis test in which rejection of the null hypothesis occurs for values of the test statistic in one tail of the sampling distribution.

Two-tailed test   A hypothesis test in which rejection of the null hypothesis occurs for values of the test statistic in either tail of the sampling distribution.

Type I error   The error of rejecting H_0 when it is true.

Type II error   The error of accepting H_0 when it is false.

Critical value   A value that is compared with the test statistic to determine whether H_0 is to be accepted or rejected.

Level of significance   The maximum probability of a Type I error that the user will tolerate in the hypothesis testing procedure.

Standard error of the difference between two means

$$\sigma_{\bar{X}_1 - \bar{X}_2} = \sqrt{\frac{\sigma_1^2}{n_1} + \frac{\sigma_2^2}{n_2}} \text{ when } \sigma_1 \text{ and } \sigma_2 \text{ are known}$$

$$s_{\bar{X}_1 - \bar{X}_2} = \sqrt{\frac{s_1^2}{n_1} + \frac{s_2^2}{n_2}} \text{ when } \sigma_1 \text{ and } \sigma_2 \text{ are unknown}$$

EXERCISES

Terminology and test procedures

1 In each of the following test situations say whether a one-tailed or a two-tailed test is appropriate and then state the null and alternative hypotheses:
(a) A study to test whether the durability of a product has changed.
(b) A study to check an assumption that the average hours of overtime worked per employee are more than 5 hours per week.
(c) A bank manager wishes to test whether the average number of cheques written by current account holders per quarter has decreased.
(d) A test to check whether a machine is running out of control and producing too large a number of items which fail to meet specification.
(e) A study to test the view that the average number of miles driven by 'senior citizens' is less than the average for the population as a whole.

2 State the critical values of Z in the following test situations, where α denotes the level of significance:
(a) Two-tailed test, $\alpha = 0.05$.
(b) One-tailed test, $\alpha = 0.05$.
(c) Two-tailed test, $\alpha = 0.10$.
(d) One-tailed test, $\alpha = 0.10$.
(e) $H_0: \mu = \mu_0$; $H_1: \mu \neq \mu_0$; $\alpha = 0.01$.
(f) $H_0: \mu = \mu_0$; $H_1: \mu < \mu_0$; $\alpha = 0.05$.
(g) $H_0: \mu = \mu_0$; $H_1: \mu > \mu_0$; $\alpha = 0.01$.

3 For (a) and (b) in 2. state the critical value(s) of $\overline{X}$ and define the region of acceptance given that $\mu_0 = 80$, population standard deviation is 20, $n = 100$.

Examples involving the normal distribution

4 Income tax returns show that the mean income of self-employed persons in a particular year was £15,000 with a standard deviation of £975. A random sample of 169 returns from people in the clothing industry gave a mean income of £14,500. Did this indicate that income from self-employment in the clothing industry was significantly different? (Note, in this example the hypothesis to be tested is that there is a difference in income, therefore a two-tailed test is needed. Use of the normal distribution, and therefore a Z test, is appropriate because σ is known and the sample is large.)

5 A manufacturer of TV tubes has for many years used a process giving a mean tube life of 4700 hours and a standard deviation of 1460 hours. A new process is tried to see if it will increase the life significantly. A sample of 100 new tubes gave a mean life of 5000 hours. Is the new process better than the old at the 1 per cent level of significance? (Note, a one-tailed test is required here since the question concerns an *increase* in tube life. As above, a Z test is appropriate because the sample is large and σ is known.)

6 In a study of business trends it is desired to test whether the duration of new firm starts that end in bankruptcy has declined over a period of time at the beginning of which the mean was known to be 12.8 months. A random sample of 84 bankruptcy records gives a mean of 10.4 months and a standard deviation of 6.7 months. Can one conclude that there has been a significant decline? (Note, a one-tailed test is required because the hypothesis is that there has been a decline in duration. In this example σ is unknown, but the sample is large, and so the Central Limit Theorem may be invoked and Z may be used as an approximation of t.)

7 Experience has shown that workers in an industry take an average of 24 minutes to complete a particular task. Certain design changes are made and the time taken by a random sample of 36 workers is recorded. This gave a mean of 23 minutes. How big a standard deviation would be acceptable for one to conclude that the true population mean was less than 24 minutes at the 5 per cent level of significance? (Note, this example has the same features as the question above, but the problem is set up differently by focusing on the maximum size of standard deviation that could be tolerated for one to conclude that an improvement had been achieved.)

8 In 1975 the mean size of firms in an industry, as measured by the number of employees per firm, was 307.8. Over the next 20 years considerable changes took place in demand and the technology of production and the number of firms in the industry declined to 241. A random sample of 36 of the firms in 1995 gave a mean size of 351.6 and standard deviation of 42.3. Is it fair to say that a significant change occurred in the mean size of firms? Note: it is required to test whether a significant *change* has occurred (therefore a two-tailed test is required); the population standard deviation, σ, is unknown but the sample is large and Z may be used (invoking the Central Limit Theorem). However, the sample is drawn in this example from a finite population with a fairly large sample fraction (i.e. $n/N > 0.05$) and it is therefore important to apply the finite population correction factor in estimating the standard error of the mean.

Examples involving quality control and acceptance sampling

9 A firm operates a systematic procedure to control the quality of the components coming off its production line by checking the dimensions of regular samples, four components being included in each sample. The process is set to produce components to a mean diameter of 5.0 cm with a standard deviation of 0.16 cm. Warning and control limits are set at two and three standard errors respectively. The mean values of eight consecutive samples were as follows:

   4.92, 5.10, 5.04, 4.80, 4.94, 5.25, 4.71, 4.80 cm

Comment on these results and state what action, if any, is necessary.

Examples involving the t distribution

10 An intelligence test, used for staff recruitment, is devised so as to give a normal distribution of scores with a mean of 100. A random sample of 20 people who are given the test achieve a mean score of 121 with a standard deviation of 14. Does this suggest that they are an unusual group? (Note, a two-tailed test is required since the test simply concerns a difference from the hypothesized mean. The t distribution is appropriate since the sample is small and σ is unknown but the population distribution is known to be normal.)

11 A brand of matches is sold in boxes on which it is claimed that the average contents are 40 matches. A check on a pack of 5 boxes gives the following results:

   41, 39, 37, 40, 38

Is the manufacturer's claim justified? (Note, a two-tailed test is required since the average contents are not claimed to be a minimum or a maximum. A t test is appropriate since the sample is small and σ is unknown. It is assumed, in this case, that the population distribution is normal.)

Examples involving the difference between sample means

12 Analyses of a national sample survey of earnings of manual workers broken down according to region and occupation include the following results:

	Region 1	Region 2
Bricklayers (nos):	$n_1 = 184$	$n_2 = 210$
Average hourly earnings	$X_1 = £3.30$	$X_2 = £3.22$
Standard deviation	$s_1 = £0.34$	$s_2 = £0.28$

Is the difference in the average hourly earnings of bricklayers in these two regions statistically significant? (Note, in this example the hypothesis to be tested is that there is no difference in earnings: therefore a two-tailed test is needed. Use of the normal distribution, and therefore a Z test, is appropriate because, although the population standard deviations (σ_1 and σ_2) are unknown, the samples are large and the Central Limit Theorem may be invoked.)

13 Is the difference in earnings in Exercise 12 statistically significant at the 1 per cent level?

14 The purity of a chemical produced by two companies varies. A potential purchaser obtains 10 samples from each company and measures the mean percentage purity from each company with the following results:

Company 1	Company 2
$X_1 = 72$	$X_2 = 74$
$s_1 = 2.1$	$s_2 = 3.2$

Is there a significant difference in the purity of the chemicals produced by the two companies? (Note, a two-tailed test is required using the t statistic because the samples are small and the population variances (σ_1^2 and σ_2^2) are unknown. We assume that the populations are normally distributed with equal variances.)

15 A car fleet operator chooses to equip his cars with tyres produced by company 1 rather than company 2, even though they are more expensive, because tests have shown that on average they last for 10,000 miles longer. Tests are conducted periodically to see whether this difference in life is being maintained. Samples of 40 tyres of each make replaced in the last year gave the following results:

Company 1	Company 2
$X_1 = 39,000$	$X_2 = 31,000$
$s_1 = 5,400$	$s_2 = 4,800$

Do these results allow one to conclude, at the 1 per cent level of significance, that the difference is being maintained? (Note, the null hypothesis is that there is a difference between the two population means equal to 10,000 miles. The population variances (σ_1^2 and σ_2^2) are not known but the samples are large, the Central Limit Theorem may be invoked and Z may be used as an approximation to t.)

9

Tests of goodness-of-fit and independence

The essence of tests of goodness-of-fit and independence in business

In this chapter we now turn our attention to a very important kind of significance test that is used when the investigation concerns *category variables* rather than *quantity variables*, i.e. when we are concerned not with a measurement of quantity for each observation in a sample but with counting how many observations fall into each of a number of *descriptive categories*. For example, consider the case of a firm employing 200 people, which is accused of sexual discrimination in its employment practices. The numbers of males and females employed are:

Male	Female	Total
150	50	200

So, in this case, we have two descriptive categories: male and female. To examine the accusation, we would need to consider how many employees one would *expect* in these two categories if there were no discrimination. In other words, we would have to compare *expected* frequencies with the actual number of *observed* frequencies. This gives rise to a *goodness-of-fit test*, i.e. if there is a 'good' fit between observed and expected frequencies, it is possible to conclude, with a specified degree of confidence (on the basis of the statistical test considered in this chapter), that there is no discrimination. This test is known as the χ^2 test (chi-squared test, where 'chi' is pronounced 'ki' as in kite). It is important to note that this test requires information about the *absolute* frequency and not merely the relative frequency in each sub-category.

The test can be readily extended to situations involving cross-tabulations of variables, e.g. the data above could be cross-classified according to, say, marital status. We could then address the question of whether or not the employment of males and females is independent of their marital status – a *test of independence*. This is dealt with later in the chapter.

The χ^2 test differs very much from those considered in Chapter 8. In that chapter, statistical tests were centred around the properties of normal distributions and the estimation and testing of population parameters – hence the tests are often known as *parametric* tests. In contrast, the χ^2 test is referred to as a *non-parametric* test because, unlike its parametric counterpart, it is applicable to situations in which we do not need to make any assumptions regarding the normality of populations.

We now turn to consider the application of the χ^2 test to the two types of problem outlined above, involving goodness-of-fit and independence. It will be seen that it has many applications in the business world.

Goodness-of-fit tests

By way of introducing the principles behind goodness-of-fit tests, we turn back to the discrimination problem posed above. Recall that there were 150 males and 50 females employed by a firm. We need to determine how many of each sex would be 'expected' to be employed if there were no discrimination. One approach might be to consider the proportion of males and females in the working population as a whole – say this is 60 per cent and 40 per cent respectively. This would mean that we would expect 120 men (60 per cent of 200) and 80 females to be employed by this firm. So we have:

	Male	Female
Observed frequency (O)	150	50
Expected frequency (E)	120	80

Naturally, if there were no difference between the observed and expected frequencies in each sex category, then this would be good evidence that there is no discrimination. If there is a difference (as here), the question to be addressed is whether the difference has arisen merely by chance or whether it is just too big to have arisen by chance alone. A χ^2 statistic, which forms the basis of the test to be carried out, needs to be calculated. This is based on the differences between the observed and expected frequencies as follows:

χ^2 statistic:

$$\chi^2 = \Sigma\left(\frac{(O_i - E_i)^2}{E_i}\right)$$

where the summation is conducted over all pairs of observed and expected frequencies $(O_i - E_i)$ relative to the expected frequency E_i for each pair.

Using the above data, we have

$$\chi^2 \text{ statistic}^* = \frac{(150 - 120)^2}{120} + \frac{(60 - 80)^2}{80}$$

$$= \frac{900}{120} + \frac{400}{80}$$

$$= 7.5 + 5$$

$$= 12.5$$

We showed in the last chapter that to conduct a test of a statistical hypothesis, knowledge of a sampling distribution is essential. The sampling distribution of χ^2 statistics follows a special distribution known as the χ^2 *distribution*. This is in fact a whole family of distributions, each of which depends on the number of degrees of freedom available. The degrees of freedom are related to the number of categories (k) into which each variable under consideration is subdivided. In the example above involving *one* variable (employment) and two categories (male and female), the number of degrees of freedom is $k - 1 = 2 - 1 = 1$. A graph of a χ^2 sampling distribution is given in Figure 9.1, while Figure 9.2 shows a 'family' of distributions for different degrees of freedom.

As with the normal and t distributions, probabilities are measured by areas under a χ^2 curve and a χ^2 test is conducted by comparing the actual

---

*Strictly speaking, a so-called 'Yates' continuity correction factor' should be applied because there are only two categories of the variable sex. For the sake of simplicity we ignore it here because we are only presenting general principles. Details of the correction factor are given later.

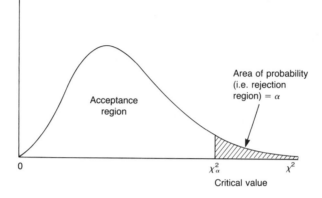

Figure 9.1 χ^2 distribution.

(calculated) value of the χ^2 statistic with some critical χ^2 value given in χ^2 tables – see Appendix A5. It will be seen from Figures 9.1 and 9.2 that χ^2 distributions all have a minimum value of zero and hence all hypothesis tests are, by definition, one-tailed tests.

Having explained the χ^2 distribution and tables, we can now return to complete the example of testing for discrimination above. If we test at the 5 per cent level of significance ($\alpha = 0.05$), the critical value of χ^2, with one degree of freedom, equals 3.84 from Appendix A5. As the actual (computed) χ^2 statistic (equal to 12.5) is greater than the critical value (3.84), we must reject the null hypothesis (i.e. the hypothesis of no difference between actual and expected frequencies) and conclude, therefore, that the difference is statistically significant. This provides supporting evidence for the accusation of discrimination. However, it is, of course, not *absolute proof* because our conclusion has a 5 per cent chance of being wrong and because it could be argued that the basis of calculating the expected frequencies is inappropriate owing to the special labour requirements of this firm.

For purposes of exposition, the example above was made simple in that we had only two categories. Let us now illustrate the use of the χ^2 test to deal with the breakdown of a variable involving more than two categories.

Example
A motor car manufacturer produces identical types of cars in five factories, each employing the same number of workers and the same technology. The chairman is considering expanding production at one factory to meet anticipated future growth in demand for cars. In deciding which factory to expand, it has been suggested by a manager that although the records

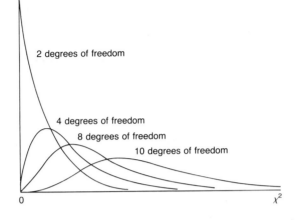

Figure 9.2 χ^2 distributions for different degrees of freedom.

indicate different production levels in the five factories, the differences are not significant and therefore that the choice is not important from an efficiency viewpoint. The chairman, rather than accept this view outright, decides to conduct a test to determine whether or not it is statistically justifiable. Given the production figures below for one week at each of the five factories, what advice would you give to the chairman?

Factory	Production levels (number of cars)
A	185
B	210
C	190
D	200
E	215
Total	1000

Solution
The problem reduces to one of conducting a χ^2 test of the hypotheses:

H_0: the production levels are the same in all five factories.

H_1: the production levels are not the same in all five factories.

The figures above represent *observed* frequencies. We also need a set of *expected* frequencies in order to compute the χ^2 test statistic. These expected values are calculated on the assumption that H_0 is true, i.e. expected production levels are the same and therefore equal to $1000/5 = 200$ at each factory. Table 9.1 sets out the computations to derive the actual χ^2 statistic. Thus:

$$\chi^2 \text{ statistic} = 3.25$$

The number of degrees of freedom is given by the number of categories minus one, i.e.

$$k - 1 = 5 - 1 = 4$$

Finally, the critical value of χ^2 with 4 degrees of freedom (for a significance level of 5 per cent, i.e. $\alpha = 0.05$) is obtained from the χ^2 tables. We find:

$$\chi^2_\alpha = \chi^2_{0.05} = 9.49$$

Decision: The calculated value of χ^2 is compared with the critical value: since $3.25 < 9.49$, the null hypothesis is accepted. That is, we should advise the chairman that production levels are *not* significantly different at the five factories.

Table 9.1 Calculation of the χ^2 statistic for production levels

Factory	Observed (O_i)	Expected (E_i)	$O_i - E_i$	$(O_i - E_i)^2$	$\dfrac{(O_i - E_i)^2}{E_i}$
A	185	200	−15	225	1.125
B	210	200	10	100	0.5
C	190	200	−10	100	0.5
D	200	200	0	0	0
E	215	200	15	225	1.125
Summations	1000	1000			$3.25 = \chi^2$

A condition for applying the χ^2 test

In χ^2 tests, no value of E_i should be less than 5. If this should arise in a particular problem, then it is necessary to combine the expected frequencies in adjacent categories as appropriate – inevitably reducing the number of categories – until the combined expected frequency is at least 5. Before applying χ^2 tests, therefore, it is important to see that this condition is fulfilled. This adjustment is illustrated in the next example which deals with a further application of χ^2 in goodness-of-fit tests.

Testing a distribution for normality

The χ^2 distribution may also be used to test whether or not a set of observed frequencies is consistent with a given probability distribution, such as the normal, Poisson or binomial distributions. In this section we shall illustrate the procedural steps with regard to the normal distribution only. It is very common to test whether a distribution is normal or not.

Example
A firm supplying sand to builders' merchants inspects the records for a random sample of 250 orders. These records produce the distribution of size of orders as shown in Table 9.2. The firm needs to take decisions about stock-holding in order to meet the patterns of demand for sand that it faces. It is suggested that the pattern of order sizes follows that of a normal distribution. Test this belief.

Table 9.2 Testing for normality in the distribution of sand orders

Order size (cubic metres) X	Observed frequency O_i	Expected frequency E_i	$(O_i - E_i)^2$	$\dfrac{(O_i - E_i)^2}{E_i}$
Under 7.5	2 ⎫ 12	3.2 ⎫ 14.6	6.76	0.46
7.5 but under 9.5	10 ⎭	11.4 ⎭		
9.5 but under 11.5	25	31.5	42.25	1.34
11.5 but under 13.5	45	56.3	127.69	2.27
13.5 but under 15.5	65	64.7	0.09	0.00
15.5 but under 17.5	60	49.3	114.49	2.32
17.5 but under 19.5	35	24.1	118.81	4.93
19.5 but under 21.5	5 ⎫ 8	7.8 ⎫ 9.6	2.56	0.27
21.5 and over	3 ⎭	1.8 ⎭		
Summations:	250	250		$11.59 = \chi^2$

Solution
In order to calculate expected frequencies, we must first calculate the sample mean ($\bar{X}$) and standard deviation (s) to use as estimates of the unknown

population mean and standard deviation. These are computed from the raw data as:

$$\bar{X} = 14.192, \ s = 2.993$$

From the table of areas for the standard normal curve we can now calculate the class frequencies we would *expect* if the hypothesis that the sample has been drawn from a normal population were true. These expected frequencies are shown in the E_i column of Table 9.2. To demonstrate how these have been calculated, let us examine one class (19.5 but under 21.5) which gives an expected frequency of 7.8. This is arrived at by first calculating the value of Z which corresponds to each class limit and the corresponding probability (i.e. area obtained from the standard normal tables). Thus, for the class (19.5 but under 21.5), we have:

X	$Z = \dfrac{(X - \bar{X})}{s}$	Area to the left
21.5	2.44	0.4927
19.5	1.77	0.4616

Hence, by subtraction, the area between 19.5 and 21.5 = 0.0311. This is illustrated in Figure 9.3. So the expected frequency in this class is $0.0311 \times 250 = 7.8$ (approximately).

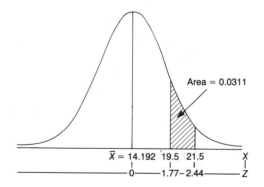

Figure 9.3 Testing a distribution for normality using a χ^2 test.

Having calculated expected frequencies for all classes and taken the appropriate action in those cases where expected frequencies fall below 5 by summing the E_is of adjacent classes (as shown in the table), we then proceed to calculate $(O_i - E_i)^2/E_i$ for each. The sum of these, it will be seen – the χ^2 statistic – is 11.59. We can now test the following hypotheses:

H_0: the population of order sizes is normally distributed.

H_1: the population is not normally distributed.

In determining the critical value of χ^2 in this example, it should be noted that the number of degrees of freedom is $k - p - 1$, where k is the number of classes (after ensuring that the 'at least' 5 condition has been satisfied) and p is the number of parameters that have had to be used in calculating expected frequencies. In this case $p = 2$ because we have had to use the mean and standard deviation in arriving at the E_i values. Therefore, the number of degrees of freedom is $7 - 2 - 1 = 4$. Thus:

Critical χ^2: $\chi^2_{0.05} = 9.49$

Conclusion: $\chi^2 > \chi^2_{0.05}$, so we can reject the null hypothesis. That is, the distribution of the sample of order sizes cannot be regarded as approximately a normal distribution.

Tests of independence

As noted in the introduction to this chapter, the χ^2 test can also be applied to situations in which observations are cross-classified among different variables. In such cases, the test involves a test of the independence of the classificatory variables. Examples of the sorts of questions that may then be addressed are:

□ Is there a relationship between the educational backgrounds of new employees and the various salary scales on which they are placed?
□ Is there a significant difference in the pattern of housing tenure (owning or renting) of people from different social classes?
□ Does the degree of customer satisfaction with, say, three models of food-mixer depend on the type of mixer purchased?

To address such questions, we can cross-classify the observations or responses according to the classificatory variables in a *contingency table*.

A 2×2 contingency table arises from the breakdown of two categorical variables into two classifications each. In general, an $r \times c$ contingency table corresponds to a breakdown of one variable into r classes ('rows') and the other into c classes ('columns'), giving rise to $r \times c$ 'cells'. The number of degrees of freedom in this case is now equal to $(r-1)(c-1)$. (Recall that, as with the one-variable case, the data used must relate to *absolute* frequencies and *not* simply relative frequencies.)

We now proceed to illustrate the conduct of the χ^2 test in this context and the conclusions that may be drawn.

Example: 2 × 2 contingency table
Here we extend our earlier example of sex discrimination in employment. The 200 employees were sub-classified according to sex. We could now sub-classify them further according to marital status – see Table 9.3. The question to be addressed is as follows: 'Is the pattern of employment between male and female employees independent of marital status?'

Table 9.3 Breakdown of employees by sex and marital status

Marital status of employees	Sex of employees		Total
	Male	Female	
Married	90	40	130
Single	60	10	70
Total	150	50	200

Solution
To answer this question we must first assign expected frequencies to each of these observed cell frequencies. These represent the numbers that would have occurred if, for example, the ratio between the number of married males and single males, was the same as the ratio for all employees and likewise for the female workforce. The computations are shown in Table 9.4.

Before applying the χ^2 test to these observed and expected frequencies, note that the number of degrees of freedom $(r-1)(c-1)$ is $(2-1)(2-1) = 1$ in this example. Therefore, the Yates' continuity correction factor needs to be applied. This is briefly explained below.

Yates' continuity correction factor
When there is only one degree of freedom we must introduce Yates' continuity correction factor, as noted earlier. This arises because the χ^2 tables are calculated from χ^2 probability distributions which are continuous, whereas the approximations (χ^2 statistics) are discrete. This creates a

Table 9.4 Observed and expected breakdown of employees by sex and marital status

Marital status	Male O_i	Male E_i	Female O_i	Female E_i	Total
Married	90	$\frac{130}{200} \times 150 = 97.5$	40	$\frac{130}{200} \times 50 = 32.5$	130
Single	60	$\frac{70}{200} \times 150 = 52.5$	10	$\frac{70}{200} \times 50 = 17.5$	70
Total	150	150	50	50	200

tendency to underestimate the probability. Yates showed that when the following expression is used:

$$\chi^2 = \sum \left[\frac{(|O_i - E_i| - \frac{1}{2})^2}{E_i} \right]$$

the χ^2 statistic approximation improves. But note that it is *only* necessary to introduce the correction factor when the number of degrees of freedom is 1. When the total number of observations is large, say $n > 50$, the correction factor has little effect on the outcome and can be ignored.

Returning to the example, we can now calculate the χ^2 statistic. This is shown in Table 9.5. The χ^2 test is conducted as follows:

Hypotheses: H$_0$: the employment by sex is not related to marital status.

H$_1$: the employment by sex is related to marital status.

Critical χ^2 value: $\chi^2_{0.05} = 3.841$ with 1 degree of freedom.

Decision: $\chi^2 > \chi^2_{0.05}$ (i.e. $5.744 > 3.841$). Therefore, we *reject* the null hypothesis and conclude that there is a relationship between the pattern of employment according to sex and the marital status of employees.

Example: 3 × 3 contingency table
A large consultancy firm regularly recruits MBA graduates. The personnel director has categorized each business school producing MBA graduates as 'top-rate', 'adequate' or 'bad' to assist their recruitment strategy. A survey

Table 9.5 Computation of χ^2 statistic for a 2×2 contingency using Yates' correction

	O_i	E_i	$O_i - E_i$	$\|O_i - E_i\| - \frac{1}{2}$	$\dfrac{[\|O_i - E_i\| - \frac{1}{2}]^2}{E_i}$
Males:					
Married	90	97.5	−7.5	7.0	0.503
Single	60	52.5	7.5	7.0	0.933
Females:					
Married	40	32.5	7.5	7.0	1.508
Single	10	17.5	−7.5	7.0	2.800
					$5.744 = \chi^2$

of the performance of 100 recent recruits has rated them as 'excellent', 'average' or 'poor'. A cross-classification of the results of the survey is shown in Table 9.6. Is there a relationship between the rating of these recruits and the business school at which they were trained?

Solution
Expected frequencies are calculated in the same way as before and are also shown in Table 9.6 (in parentheses). The χ^2 statistic is calculated as follows:

$$\chi^2 = \frac{(10-5)^2}{5} + \frac{(10-15)^2}{15} + \frac{(5-5)^2}{5} + \frac{(7-9)^2}{9}$$

$$+ \frac{(30-27)^2}{27} + \frac{(8-9)^2}{9} + \frac{(3-6)^2}{6} + \frac{(20-18)^2}{18}$$

$$+ \frac{(7-6)^2}{6}$$

$$= 5.0 + 1.67 + 0.0 + 0.44 + 0.33 + 0.11 + 1.5 + 0.22 + 0.17$$

$$= 9.44$$

Hypotheses: H_0: the rating of business schools and the performance of graduates are independent.
H_1: the ratings are not independent.

Critical χ^2 *value:* $\chi^2_{0.05} = 9.49$ with $(3-1)(3-1) = 4$ degrees of freedom.

Table 9.6 3×3 contingency table: cross-classification of MBA graduates (observed and expected* frequencies)

Rating of business schools	Rating of graduates			
	Excellent	Average	Poor	Total
Top-rate	10 (5)	10 (15)	5 (5)	25
Adequate	7 (9)	30 (27)	8 (9)	45
Bad	3 (6)	20 (18)	7 (6)	30
Total	20	60	20	100

*Expected frequencies are shown in parentheses.

Decision: $\chi^2 < \chi^2_{0.05}$ (i.e. $9.44 < 9.49$). Therefore, we accept H_0, i.e. there is no relationship between the performance of graduates and the business school at which they were trained, though note that H_0 is only *just* accepted.

In the second part of this chapter we have been dealing with tests of independence, concerning situations in which we were interested in testing for the association between categorical variables. In the next chapter, we will take a further step forward in considering the nature of the relationship between variables. This involves the techniques of regression and correlation.

Use of MINITAB

An illustration of the use of the statistical package MINITAB to conduct a χ^2 test, using the example of the test of independence given above, is shown in Computer illustration 9.1.

Computer illustration 9.1   MINITAB and chi-squared test of independence (compare with the example on pages 173–5)

```
MTB > NAME  C1 'Excell' C2 'Average' C3 'Poor'
MTB > READ C1-C3
DATA> 10 10 5
DATA> 7 30 8
DATA> 3 20 7
DATA> END
        3 ROWS READ
MTB > CHISquared test on table in C1-C3

Expected counts are printed below observed counts
```

	Excell	Average	Poor	Total
1	10 5.00	10 15.00	5 5.00	25
2	7 9.00	30 27.00	8 9.00	45
3	3 6.00	20 18.00	7 6.00	30
Total	20	60	20	100

```
ChiSq =   5.000 +   1.667 +   0.000 +
          0.444 +   0.333 +   0.111 +
          1.500 +   0.222 +   0.167 = 9.444
df = 4
```

Authors' note: The computed chi-squared value (9.444) is then compared with the critical value according to the desired level of signficance as in Appendix A5. For the decision, see page 175.

Key learning points

Goodness-of-fit test   A statistical test conducted to determine whether to accept or reject a hypothesized probability distribution for a population.

Chi-squared (χ^2) statistic   This forms the basis of the goodness-of-fit test to be carried out and is based on the differences between the observed and expected frequencies.

$$\chi^2 = \sum \left(\frac{(O_i - E_i)^2}{E_i} \right)$$

Chi-squared (χ^2) distribution   The sampling distribution of χ^2 statistics; there is in fact a whole family of distributions, each of which depends on the number of degrees of freedom available.

Test of independence A statistical test of the independence of classificatory variables.

Contingency table A table used to summarize observed and expected
frequencies for a test of independence of population characteristics.

Yates' continuity correction factor Used to adjust the value of the χ^2
statistic when there is only one degree of freedom present; thus, the
expression for the χ^2 statistic is:

$$\chi^2 = \sum \left[\frac{(|O_i - E_i| - \frac{1}{2})}{E_i} \right]^2$$

EXERCISES

Tests of goodness-of-fit

1 The new owner of a company has been informed by the previous owner that,
historically, sales of microwave ovens have been distributed across the model
range as follows:

　　Model 1　40%;　　　Model 2　60%;　　　Model 3　10%.

The new owner, in trying to decide whether or not he should reduce the range
of models produced, decides to take a random sample of 100 sales of
microwave ovens. He finds that sales are distributed as follows:

　　Model 1　20%;　　　Model 2　50%;　　　Model 3　20%.

Test the null hypothesis that the historical pattern of model sales still prevails
(at the 1 per cent level of significance).

2 A company expects 20 per cent of the door-to-door calls made by a salesman
to result in an actual purchase. During a trial period, a newly appointed
salesman makes 40 door-to-door visits and achieves only 4 sales. Test
whether or not the performance of the new salesman in achieving sales differs
significantly from the general performance expected by the company. (Note,
since there is only one degree of freedom, i.e., $k - 1 = 1$, Yates' continuity
correction factor should be applied here.)

3 A consumer protection group has carried out a survey on the reliability of
washing machines. Using a sample of 100 machines, researchers recorded the
number of months that passed before a machine had a major breakdown. The
actual distribution of breakdowns, according to the number of months that
elapse (in classes), is shown below, along with the expected frequencies if the
distribution of breakdowns follows a normal distribution. Test whether or not the
actual distribution of breakdowns differs significantly from a normal distribution.

Months before breakdown (classes)	Actual number of machine breakdowns	Expected number of machine breakdowns
under 17	6	9
18–20	24	17
21–23	28	27
24–26	18	25
27–29	14	15
30 or over	10	7
	Total 100	Total 100

Tests of independence

4 A firm conducts a sample survey of 500 households to see if preferences for two of its brands are related to socio-economic group and obtains the following results:

Brand	Socio-economic group			
	A	B	C	Total
1	125	110	90	325
2	75	60	40	175
Total	200	170	130	500

Test whether or not there is a significant relationship at the 5 per cent level of significance.

5 The following information shows the production levels for 100 workers (categorized as low, medium and high) for three age groups.

Age group	Production level			
	Low	Medium	High	Total
18–30	12	15	13	40
31–45	11	13	11	35
45–65	8	10	7	25
Total	31	38	31	100

Test whether or not there is a significant relationship between production levels and age.

10

Simple regression and correlation analysis

The essence of simple regression and correlation in business

There are many instances in business in which observations on two or more variables appear to be related to one another. For example, sales may seem to be related to advertising expenditure, profits may seem to be related to prices, absenteeism may seem to be related even to the weather! However, it would hardly seem appropriate to make major business decisions regarding advertising expenditure, for example, based on such flimsy evidence without further investigation concerning the form and degree of any relationship – if indeed any relationship exists at all!

In this chapter, we introduce two techniques which are aimed at measuring such relationships and testing their significance. These techniques are referred to as:

□ Regression analysis.
□ Correlation analysis.

Regression analysis is concerned with measuring the way in which one variable is related to another, i.e. how differences in one or more variables help to explain differences in another variable. *Correlation analysis*, on the other hand, is simply concerned with providing a statistical measure of the strength of any relationship between variables. When the relationship between only two variables is being considered the term *simple* regression and correlation analysis is used. This is in contrast to *multiple* regression and correlation analysis which is concerned with the relationship between one variable and two or more other variables. This chapter is concerned with

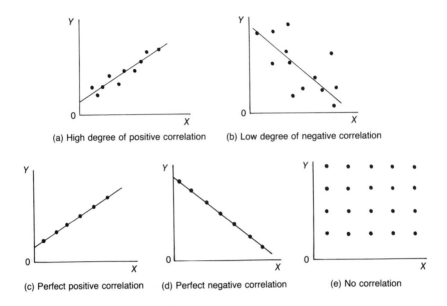

Figure 10.1 Scatter diagrams.

simple regression and correlation while the next chapter is concerned with multiple regression and correlation.

Figure 10.1 is meant to convey the essence of simple regression and correlation analysis. Each of the diagrams (known as *scatter diagrams*) consists of a set of points of paired observations on two variables, X and Y (e.g. these could be advertising expenditure and sales, respectively). It will be seen that straight lines have been drawn through the points in each diagram, except the last one. The objective of simple regression analysis is to arrive at an expression which defines the line which 'best' fits each set of plotted points; such lines are referred to as *regression lines*. No such line is drawn in the last diagram because the scatter of points is such that there is no unique best-fitting regression line.

With regard to correlation, the diagrams illustrate different degrees of simple correlation, ranging from perfect correlation in diagrams (c) and (d) to no correlation at all in diagram (e). The objective of simple correlation analysis is to arrive at a single summary measure of the degree of correlation between any two variables such as X and Y.

In this chapter we set out the general principles underlying these techniques, confined to cases involving two variables. This is sufficient to provide a sound understanding of the principles involved in the application of the techniques and their use in more complex applications involving more than two variables.

Simple regression analysis

The notion of a regression line was introduced above. For the purpose of illustration we have assumed that the best-fitting regression lines in Figure 10.1 are straight lines. it should be appreciated that regression analysis is not restricted to such linear relationships, but can be readily extended to non-linear relationships. The principles, however, are the same and hence we consider only linear regression analysis here. The central problem of simple regression analysis is to employ criteria which will allow us to identify the best-fitting line passing through any set of paired observations on X and Y, and hence to determine its equation in mathematical terms.

In general, the equation of any straight line is given by the expression:

$$Y = a + bX$$

It is conventional to assume that Y varies as X varies, rather than the other way round, i.e., that Y depends on X. Hence, Y is known as the *dependent* variable and X as the *independent* (or *explanatory*) variable. The interpretation of this equation is that as X changes, Y changes by b times the change in X, and therefore b measures the *slope* or *gradient* of the line. When X takes the value of zero, Y has the value a, which is referred to as the *intercept*. Examples are given in Figure 10.2. In Figure 10.2(a), the three lines have a zero intercept ($a = 0$) with the slopes increasing as the value of b increases. In Figure 10.2(b), the three lines have the same positive intercept. Given the equations for these various lines (shown in Figure 10.2), we can now 'predict' values of Y for any given value of X. Thus, for car 1, if 2 gallons of petrol are consumed ($X = 2$), the number of miles travelled will be 60. The relationships above, of course, are shown as precise relationships. In practice we have a scatter of points as in Figure 10.1.

Criteria for a best-fitting regression line: the method of least squares

A scatter diagram of sales per month and advertising expenditure per month is shown in Figure 10.3 along with the line of best fit. This line is determined

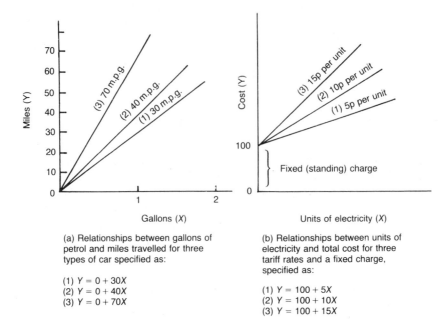

Figure 10.2 Intercepts and gradients.

(a) Relationships between gallons of petrol and miles travelled for three types of car specified as:

(1) $Y = 0 + 30X$
(2) $Y = 0 + 40X$
(3) $Y = 0 + 70X$

(b) Relationships between units of electricity and total cost for three tariff rates and a fixed charge, specified as:

(1) $Y = 100 + 5X$
(2) $Y = 100 + 10X$
(3) $Y = 100 + 15X$

using the method of *least squares*. The method allows us to derive the equation for this line, which we shall denote by:

$$Y_c = a + bX$$

where Y_c stands for the value of the variable Y *computed* from the relationship for a given value of the variable X. (Y_c is therefore distinguished from Y which represents actual, observed values.) The line $Y_c = a + bX$ expresses the average relationship between the two variables; it is called the *linear regression of Y on X* and the slope constant b is referred to as the *regression coefficient*. The problem remaining is to determine the values of a and b – these will then give us the equation for the best-fitting line.

The values of a and b must be calculated in such a way that the fitted line is as close as possible to the plotted points, corresponding to the observed values of X and Y (i.e. X_i, Y_i). Consider, for example, the point A in Figure 10.3. This point corresponds to a specific pair of observed values X_i and Y_i. The computed Y value (Y_c), corresponding to the given value X_i, can be determined from the relationship $Y_c = a + bX_i$. There will usually be differences between the actual values of Y and their computed values, depending on the closeness of the relationship. These

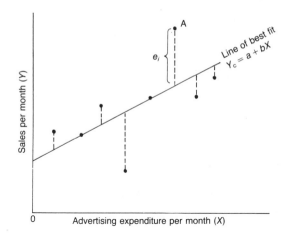

Figure 10.3 Sales and advertising expenditure: line of best fit.

differences (or 'deviations') between the actual and computed Y values are measured by

$$e_i = Y_i - Y_c$$

where the deviations, e_i, are known as *residuals*. As illustrated in Figure 10.3, they can take positive and negative values for different points; that is, actual points may be above the fitted line (e_i positive) or below it (e_i negative). The relevance of this analysis of deviations is that the best-fitting line can be obtained by ensuring that the sum of the *squared* residuals (Σe_i^2) is as small as possible. This is the basis of the method of least squares. The deviations are squared in order to give weight to both positive and negative values; otherwise they would cancel each other out.

The procedure for finding a and b from first principles, using the method of least squares, is rather complicated, involving differential calculus, and its demonstration is not essential to understanding the essence of statistics. It leads to the following expressions for determining the values of a and b. These are:

Formulae for regression coefficients:

$$b = \frac{\Sigma X_i Y_i - n\bar{X}\bar{Y}}{\Sigma X_i^2 - n\bar{X}^2}$$

$$a = \bar{Y} - b\bar{X}$$

where $\bar{Y}$ and $\bar{X}$ are the arithmetic means of the Y_i and X_i values respectively.

Once a and b have been determined, we can then deduce the equation for the best-fitting line, i.e. $Y_c = a + bX$.

Example
The following data show monthly advertising expenditure (£000s) and sales (£000s) over a period of 6 months. Estimate the relationship between sales (Y) and advertising expenditure (X).

Sales Y_i: 3   15   6   20   9   25

Advertising
expenditure X_i: 1   2   3   4   5   6

Solution
The computations involved to determine a and b are as follows (note that Y_i^2 values are not needed here but are included for use in analyzing correlation later).

X_i	Y_i	X_i^2	$X_i Y_i$	Y_i^2
1	3	1	3	9
2	15	4	30	225
3	6	9	18	36
4	20	16	80	400
5	9	25	45	81
6	25	36	150	625
$\Sigma X_i = 21$	$\Sigma Y_i = 78$	$\Sigma X_i^2 = 91$	$\Sigma X_i Y_i = 326$	$\Sigma Y_i^2 = 1376$

$$\bar{X} = 21/6 = 3.5 \quad \bar{Y} = 78/6 = 13$$

$$b = \frac{\Sigma X_i Y_i - n\bar{X}\bar{Y}}{\Sigma X_i^2 - n\bar{X}^2}$$

$$= \frac{326 - 6 \times 3.5 \times 13}{91 - 6 \times (3.5)^2}$$

$$= 3.03$$

$$a = \bar{Y} - b\bar{X}$$

$$= 13 - 3.03 \times 3.5$$

$$= 2.40$$

Hence, the estimated relationship between sales and advertising expenditure is:

$$Y_c = 2.40 + 3.03X$$

The interpretation of this equation is that, assuming a linear relationship, for every £1000 increase in advertising expenditure, sales can be expected to increase by 3.03 thousand units on average. With no expenditure on advertising, average sales are likely to be 2.40 thousand units.

We referred in Figure 10.1 to positive and negative correlation and illustrated the corresponding regression lines. In the case of negative (i.e. inverse) relationships, it will be appreciated that the regression coefficient b is negative.

A note on causation

In the example above, it is implicitly assumed that sales *depend* upon advertising expenditure – and not the other way round. In other words, variations in advertising expenditure are assumed to *cause* variations in sales. While this may appear reasonable, we have not *proved* the direction of causation, i.e. the estimated regression equation measures the relationship but does not, in itself, prove causation.

Testing the significance of b

It should be appreciated that while we have calculated a regression equation, we have not as yet considered its statistical significance. This naturally depends on the statistical significance of a and b. Most commonly we are concerned with testing the significance of b because the intercept a is of little interest in its own right. We now turn to this issue.

The data set (X_i, Y_i) represents a sample of observations from all possible values of the two variables; that is, from the population of all paired values (X_i, Y_i). In this case the sample regression coefficients a and b represent *estimates* of the corresponding intercept and slope coefficients for the population from which the sample has been drawn. We shall denote these population coefficients by A and B respectively. The population coefficients are, of course, unknown and the sample coefficients represent only one result among a number of possible results that could have been obtained depending on the sample. However, we are still able to use the sample results to test the significance of the relationship between the variables X and Y.

Most commonly we are concerned with testing the null hypothesis H_0: $B = 0$; that is, that the slope of the population regression line is zero. Acceptance of this hypothesis means that the population regression line is a horizontal line (i.e. with slope $B = 0$). In this case, information about X would be of no value in helping us to predict values of Y. On the other hand, if we reject this hypothesis and accept one of the possible alternative hypotheses that we may wish to test (e.g. $B \neq 0$, $B > 0$ or $B < 0$), then the population regression line must slope upwards (or downwards) such that information about X will help us to predict values of Y.

To test these hypotheses we must turn to the only information available, namely the sample regression equation and test H_0 against the sample result, e.g. to compare b with the hypothesized value, B. In order to do this we first need to be able to measure the standard error of b (just as we used the standard error of the mean in testing the significance of sample means – see Chapter 8). This is given by the expression:

Standard error of b (denoted s_b):

$$s_b = \frac{\text{s.e.e.}}{\sqrt{\Sigma X_i^2 - n\overline{X}^2}}$$

where s.e.e. denotes the 'standard error of estimate' and is equal to

$$\text{s.e.e.} = \sqrt{\frac{\Sigma Y_i^2 - a\Sigma Y_i - b\Sigma X_i Y_i}{n - 2}}$$

The test statistic can be either Z or t but a t test is normally required and we confine our attention here to this case. The value of t as the test statistic is defined as:

$$t = \frac{b - B}{s_b}$$

This has a t distribution with $n - 2$ degrees of freedom, where n is the number of paired observations (X_i, Y_i). This is then compared with the critical value of t from the t tables (Appendix A4) for the required level of significance, α.

Note that since under H_0, $B = 0$ is being tested, this is equivalent to testing $t = b/s_b$. As with the other tests of significance, if the calculated value of t falls outside the critical limits t_α (one-tailed test) or $t_{\alpha/2}$ (two-tailed test), we reject the null hypothesis that $B = 0$, and conclude that $B \neq 0$ (two-tailed test) or $B > 0$ or $B < 0$ (as appropriate for one-tailed tests).

Example

In the example above we estimated the regression equation for the relationship between sales and advertising expenditure as:

$$Y_c = 2.40 + 3.03X$$

The question now arises whether or not the regression coefficient b (3.03) is significantly greater than zero (a *positive* one-tailed test since we have a prior expectation in this case that sales rise with advertising expenditure).

The data required are the summations from the earlier calculations; these are:

$$\Sigma X_i = 21; \quad \Sigma Y_i = 78; \quad \Sigma X_i^2 = 91; \quad \Sigma X_i Y_i = 326; \quad \Sigma Y_i^2 = 1376.$$

In addition,

$$\bar{X} = 3.5, \ \bar{Y} = 13, \ a = 2.40, \ b = 3.03, \ n = 6$$

Hypotheses: $\quad H_0: \quad B = 0$
$\qquad\qquad\quad H_1: \quad B > 0$

Test statistic: $\quad t = \dfrac{b}{s_b}$

$$\text{where } s_b = \frac{\sqrt{[(\Sigma Y_i^2 - a\Sigma Y_i - b\Sigma X_i Y_i)]/(n - 2)}}{\sqrt{\Sigma X_i^2 - n\bar{X}^2}}$$

$$= \frac{\sqrt{[(1376 - (2.40 \times 78) - (3.03 \times 326)]/(6 - 2)}}{\sqrt{91 - (6 \times 3.5^2)}}$$

$$= \frac{7.089}{4.183}$$

$$= 1.69$$

$$\text{Thus, } t = \frac{3.03}{1.69}$$

$$= 1.79$$

Critical t value: $\quad t_{0.05} = 2.132$ with 4 degrees of freedom (i.e. $n - 2$)
Decision: $\quad t < t_{0.05}$, i.e. $1.79 < 2.132$

Therefore, we must accept H_0, i.e. we cannot conclude that the relationship between sales and advertising expenditure is significant at the 5 per cent level of significance.

Forecasting and regression analysis

Up to this point our aim has been to derive the best-fitting regression equation explaining the relationship between the two variables X and Y. Undoubtedly, this is the main purpose of simple regression analysis for it enables us to specify by how much the dependent variable changes in response to a change in the independent variable: for example, by how much sales increase as advertising expenditure increases; by how much a consumer increases expenditure on 'luxury' goods (such as overseas holidays) as his or her income rises; by how much profits in the ice-cream industry might vary during certain weeks of the year as the number of hours of sunshine varies, etc. Perhaps just as important, however, is the use of regression analysis to make *forecasts* or *projections* of changes in the dependent variable as the dependent variable changes. For example, by how much will prices rise in the shops if trade unions obtain a 10 per cent rise in wages for shop assistants?

If we derive the equation for the best-fitting regression line, between, say, prices (P) and wages (W), we can then project what will happen to prices as wages rise, by substituting the corresponding values of W into the resultant best-fitting regression equation:

$$P_c = a + bW$$

where, in keeping with our earlier notation, P_c represents the computed values of P lying along the best-fitting line. We can obtain 'forecasts' for P by substituting any value of W into this equation (including values which may not even have been observed or used previously to derive the regression line). It is common to denote forecasted values of the dependent variable by a superscript 'f'; i.e. P^f. However, needless to say, to make such forecasts requires the assumption (and perhaps a heroic assumption!) that the linear relationship computed for the past will continue to hold true for all time. Caution is clearly necessary in the use of regression results in this context. Further discussion of forecasting is given in Chapter 12.

Extrapolation versus interpolation

Computing values for the dependent variable (Y_c) *within* the range of recorded observations on the independent variable is referred to as *interpolation*. In contrast, projecting values (backwards as well as forwards) outside this range, giving rise to Y^f values, is referred to as *extrapolation*.

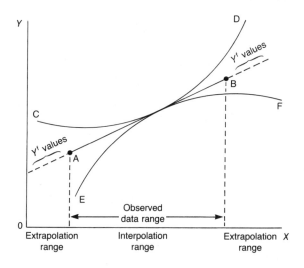

Figure 10.4 Extrapolation and interpolation.

This distinction is illustrated in Figure 10.4. Thus, computed values of Y within the range AB in Figure 10.4 give rise to interpolation, while any projection outside this range gives rise to extrapolation.

A further warning is in order. It must be stressed that extrapolation may, in some circumstances, give rise to very inaccurate or dubious forecasts. This is because a *linear* relationship which may be a true or reasonably good approximation for a particular range of observations (such as between A and B) may not be true for observations outside this range, as illustrated in Figure 10.4 by the curves CD and EF. Forecasts are only estimates, and so a *forecast error* is likely to arise in almost every case. It is for this reason that such forecasts are often referred to as *projections* rather than *predictions*. True predictions would attempt to take account of other factors not reflected in the data. The error is equal to the difference between the actual value of Y_i (if or when it occurs) and the forecasted value, Y_i^f, i.e. $(Y_i - Y_i^f)$. Hence the greatest of care must be exercised when making judgements based on extrapolation. Governments, statisticians, scientists, managers, economists, etc. frequently make forecasts by extrapolating, but awareness of the limitations of the technique should enable one to appreciate and view such forecasts with caution.

The burden of computation in regression analysis: the use of computers

Computations in regression analysis, if done manually, are burdensome. This is an area of statistics in which the introduction of computers has probably made one of the biggest impacts. Nowadays, statistical computer software will produce all the regression results needed in a matter of seconds, even for very large data sets. There is a danger, however, of using these packages mechanically without being aware of the nature of the results and the pitfalls. The objective so far in this chapter has been to develop this awareness. At the end of this chapter we present an illustration of the regression output that would be produced by one of the most popular, and user-friendly, statistical packages, MINITAB.

Simple correlation analysis

Simple correlation analysis, as we explained in the introduction to this chapter, is a means of measuring the strength or 'closeness' of the relationship between two variables. It should be clear that the concept of correlation is very closely linked to regression analysis – if all the paired points (X_i, Y_i) lie on a straight line then the correlation between the variables X and Y is perfect. Whether the correlation is perfectly *positive* or *negative* depends, of course, on whether the straight line through the points has a positive or negative slope. In Figure 10.1, discussed earlier, diagram (d) illustrates perfect negative correlation while diagram (c) illustrates perfect positive correlation. The more scattered and random are the points (X_i, Y_i), the less the degree of correlation, as in diagrams (a), (b) and (e).

Correlation analysis provides a numerical summary measure of the degree of correlation between two variables X and Y. This is termed a *correlation coefficient, r*, which is defined as follows:

$$r = \frac{s_{XY}}{s_X s_Y}$$

where s_{XY} = sample covariance, given by:

$$\frac{\Sigma(X_i - \bar{X})(Y_i - \bar{Y})}{n - 1}$$

s_X = sample standard deviation of X values
s_Y = sample standard deviation of Y values

Computing the values of r, using this definition, is tedious. However, it reduces to a quicker, more convenient formula:

$$r = \frac{n\Sigma X_i Y_i - (\Sigma X_i)(\Sigma Y_i)}{[\sqrt{n\Sigma X_i^2 - (\Sigma X_i)^2}][\sqrt{n\Sigma Y_i^2 - (\Sigma Y_i)^2}]}$$

By definition, the value of r must lie within the range -1 and $+1$. Hence:

□ $r = +1$ denotes perfect positive correlation, as in Figure 10.1(c).
□ $r = 0$ denotes no correlation, as in Figure 10.1(e).
□ $r = -1$ denotes perfect negative correlation as in Figure 10.1(d).

We illustrate the calculation and comment on the interpretation of r below, using the data for sales and advertising expenditure given on pages 184–5.

Example
The data and corresponding summations are reproduced below:

X_i	Y_i	X_i^2	$X_i Y_i$	Y_i^2
1	3	1	3	9
2	15	4	30	225
3	6	9	18	36
4	20	16	80	400
5	9	25	45	81
6	25	36	150	625
$\Sigma X_i = 21$	$\Sigma Y_i = 78$	$\Sigma X_i^2 = 91$	$\Sigma X_i Y_i = 326$	$\Sigma Y_i^2 = 1376$

$$r = \frac{n\Sigma X_i Y_i - (\Sigma X_i)(\Sigma Y_i)}{[\sqrt{n\Sigma X_i^2 - (\Sigma X_i)^2}][\sqrt{n\Sigma Y_i^2 - (\Sigma Y_i)^2}]}$$

$$= \frac{(6 \times 326) - (21 \times 78)}{[\sqrt{(6 \times 91) - (21)^2}][\sqrt{(6 \times 1376) - (78)^2}]}$$

$$= \frac{318}{10.247 \times 46.605}$$

$$= 0.667 \text{ (approximately 0.67)}$$

This suggests a fairly high degree of correlation between sales and advertising expenditure. However, as with regression analysis, we have to test whether this degree of correlation is significant, i.e. what is the probability that it has occurred by chance when there may be little correlation in the populations of X and Y from which the sample has been drawn? We conduct the test below after first considering a useful related aspect of the interpretation of r in terms of the measurement of the *overall* explanatory power of a regression equation, known as the *coefficient of determination*.

Coefficient of determination

The coefficient of determination is simply the squared value of the correlation coefficient above, i.e. r^2. It is particularly useful in describing the closeness of the relationship between X and Y, i.e. how closely the actual points cluster around the regression line (how 'good' the fit is). In the estimated regression of Y on X ($Y_c = a + bX$), we are trying to explain the total variation in the observations of Y by variations in X. Rarely, however, is *all* of the variation in Y explained by the variation in X alone – there is usually an 'explained' proportion of variation and an 'unexplained' proportion. That is,

Total variation in Y = explained variation + unexplained variation

where: total variation = $\Sigma(Y_i - \bar{Y})^2$

explained variation = $\Sigma(Y_c - \bar{Y})^2$

unexplained variation = $\Sigma(Y_i - Y_c)^2$,   i.e. Σe_i^2.

Thus:

$$\Sigma(Y_i - \bar{Y})^2 = \Sigma(Y_c - \bar{Y})^2 + \Sigma(Y_i - Y_c)^2$$

The coefficient of determination, r^2, measures the proportion of total variation that is explained, i.e. it is equivalent to the following:

$$\frac{\text{Explained variation in } Y}{\text{Total variation in } Y} = \frac{\Sigma(Y_c - \bar{Y})^2}{\Sigma(Y_i - \bar{Y})^2}$$

Naturally, it is easier to measure r^2 by simply taking the squared value of r. By definition, the unexplained proportion is measured by $(1 - r^2)$. In the example above, where $r = 0.667$, $r^2 = (0.667)^2 = 0.44$. We are able to say, therefore, that 44 per cent of the variation in sales is 'explained' by variation in advertising expenditure, while 56 per cent is 'unexplained' (i.e. due to other factors). Remember again, however, that this conclusion and the use of this terminology should not be taken to imply *causation*, i.e. that X causes Y. It is merely stating a statistical relationship.

Testing the significance of r

Once again, we must test the significance of a sample coefficient – in this case the value of r – just as we did in the case of the regression coefficient *b.* It is worth noting that, in the case of only two variables X and Y, a significance test on *r* is equivalent to a significance test on the regression coefficient *b.*

The test involves the difference between the value of *r* calculated for the sample data and the corresponding unknown value for the population correlation coefficient, conventionally denoted by the Greek letter ρ (pronounced 'rho'). As in the case of the regression coefficient, *b*, we need to determine the probability of this difference occurring, and thus whether the difference is statistically significant. Hence, we calculate the test statistic, *t*, as:

$$t = \frac{r - \rho}{\text{standard error of } r}$$

In correlation analysis, we are usually concerned with testing whether the value of *r* could have come from a population in which there was no linear correlation between X and Y (i.e. $\rho = 0$). Hence, the above expression reduces to:

$$t = \frac{r}{\text{standard error of } r}$$

where the standard error of *r* is given by:

$$\text{Standard error of } r = \sqrt{\frac{1 - r^2}{n - 2}}$$

Thus, the test statistic for the null hypothesis that $\rho = 0$ reduces to:

$$t = \frac{r}{\sqrt{\dfrac{1 - r^2}{n - 2}}}$$

which will have a *t* distribution with $n - 2$ degrees of freedom.

Example

In the example above, where $r = 0.667$, the procedural steps for testing whether there is a significant degree of positive correlation between X and Y are as follows:

Null hypothesis: $H_0: \rho = 0$
$H_1: \rho > 0$

Test statistic: $t = \dfrac{r}{\sqrt{\dfrac{1-r^2}{n-2}}}$

$ = \dfrac{0.667}{\sqrt{\dfrac{1-(0.667)^2}{(6-2)}}}$

$ = \dfrac{0.667}{0.373}$

$ = 1.79$

Critical t *value:* $t_{0.05} = 2.132$ with 4 degrees of freedom (i.e. $n-2$)
Decision: $t < t_{0.05}$ i.e. $(1.79 < 2.132)$

Therefore, we conclude that H_0 is accepted, i.e. one cannot conclude that the degree of correlation between sales and advertising expenditure is significant at the 5 per cent level of significance – the same conclusion reached earlier where we tested the significance of the regression coefficient b.

Note that, if we are testing for a significant degree of *negative* correlation between X and Y, then the alternative hypothesis above would be H_1: $\rho < 0$.

Extensions of simple regression and correlation analysis

In this chapter we have only presented the essence of simple regression and correlation. We comment on three extensions of the analysis presented here.

Non-linear relationships

We have illustrated the concepts of regression and correlation by reference to a simple linear relationship involving only two variables, X and Y. It should be appreciated, however, that the techniques can be readily extended to situations in which the form of the relationship is *non-linear* (commonly referred to as 'curvilinear'). For this reason it is usually desirable to plot data as a scatter diagram, as in Figure 10.1, to obtain a visual impression of the relationship before carrying out any calculations. For ease of analysis in the case of a non-linear relationship it is often possible to convert the relationship to a linear one by mathematical transformation of the variables (such as taking logarithms).

Multiple regression and correlation analysis

We have dealt in this chapter with relationships involving *one* independent (explanatory) variable, X, which gives rise to *simple* regression and correlation analysis. Again, the techniques of regression and correlation analysis can be extended to include more than one explanatory variable, giving rise to *multiple* regression and correlation analysis. Multiple regression and correlation analysis is dealt with in the next chapter.

Other measures of correlation

In this chapter we have introduced one measure of correlation – the simple correlation coefficient, r – where the variables have a numerical value. Other situations may only involve *rankings*, as in the ranking of preferences for different product brands. Measures of *rank correlation* have been devised to deal with this situation. One such measure is *Spearman's rank correlation*. When more than two sets of ranks are involved, an appropriate measure of correlation between the rankings is *Kendall's coefficient of concordance*.

Use of MINITAB

In Computer illustration 10.1 we show the output provided by the statistical computer package, MINITAB, based on the data for sales and advertising expenditure used throughout this chapter. It will be noted that the standard printout from MINITAB includes more information than we have discussed. We have highlighted the key results:

☐ The estimated least squares regression equation (showing the values of a and b)

☐ The standard deviation of the regression coefficient (i.e. standard error, s_b)

☐ The standard error of estimate (s.e.e.)

☐ The coefficient of determination (r^2 – the correlation coefficient squared)

□ t statistics relating to both regression coefficients a and b (although we have only discussed the latter in this chapter)

□ Computed values for Y, i.e. Y_c

□ Residuals, e_i, given by $(Y - Y_c)$

Computer illustration 10.1 MINITAB and regression and correlation analysis (compare with the examples on pages 184–5, 191–2 and 193–4.

```
            REGRESSION OF SALES (Y) ON ADVERTISING EXPENDITURE (X)

MTB > NAME C1 'X'
MTB > NAME C2 'Y'
MTB > SET C1
DATA> 1 2 3 4 5 6
DATA> END
MTB > SET C2
DATA> 3 15 6 20 9 25
DATA> END

MTB > BRIEF 3   (This command gives computed Y_c values.)

MTB > REGRESSION OF 'Y', USING 1 PREDICTOR, ON 'X'
```

The regression equation is ← [Least squares line]
$Y = 2.40 + 3.03\ X$

Predictor	Coef	Stdev	t-ratio	p
Constant	2.400	6.607	0.36	0.735
X	3.029	1.697	1.79	0.149

[s.e.e.]

$s = 7.097$ ◄   R-sq = 44.3%   R-sq(adj) = 30.4%

Analysis of Variance r^2 s_b $t = b/s_b$

SOURCE	DF	SS	MS	F	p
Regression	1	160.51	160.51	3.19	0.149
Error	4	201.49	50.37		
Total	5	362.00			

Obs.	X	Y	Fit	Stdev.Fit	Residual	St.Resid
1	1.00	3.00	5.43	5.14	-2.43	-0.50
2	2.00	15.00	8.46	3.86	6.54	1.10
3	3.00	6.00	11.49	3.02	-5.49	-0.85
4	4.00	20.00	14.51	3.02	5.49	0.85
5	5.00	9.00	17.54	3.86	-8.54	-1.43
6	6.00	25.00	20.57	5.14	4.43	0.90

Y_c $e = Y - Y_c$

Comparing the results computed manually with those from MINITAB, it will be seen that there are some very small differences. These are merely due to the fact that MINITAB computes to a larger number of decimal places than we have used earlier.

Key learning points

Regression analysis   Concerned with measuring the way in which one variable is related to another.

Correlation analysis   Concerned with providing a statistical measure of the strength of any relationship between variables.

Scatter diagram   A diagram which consists of a set of points of paired observations on two variables.

Dependent variable   The variable that is being predicted or explained. It is denoted by Y in the regression equation.

Independent (or explanatory) variable   The variable that is doing the predicting or explaining. It is denoted by X in the regression equation.

Residual   The difference between the actual value of the dependent variable and the value computed using the estimated regression equation.

$$e_i = Y_i - Y_c$$

The method of least squares   The approach used to develop the estimated regression equation which minimizes the sum of squares of the deviations between the actual and computed (i.e. estimated) values of the dependent variable:

Minimize Σe_i^2

Estimated regression equation   The estimate of the regression equation obtained by the method of least squares.

$$Y_c = a + bX$$

Formulae for regression coefficients

$$b = \frac{\Sigma X_i Y_i - n\bar{X}\bar{Y}}{\Sigma X_i^2 - n\bar{X}^2}$$

$$a = \bar{Y} - b\bar{X}$$

Standard error of b

$$s_b = \frac{\text{s.e.e.}}{\sqrt{\Sigma X_i^2 - n\bar{X}^2}} \quad \text{where s.e.e.} = \sqrt{\frac{\Sigma Y_i^2 - a\Sigma Y_i - b\Sigma X_i Y_i}{n-2}}$$

Testing the significance of b

$$t = \frac{b - B}{s_b}$$

Correlation coefficient (r)   Provides a numerical summary measure of the degree of correlation between two variables.

$$r = \left[\frac{n\Sigma X_i Y_i - (\Sigma X_i)(\Sigma Y_i)}{\sqrt{n\Sigma X_i^2 - (\Sigma X_i)^2}\,[\sqrt{n\Sigma Y_i^2 - (\Sigma Y_i)^2}} \right]$$

Coefficient of determination (r^2)   A measure of the variation explained by the estimated regression equation. It is a measure of how well the estimated regression equation fits the data.

$$r^2 = \frac{\text{Explained variation in } Y}{\text{Total variation in } Y} = \frac{\Sigma(Y_c - \bar{Y})^2}{\Sigma(Y_i - \bar{Y})^2}$$

Testing the significance of r

$$t = \frac{r}{\sqrt{\dfrac{1 - r^2}{n - 2}}}$$

EXERCISES

1 The data show the commission earnings last month achieved by 9 salesmen in relation to their years of experience in selling.

Sales commission (£)	Numbers of years' experience
50	6
100	13
140	27
110	15
70	9
90	11
140	21
100	14
80	12

(a) Compute the best-fit regression equation between these two sets of data, assuming that sales commission is dependent on years of selling experience.
(b) Test whether the regression coefficient, b, is significantly greater than zero (at the 5 per cent level of significance).
(c) What is the degree of correlation between the two data sets?
(d) What proportion of the variation in commission earnings is explained by factors *other than* years of selling experience?
(e) What commission would be expected for a salesman with 10 years of experience?

2 A central heating fuel distributor records the following sales of fuel oil (000s of litres) over 10 winter weeks along with the average temperature (°C) for each week.

Week:	1	2	3	4	5	6	7	8	9	10
Fuel oil sales (000s of litres):	26	17	7	12	30	40	20	15	10	5
Average temperature (°C):	4	10	14	12	4	5	8	11	13	15

(a) Compute the best-fit regression equation between fuel oil sales and temperature, assuming that fuel oil sales are dependent on temperature.
(b) Test the significance of the regression coefficient, b, at the 5 per cent level of significance.
(c) What is the degree of correlation between sales and temperature?
(d) What proportion of the variation in fuel oil sales is explained by variations in temperature?
(e) What fuel oil sales would be expected if the temperature rose to 12 °C?

3 A firm has decided to devise an aptitude test to give to applicants for jobs as assemblers. Aptitude scores for 10 current employees are compared below with times they take on an assembly task.

Aptitude test score:	40	30	50	20	22	35	10	10	15	50
Assembly time (minutes):	6	7	2	6	7	5	8	9	9	3

(a) Regress assembly times on aptitude scores and say whether or not assembly times are positively related to aptitude scores.
(b) Measure the degree of correlation and say whether it is significant.
(c) Interpret the results.

11

Multiple regression and correlation analysis

The essence of multiple regression and correlation in business

In Chapter 10 we considered the essence of simple linear regression and correlation analysis involving a dependent variable (Y) and only one explanatory variable (X). In this chapter we turn to consider the extension of the simple model to applications involving two or more explanatory variables as the basis for estimating the value of Y. This extension gives rise to *multiple* linear regression and correlation.

Multiple regression and correlation analysis has a wide range of applications. It is the basis of all macroeconomic forecasting models. In a business context, an example of its application would involve the prediction of sales which it is thought are related to a number of explanatory variables such as: advertising expenditure, number of sales representatives, price of the product, as well as perhaps seasonal factors (measured by rainfall, temperature, etc.).

It will be appreciated that in the case of multiple regression which involves more than one explanatory variable, the estimated regression line cannot be represented in a simple two-dimensional diagram (as in Figure 10.1, page 180). The multiple regression line is a line in multi-dimensional space. The calculations required for determining the estimated regression equation and for measuring correlation are much more tedious than in the case of simple regression and correlation. These calculations are not normally carried out manually. Nowadays, the use of computers and appropriate statistical packages, such as MINITAB, makes the estimation of the regression equation and correlation coefficient a simple task.

In this chapter, therefore, after examining the key concepts involved in multiple linear regression and correlation analysis, we focus on the interpretation of the results and the application of MINITAB to various situations. In practice, the use of multiple linear regression involves a number of technical issues which are beyond the scope of this book. We refer to these briefly below but do not develop them in detail.

———

Multiple regression analysis

The multiple linear regression equation takes the following general form for the case of k explanatory variables:

$$Y_c = a + b_1 X_1 + b_2 X_2 + b_3 X_3 + \ldots + b_k X_k$$

where Yc is the computed (i.e. estimated) value of Y, a is the value of the intercept term and $b_1, b_2, b_3, \ldots, b_k$ are the values of the estimated regression coefficients corresponding to each of the explanatory variables $X_1, X_2, X_3, \ldots, X_k$.

The coefficients are naturally estimates (based on sample data) of their corresponding population parameters which may be denoted, using capital letters, as:

$A, B_1, B_2, B_3, \ldots, B_k.$

The values of the b_k coefficients are derived using the principle of the method of least squares (described in the context of simple linear regression in Chapter 10). The b_k regression coefficients are defined such that the sum of the squares of the residuals (i.e. the differences between the actual values of Y and the computed values, Y_c) is as small as possible. Thus, the objective is to minimize $\Sigma(Y - Y_c)^2$ as before. The calculations involved in deriving values for a, b_1, b_2, etc., are carried out nowadays automatically and speedily using appropriate computer software packages. As noted above, we therefore confine our attention here to the interpretation of results, their statistical significance and the pitfalls and limitations associated with multiple regression and correlation analysis.

As in the case of simple regression analysis, there are four aspects of the results to consider in the case of multiple regression:

☐ interpretation of the individual regression coefficients
☐ statistical significance of the regression coefficients

☐ overall explanatory power of the estimated equation
☐ statistical significance of the overall explanatory power

We discuss the essence of each of these in turn.

Interpretation of regression coefficients

In the multiple regression case, the intercept term a is the estimated value of Y (i.e. Y_c) when the values of *all* explanatory variables are zero. Thus, for the case of three explanatory variables:

$Y_c = a$, when $X_1 = X_2 = X_3 = 0$.

The interpretation of any b_i coefficient in multiple regression analysis is as follows: b_i represents the change in Y_c corresponding to a unit change in X_i when all other independent variables are held constant. For example, consider the case where the monthly sales of sunglasses (S) can be explained by three variables: price P, advertising expenditure E and hours of sunshine H for each month. Thus, the estimated relationship between sales and the explanatory variables can be expressed as:

$S_c = a + b_1 P + b_2 E + b_3 H$

where S_c now represents the value of monthly sales as predicted by the equation. The coefficients a, b_1, b_2 and b_3 are derived from a data set providing past monthly observations of the number of sales and the three explanatory variables over a period of time.

The interpretation of the intercept a in this context simply denotes the average number of sales when each of the three explanatory variables has a value of zero simultaneously. The coefficient b_1 represents the average change in sales associated with a unit change in the price variable P when the other independent variables are held constant. Similarly, b_2 represents the average change in sales associated with a unit change in advertising expenditure E when the other independent variables are held constant (and so on for b_3). By this means of control, we are able to separate out the effect of each explanatory variable on sales, free of any distorting influences from the other explanatory variables. For this reason, the b_1, b_2 and b_3 values are referred to as *partial regression coefficients*.

Statistical significance of individual regression coefficients

As in Chapter 10, to test whether or not a partial regression coefficient (say b_1) is significantly different from zero, we set up the null hypothesis which states that the variable associated with b_1, i.e. X_1, does not influence the dependent variable Y. Thus:

$$H_0: \quad B_1 = 0$$

where B_1 represents the hypothesized population parameter. To say, as here, that $B_1 = 0$ means that it is being hypothesized that the variable X_1 has no effect on the dependent variable Y. We are thus using the sample coefficient, b_1, which may have a non-zero value simply as a result of sampling error, to test the likelihood that the true population parameter B_1 is really zero. The alternative hypothesis, H_1, may be stated, as before, in either a one-tailed or a two-tailed form:

Two-tailed test $\quad$ $H_1: \quad B_1 \neq 0$

One-tailed tests $\quad$ $H_1: \quad B_1 < 0$ $\quad$ or $\quad$ $H_1: \quad B_1 > 0$

Similar hypotheses may be set up for the other regression coefficients.

These hypotheses may be tested using a t test (as before), where the calculated value of the test statistic is defined as:

Test statistic

$$t = \frac{b_i - B_i}{S_{b_i}}$$

where, as before, S_{b_i} is the standard error of b_i.

Since under the null hypothesis $H_0: B_i = 0$, this reduces to:

$$t = \frac{b_i}{S_{b_i}}$$

This calculated value of t is then compared with its critical value, given in the t table (see Appendix A4). Note that the degrees of freedom for the t statistic in the multiple regression case, however, are:

Degrees of freedom

$$n - k - 1$$

where n is the number of observations on the dependent variable and k is the number of independent variables

Note that if any individual regression coefficient is found not to be significant based on the t test, the corresponding explanatory variable would normally be excluded from the final regression model or replaced in modified form (e.g. a non-linear form such as its value squared) and its significance re-tested.

The fact that individual regression coefficients may be found to be statistically significant does not necessarily mean that the *overall* explanatory power of the regression model is high. This involves the analysis of multiple correlation.

Multiple correlation analysis

The focus of this section is measuring and testing the overall explanatory power of a multiple regression model.

Overall explanatory power of the estimated regression equation

Multiple coefficient of determination, R^2

In discussing simple correlation analysis in the last chapter we explained that the coefficient of determination r^2 provides a measure of the overall explanatory power of a simple regression model $Y_c = a + bX$. Thus, an r^2 value of 0.81 would indicate that 81 per cent of the variation in the dependent variable Y is explained by variation in the independent variable X. In the case of multiple regression analysis we compute a similar measure which shows how much of the variation in Y is explained by the *joint* variation in all of the explanatory variables. This measure is known as the *multiple coefficient of determination*, denoted now as R^2 (rather than r^2). It is thus a measure of *overall* explanatory power (i.e. goodness-of-fit for the regression model as a whole). It is defined in the same way as r^2. Thus the value of R^2 is given by:

Multiple coefficient of determination

$$R^2 = \frac{\textbf{Explained variation in } Y}{\textbf{Total variation in } Y} = \frac{\Sigma(Y_c - \bar{Y})^2}{\Sigma(Y_i - \bar{Y})^2}$$

The value of R^2 is automatically calculated by MINITAB and other computer packages. The range for R^2 is from 0 to 1. If $R^2 = 1$, then 100 per cent of the total variation in the dependent variable Y has been explained by the model. This rarely, if ever, occurs in practice, but in general a large value of R^2 is desirable. The fit of the model is said to be 'better' the closer the value of R^2 is to 1. Naturally, judgements of overall explanatory power also require a test of the statistical significance of R^2 (see below).

Coefficient of multiple correlation, R

The square root of the multiple coefficient of determination is the *coefficient of multiple correlation*, denoted by R. It is a measure of the degree of association between Y and all the explanatory variables jointly. Conceptually, it is thus akin to the coefficient of correlation r in the simple regression case but, whereas r can be positive or negative, R is always taken to be positive. Note, however, that in practice R is of little importance and can be ignored. Most attention is paid to the multiple coefficient of determination, R^2.

Adjusted multiple coefficient of determination, $\bar{R}^2$

It can be shown that adding additional explanatory variables to a multiple regression model will generally increase the value of R^2. In view of this, in comparing two regression models with the *same dependent variable (Y)* but a different number of explanatory X variables, one must be very wary of choosing that model which has the highest R^2 value. To compare two R^2 values, it is necessary to take into account the number of X variables included in each model. This is done by computing an *adjusted R^2 value*, denoted $\bar{R}^2$ (pronounced 'R-bar squared'), in order to avoid overestimating the impact of any additional explanatory variable on the amount of explained variation. This adjusted R^2 value is known as the *adjusted multiple coefficient of determination* and is measured as:

Adjusted multiple coefficient of determination

$$\bar{R}^2 = 1 - (1 - R^2)\,\frac{n-1}{n-k-1}$$

where *n* is the sample size and *k* is the number of independent variables.

Statistical significance of overall explanatory power

We showed above how the statistical significance of each of the partial regression coefficients b_k may be tested using a t test. Similarly, we can test the statistical significance of the regression model as a whole, i.e. its *overall explanatory power*, given by R^2. This requires a different procedure involving a test statistic known as the F *statistic*.

Whereas the test of the statistical significance of an individual coefficient (b_k) involves a test of the null hypothesis, $H_0: B_k = 0$, a test of *overall explanatory power* is a test of whether or not *all* the Bs are equal to zero. The relevant test statistic, the F *statistic*, is again calculated automatically by computer packages, such as MINITAB, and there is no need to be concerned with its actual measurement. In brief, however, it is defined as the ratio of the explained to the unexplained *variance*. Recall that the total variation in the dependent variable $\Sigma(Y_i - \bar{Y})^2$ may be decomposed into a part explained by the regression, $\Sigma(Y_c - \bar{Y})^2$ and a residual (unexplained) part $\Sigma(Y_i - Y_c)^2$. The relevant expressions for *explained variance* and *unexplained variance* are simply the total explained and unexplained *variation* divided by their respective degrees of freedom (k and $n - k - 1$ respectively).

F test

Having measured the F statistic, the test of statistical significance – the F *test* – follows the usual procedures. In summary, in the present context, these procedures involve first specifying the test hypotheses and then comparing the calculated F statistic with a critical value obtained from F tables of the probability distribution of F (Appendix A6) with a given level of probability (the F *tables* are explained below).

The hypotheses may be stated as:

H_0: $B_1 = B_2 = \ldots = B_k = 0$

H_1: one or more of the B coefficients is not equal to zero.

If we reject H_0, we can conclude that there is a significant relationship between the dependent variable and at least one of the independent (explanatory) variables and that the regression equation *as a whole* is significant. But note that even if the regression as a whole is significant, some of the individual regression coefficients may not be statistically significant and thus it is important to test the statistical significance of each of the individual explanatory variables and not to rely solely on the test of overall explanatory power. It is worth noting too that in the case of simple regression analysis, with only one explanatory variable, an F test of overall explanatory power is necessarily equivalent to a t test of the single regression coefficient B. In this case, it may be shown that $F = t^2$.

F tables and the F distribution

It remains to explain the use and layout of the F tables. The form of the F distribution is illustrated in Figure 11.1. Note that the distribution is non-symmetrical and the F values cannot be negative. The actual shape of the distribution depends upon the degrees of freedom of the corresponding numerator and denominator of the expression for calculating the F *statistic* referred to above (i.e. k and $n - k - 1$ respectively). Tables of the F statistic for probability values (α) of 0.05 and 0.01 with degrees of freedom, denoted v_1 and v_2 for the numerator and denominator respectively, ranging from 1 to ∞ are given in Appendix A6. Thus, for example, it will be seen that, with $v_1 = 9$ and $v_2 = 12$, the critical F statistic (denoted F_α) is equal to 2.80

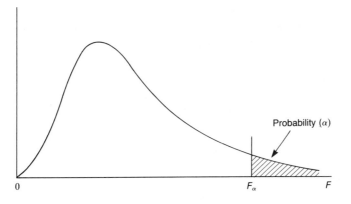

Figure 11.1 *F* distribution.

at the 5 per cent level of significance and 4.39 at the 1 per cent level; that is, there is only a 5 per cent chance of obtaining a value of the F statistic greater than 2.80 and a 1 per cent chance of it exceeding 4.39. Note that Appendix A6 is in two parts, the first corresponding to $\alpha = 0.05$ and the second to $\alpha = 0.01$. So, returning to the conduct of the F test, if the computed F statistic exceeds the critical F value then we reject the null hypothesis and conclude that the overall regression is statistically significant.

Pitfalls and limitations of multiple regression analysis

A number of pitfalls face the unwary in the use of multiple regression. Detailed consideration of these, and the limitations which they pose, is beyond the scope of this book. We comment on them briefly here in order to sound a note of caution. Detailed discussions will be found in specialized books on regression analysis.

The main problems are associated with the following issues:

□ the choice of an inappropriate *functional form* for the estimated regression equation (i.e. linear versus non-linear relationships), referred to as *functional form misspecification*;

□ the extent to which two or more of the explanatory variables are correlated with one another, thus making it impossible to measure their separate influences reliably, a problem referred to as *multicollinearity*;

☐ the possibility that observations on the dependent variable Y are themselves correlated over time, referred to as a problem of *autocorrelation* or *serial correlation*, which affects the reliability of significance tests on the partial regression coefficients;

☐ the possibility that the prediction errors may not be constant and instead may be correlated with the size of the explanatory variables, a problem – referred to as *heteroscedasticity* – which again may affect the reliability of significance tests on the estimated regression coefficients;

☐ the possibility that the explanatory variables in the regression model include measurement errors, a problem – referred to as *errors in variables* – which leads to biased and inconsistent estimates of the regression coefficients.

Use of MINITAB

Example and computer illustration
The table below shows the monthly sales of sunglasses by a firm over a period of 12 months together with details of average prices in each month, advertising expenditure per month and the mean daily hours of sunshine in each month.

Using the data:

1. compute the regression equation which can be used to estimate the influence of the three explanatory variables (price, advertising expenditure and hours of sunshine) on sales of sunglasses,

2. interpret the results, and

3. use the results to predict sales when price is £2.50, advertising expenditure is £25,000 and the mean hours of sunshine is 5.

Month	Sales (000s)	Price (£)	Advertising expenditure (£000s)	Mean daily hours of sunshine (number)
January	75	6.8	2	2.4
February	90	6.5	5	4.0
March	148	6.0	6	5.2
April	183	3.5	7	6.8
May	242	3.0	22	8.0
June	263	2.9	25	8.4
July	278	2.6	28	10.4
August	318	2.1	30	11.5
September	256	3.1	22	9.6
October	200	3.6	18	6.1
November	140	4.2	10	3.4
December	80	5.2	2	2.0

Solution
(1) Regression equation

The MINITAB printout below shows the estimated regression equation for the multiple linear regression model:

sales = $a + b_1$ (price) + b_2 (advertising expenditure) + b_3 (hours).

The equation is:

sales = $120 - 12.2$ (price) + 2.32 (advertising expenditure) + 13.2 (hours).

(2) Interpretation

To interpret the results we pay attention to the following factors:

☐ the size and sign of the estimated regression coefficients (b_1, b_2, b_3)
☐ the statistical significance of the regression coefficients
☐ the statistical significance of the regression as a whole
☐ the overall explanatory power of the regression model
☐ the presence of unusual observations (i.e. so-called *outliers*)

Size and sign of coefficients. A priori one would expect sales to be inversely related to price (i.e. sales increase as price falls), but to be positively related both to advertising expenditure and hours of sunshine (b_3). In summary, therefore, *a priori* expectations are that the regression coefficient for price (b_1) should be negative and those for advertising expenditure (b_2) and hours of sunshine (b_3) should be positive. It will be seen from the MINITAB output that this is in fact the case. Interpretation of the size of the coefficients, bearing in mind the units of measurement of the original data, is that sales fall by 12.2 (000) for a unit increase (£1) in price, rise by 2.32 (000) for a unit increase (£1000) in advertising expenditure and rise by 13.2 (000) for a unit rise (one hour) in sunshine.

Statistical significance of the coefficients. It will be seen that the t ratio for price is -2.77. The statistical significance of this result may be judged in two ways. One is to compare the value with the critical value of t with degrees of freedom $= n - k - 1$ where k is the number of independent variables from the t tables (Appendix A4). Thus for a one-tailed test (with H_1: $B_1 < 0$) $t = -1.86$ (i.e. $t_{0.05}$ with 8 degrees of freedom). As $-2.77 < -1.86$ we reject H_0 (i.e. $B_1 = 0$) and conclude that B_1 is significantly less than zero. The alternative way of conducting the hypothesis test is to use the p values (probability values) given in the MINITAB output alongside the t ratios. The p statistic shown alongside the t ratio of -2.77 is 0.024. This indicates that

Computer illustration 11.1 MINITAB and multiple regression and correlation analysis

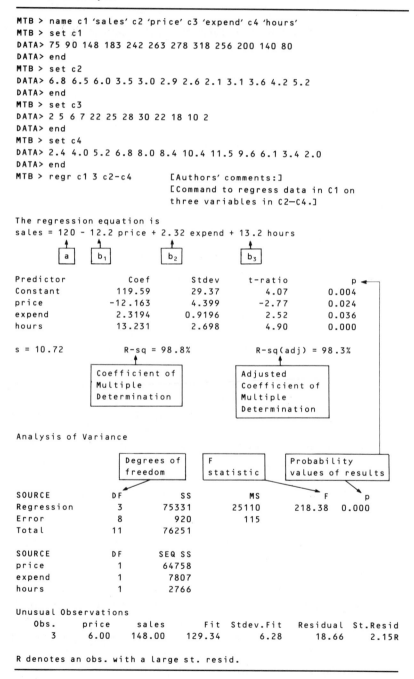

```
MTB > name c1 'sales' c2 'price' c3 'expend' c4 'hours'
MTB > set c1
DATA> 75 90 148 183 242 263 278 318 256 200 140 80
DATA> end
MTB > set c2
DATA> 6.8 6.5 6.0 3.5 3.0 2.9 2.6 2.1 3.1 3.6 4.2 5.2
DATA> end
MTB > set c3
DATA> 2 5 6 7 22 25 28 30 22 18 10 2
DATA> end
MTB > set c4
DATA> 2.4 4.0 5.2 6.8 8.0 8.4 10.4 11.5 9.6 6.1 3.4 2.0
DATA> end
MTB > regr c1 3 c2-c4          [Authors' comments:]
                               [Command to regress data in C1 on
                               three variables in C2–C4.]
```

```
The regression equation is
sales = 120 - 12.2 price + 2.32 expend + 13.2 hours
```

$$\text{sales} = \underset{a}{120} - \underset{b_1}{12.2}\ \text{price} + \underset{b_2}{2.32}\ \text{expend} + \underset{b_3}{13.2}\ \text{hours}$$

Predictor	Coef	Stdev	t-ratio	p
Constant	119.59	29.37	4.07	0.004
price	-12.163	4.399	-2.77	0.024
expend	2.3194	0.9196	2.52	0.036
hours	13.231	2.698	4.90	0.000

s = 10.72   R-sq = 98.8%   R-sq(adj) = 98.3%

Coefficient of
Multiple
Determination

Adjusted
Coefficient of
Multiple
Determination

Analysis of Variance

Degrees of freedom   F statistic   Probability values of results

SOURCE	DF	SS	MS	F	p
Regression	3	75331	25110	218.38	0.000
Error	8	920	115		
Total	11	76251			

SOURCE	DF	SEQ SS
price	1	64758
expend	1	7807
hours	1	2766

Unusual Observations

Obs.	price	sales	Fit	Stdev.Fit	Residual	St.Resid
3	6.00	148.00	129.34	6.28	18.66	2.15R

R denotes an obs. with a large st. resid.

the t value of -2.77 cuts off a tail area of 0.024 (i.e. 2.4 per cent). Thus if the test is conducted at the 5 per cent level of significance ($\alpha = 0.05$), the *p value* indicates that the value of the test statistic falls in the rejection region. In general, if the p value is·less than α, then the n test statistic must be in the rejection region, whereas if the p value is greater than or equal to α, the test statistic must be in the acceptance region.

Having explained the interpretation of the p values in the MINITAB output, we can comment on the statistical significance of the other two explanatory variables very quickly. It will be seen that the p value for the advertising expenditure variable (0.036) and the hours of sunshine variable (0.000) are both less than 0.05 and thus both variables may be regarded as statistically significant at the 5 per cent level of significance (i.e. $B_2 > 0$ and $B_3 > 0$). Note that p values are expressed to three decimal places only.

Statistical significance of the regression as a whole. It will be seen that the F statistic is 218.38 and that this has a probability value of 0.000 indicating that the regression as a whole is very highly significant.

Overall explanatory power. The R^2 value (denoted R-sq in the MINITAB printout) indicates that 98.8 per cent of the variation in sales is explained by the regression as a whole (i.e. by the joint variation in the three explanatory variables). The adjusted R^2 value (denoted R-sq(adj)) equals 98.3 per cent.

Unusual observations. MINITAB highlights those observations which have especially large residuals (observed minus predicted values) for the dependent variable. (Note that the letter R used in MINITAB to denote such observations should not be confused with the coefficient of multiple correlation referred to on p. 205.) It will be seen from the output that the third observation is highlighted as an unusual observation with respect to the price variable. The purpose of identifying such an unusual observation is to direct attention to the possibility that it may be misrecorded or simply an unusual event (which should perhaps be ignored in further modelling). Such unusual observations are often referred to as *outliers*.

(3) Prediction

Given the regression equation:

$$\text{sales} = 120 - 12.2\,(\text{price}) + 2.32\,(\text{advertising expenditure}) + 13.2\,(\text{hours}),$$

the required prediction for sales is obtained by substituting the specific values for the three explanatory variables specified in the question. This gives:

Predicted sales $= 120 - 12.2(2.5) + 2.32(25) + 13.2(5)$

$$= 120 - 30.5 + 58 + 66$$

$$= 213.5 \text{ thousand}$$

Key learning points

Multiple regression model   A regression equation in which more than one independent variable is used to explain the dependent variable. The general form of the equation is:

$$Y_c = a + b_1 X_1 + b_2 X_2 + b_3 X_3 + \ldots + b_k X_k$$

Statistical significance of the regression coefficient   Use of a t test to test whether or not the partial regression coefficients are significantly different from zero.

   Test statistic:

$$t = \frac{b_i - B_i}{s_{b_i}}$$

$$= \frac{b_i}{s_{b_i}} \text{ under the null hypothesis } H_0: B_i = 0$$

Multiple correlation analysis   Refers to the measuring and testing of the overall explanatory power of a multiple regression model.

Multiple coefficient of determination (R^2)   Provides a statistical measure of the overall goodness-of-fit for the regression model as a whole.

$$R^2 = \frac{\text{Explained variation in } Y}{\text{Total variation in } Y} = \frac{\Sigma(Y_c - \bar{Y})^2}{\Sigma(Y_i - \bar{Y})^2}$$

Coefficient of multiple correlation (R)   A statistical measure of the degree of association between the dependent variable and all the explanatory variables jointly.

$$R = \sqrt{R^2}$$

Adjusted multiple coefficient of determination ($\bar{R}^2$)   Allows comparison of the overall explanatory power of regression models which have the same dependent variable but a different number of explanatory variables. The value of R^2 is adjusted as follows:

$$\bar{R}^2 = 1 - (1 - R^2)\frac{n-1}{n-k-1}$$

F test   Test of the statistical significance of the regression model as a whole, i.e. its overall explanatory power, given by R^2, based on the F statistic which follows the F distribution.

EXERCISES

1   A car dealer believes that the number of cars sold each month is related to the number of years of sales experience and the age of the salesperson. The data for a random sample of 10 salespersons are as follows:

Y	X_1	X_2
17	2	23
23	6	33
20	8	30
18	11	35
19	4	24
22	7	49
21	7	36
28	14	40
26	12	46
12	3	51

where Y = number of cars sold per month
X_1 = number of years of sales experience
X_2 = age of salesperson (years)

The MINITAB output obtained by regressing Y on X_1 and X_2 is given below.

(a) What is the estimated regression equation?
(b) Interpret the coefficients on X_1 and X_2.
(c) State whether or not there is a significant relationship between sales and both explanatory variables, taken together, at the 5 per cent level of significance.
(d) State whether or not the explanatory variables X_1 and X_2 are statistically significant at the 5 per cent level. Be sure to state the null and alternative hypotheses and on what your conclusions are based (i.e. the test procedure used).

Computer illustration 11.2   MINITAB output for Exercise 1

```
MTB > regr c1 2 c2 c3

The regression equation is
Y = 16.4 + 0.931 X1 - 0.074 X2
```

Predictor	Coef	Stdev	t ratio	p
Constant	16.424	4.351	3.77	0.007
X1	0.9307	0.2949	3.16	0.016
X2	-0.0739	0.1189	-0.62	0.554

```
s = 3.319          R-sq = 59.1%          R-sq(adj) = 47.4%
```

Analysis of Variance

SOURCE	DF	SS	MS	F	p
Regression	2	111.31	55.65	5.05	0.044
Error	7	77.09	11.01		
Total	9	188.40			

SOURCE	DF	SEQ SS
X1	1	107.06
X2	1	4.25

Unusual Observations

Obs.	X1	Y	Fit	Stdev.Fit	Residual	St.Resid
4	11.0	18.00	24.08	1.55	-6.08	-2.07R

R denotes an obs. with a large st. resid.

(e) What proportion of the variation in sales is explained by variation in the two explanatory variables?

(f) Predict the sales of a salesperson with 10 years' sales experience who is 30 years of age.

2 A management consultant employed by a firm to examine the efficiency of the plants it operates considers that the profitability of each plant is positively related to the total sales of each plant (X_1) and capital expenditure (X_2) but inversely related to a cost efficiency index (total costs/sales), denoted X_3, and the number of employees (X_4). The MINITAB output obtained by regressing profits on the four explanatory variables using data from a random sample of plants is given below.

(a) What was the total sample size used?

(b) What are the expected signs for the parameter estimates?

(c) Do the parameter estimates have the expected signs?

(d) Test the null hypothesis that the explanatory variables, as a set, do not significantly affect profits at the 5 per cent level of significance.

(e) Taken individually, do the variables have a significant influence on profits?

Computer illustration 11.3   MINITAB output for Exercise 2

```
MTB > regr c1 4 c2-c5

The regression equation is
profits = - 27.4 + 0.0464 X1 + 8.21 X2 + 12.3 X3 + 0.109 X4

Predictor              Coef         Stdev        t-ratio              p
Constant            -27.383         3.188          -8.59          0.074
X1                 0.046369      0.002742          16.91          0.038
X2                  8.2096         0.2466          33.29          0.019
X3                  12.288          3.064           4.01          0.156
X4                  0.10928        0.02139          5.11          0.123

s = 1.139            R-sq = 100.0%         R-sq(adj) = 100.0%

Analysis of Variance

SOURCE           DF              SS           MS            F          P
Regression        4         22238.1       5559.5      4288.09      0.011
Error             1             1.3          1.3
Total             5         22239.4

SOURCE           DF          SEQ SS
X1                1         20636.2
X2                1          1531.4
X3                1            36.6
X4                1            33.8

Unusual Observations
Obs.      X1     profits         Fit    Stdev.Fit    Residual   St.Resid
   4     951     168.000     168.104        1.134      -0.104     -1.00 X
   6     554     110.000     110.066        1.137      -0.066     -1.00 X

X denotes an obs. whose X value gives it large influence.
```

12

Analyzing time series data

The essence of time series analysis in business

As the name implies, a time series is any set of numerical observations which are recorded at different points in time, such as annual profits, quarterly production figures, weekly sales, daily takings, etc. The study of time series is primarily directed at an analysis of the nature of variations in such series. The information obtained may provide a detailed picture of the underlying behaviour of the variables concerned, aid the interpretation of them and also allow us to predict future values in the time series.

It is virtually impossible nowadays to read a business report or a financial newspaper or even to enter a manager's office without seeing charts of time series, illustrating fluctuations in data such as production, share prices, interest rates, sales, exchange rates, prices, imports, etc. Graphs of such data display a wide variety of movements: some will show systematic changes as, for example, in consistent growth of production; others will vary more or less systematically according to seasons of the year; while others may appear so erratic that they give the impression of being completely random.

It is helpful to measure the systematic movements of business and economic data, and necessary to try to extract some sense of order out of those which are seemingly random so that they may be useful in managerial decision making. Time series data can be regarded as the outcome of four underlying influences or *components*. These are:

☐ **Trend (denoted T).**

☐ **Seasonal variation (denoted S).**

☐ **Cyclical variation (denoted C).**

☐ **Irregular (i.e. random) variation (denoted R).**

These four components, superimposed on one another and acting in conjunction, account for the changes in data series over time, often giving them an irregular appearance. Time series analysis breaks down the observed data values (Y_t, where t denotes time) into their components. Two fundamental approaches may be employed. One is to assume that the relationship between the components may be described by an *additive model* such that:

$$Y_t = T_t + S_t + C_t + R_t$$

The other approach is to assume that the relationship may be described by a *multiplicative model* such that:

$$Y_t = T_t \times S_t \times C_t \times R_t$$

It is common in practice, however, to regard the multiplicative model as the most appropriate and, consequently, we confine our attention to this model only. The basic principles of the analysis are the same in both cases. For convenience, we will drop the time subscript t in the exposition given below. The analysis which follows focuses on the measurement of each of the four components in turn.

———

Measurement of trend (T)

A time series may tend to move in an upward or downward direction, or perhaps remain roughly constant, over fairly long periods of time. This may be fairly evident at first sight even though the series may be overlaid with the influence of the other factors defined above. Apart from simply 'guessing' the trend by means of a freehand sketch, there are two major ways of measuring the trend:

□ The linear trend method.
□ The moving average method.

The use of the linear trend method applies, of course, when the trend is appropriately described by a straight line. The moving average method is suited to situations in which there is a greater degree of irregularity and especially to those in which there are reversals of trend from time to time. The choice is determined by visual inspection of the graphed data.

Linear trend method

The linear trend method simply applies the regression techniques outlined in the previous chapter, with time taken as the independent variable, X. A linear trend is then defined as:

$$T_Y = a + bX$$

where T_Y denotes the underlying trend value of the variable Y under consideration, measured at regular intervals, X denotes the points of time (each being numbered consecutively), a is the intercept term and b represents the change in T_Y per unit of time. Figure 12.1 shows such a trend line for car production over the years 1987–95.

The original data are as follows:

Year (X)	1987	1988	1989	1990	1991	1992	1993	1994	1995
Number of cars (000s) (Y):	21	25	24	29	35	38	40	52	63

The calculation of the trend line is shown in Table 12.1 on page 220. It will be seen from Figure 12.1 that the linear trend line represents the long-term movement of car production for this company quite well in that it fits the observed values closely and tells us that the long-term trend for car production is, on average, an increase of 4.83 thousand cars per year. If it were reasonable to presume that this trend will continue, the equation for the trend line would allow management to forecast car production at future dates and thus, perhaps, to plan labour and capital requirements, etc. However, remember the reservations about extrapolation made at the end of the last chapter.

Moving average method

In contrast to the linear trend method, the moving average method provides a trend line by smoothing out fluctuations in the time series. It has the advantage, therefore, of fitting sets of data which show irregular variation. An illustration of the application of the method, using an arbitrary set of data, is shown in Table 12.2 on page 221 to give 'three-year moving average' trend values of Y, denoted T_Y. This is produced by averaging the values for the first three years (1988, 1989 and 1990), then for the years 1989, 1990, 1991, and then for 1990, 1991, 1992, etc. Note that the moving average is 'centred' against the mid-point of the averaging period. The process of centring is straightforward when the time span (n) is an *odd* number.

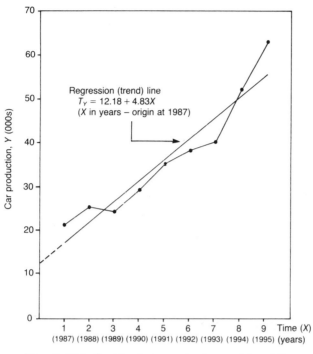

Figure 12.1 Graph of car production and trend line.

However, since data are often recorded on a quarterly, monthly, or weekly basis (for which there are *even* numbers per year), it is necessary to smooth the data on the same (yearly) basis (i.e. quarterly, monthly or weekly) – that is, to calculate a 4-, 12- or 52-period moving average respectively. In such cases, as n is an *even* number, the centring procedure above is not so straightforward (since, for example with $n = 4$, there is no single period which corresponds to the centre of the span). The problem is easily solved, however, by carrying out the centring process *twice* as illustrated in Table 12.3 on page 221, which uses quarterly data for petrol sales to show the calculation of a four-period moving average. The data and the moving average trend are graphed in Figure 12.2 on page 222.

It will be appreciated that the larger the number of terms in the moving average (i.e. the larger the value of n), then the smoother the resulting series. Over-smoothing the series, however, is a danger to be avoided, especially when the data are to be used for seasonal analysis. At the same time, the larger the value of n the more information on trend values we lose at the beginning and end of the data series (as illustrated in Tables 12.2 and 12.3). One disadvantage of the moving average trend, as opposed to a linear trend, is that it is not evident how it can be projected forward for prediction purposes.

Table 12.1 Calculation of trend for car production

Year	Time units X	Number of cars Y	X^2	XY	$T_Y = a + bX$ $= 12.18 + 4.83X$
1987	1	21	1	21	17.01
1988	2	25	4	50	21.84
1989	3	24	9	72	26.67
1990	4	29	16	116	31.50
1991	5	35	25	175	36.33
1992	6	38	36	228	41.16
1993	7	40	49	280	45.99
1994	8	52	64	416	50.82
1995	9	63	81	567	55.65
Summations (Σ)	45	327	285	1925	

$$\bar{X} = \frac{45}{9} = 5; \quad \bar{Y} = \frac{327}{9} = 36.3$$

Trend line: $\quad T_Y = a + bX$

Calculation of a *and* b*:*

$$b = \frac{\Sigma XY - n\bar{X}\bar{Y}}{\Sigma X^2 - n\bar{X}^2}$$

$$= \frac{1925 - (9 \times 5 \times 36.3)}{285 - 9 \times 5^2}$$

$$= 4.83$$

$$a = \bar{Y} - b\bar{X}$$

$$= 36.3 - (4.83 \times 5)$$

$$= 12.18$$

Trend equation:

$$T_Y = 12.18 + 4.83X$$

Measurement of seasonal variation (S)

Many series of business and economic statistics are published in two separate forms: *seasonally adjusted* and *seasonally unadjusted*. The difference arises from the fact that when data (such as output, sales, etc.) are recorded

Table 12.2 Calculation of a three-year moving average trend

Year	Y_t	Moving average trend (T_Y)
1988	15	
1989	25	= (15 + 25 + 30)/3 = 23.33
1990	30	= (25 + 30 + 35)/3 = 30
1991	35	= (30 + 35 + 45)/3 = 36.67
1992	45	= 45
1993	55	= 53.33
1994	60	= 63.33
1995	75	

Table 12.3 Calculation of a four-quarter moving average trend

Year/quarter		Petrol sales (000s of litres)	Four-quarter moving averages	Centred moving average trend
1992	Q1	9		
	Q2	11		
	Q3	15	11.75	
	Q4	12	12.25	12
1993	Q1	11	14.00	13.125
	Q2	18	15.25	14.625
	Q3	20	16.25	15.75
	Q4	16	19.75	18
1994	Q1	25	22.75	21.25
	Q2	30	25.75	24.25
	Q3	32	29.25	27.5
	Q4	30	30.00	29.625
1995	Q1	28	31.25	30.625
	Q2	35	33.25	32.25
	Q3	40	34.75	34
	Q4	36		

monthly or quarterly, they frequently exhibit strong seasonal variations and, as a consequence, considerable attention is given to adjusting the observed information to allow for this seasonal element. Hence the observed data are said to be seasonally unadjusted, while allowance for seasonal variation gives rise to seasonally adjusted data. Annual data, by definition, cannot of course exhibit seasonal variation. The purpose of seasonal adjustment is to allow the underlying movements in the series to be revealed, undistorted by any seasonal variation.

Reporting of information which has not been adjusted to allow for seasonal variation can give a very misleading impression about the underlying behaviour of the variable in question. Ice-cream sales, for

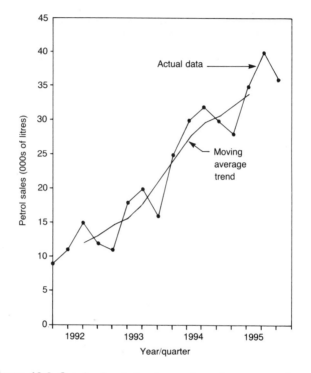

Figure 12.2 Graph of petrol sales and moving average trend.

example, generally fall in winter time. Therefore, in interpreting data on ice-cream sales, the question arises whether the trend of sales is greater or less than would be expected, given the normal seasonal effect. To answer this question requires that the data should be adjusted to remove the effect of seasonal variation on ice-cream sales. In other words, given that a time series may be regarded as the product of the four components $T \times S \times C \times R$, it is necessary to measure S and then 'de-seasonalize' the series by dividing by S. The seasonal factor S is normally measured in the form of a *seasonal index*. For example, in the case of quarterly data, the seasonal index (S) might have the values 97, 100, 102, 101, corresponding to the four quarters Q1–Q4. These would mean that, for example, for the first quarter the effect of seasonal variation reduces the value of the variable in question by 3 per cent on average relative to trend (because the index for the first quarter is 97) while, in contrast, seasonal variation increases the value by 1 per cent above trend in Q4. We now turn to describe the calculation of a seasonal index.

In essence, the calculation of a seasonal index simply consists of computing averages of actual observations relative to their trend values for

Table 12.4 Calculation of a seasonal index by the ratio-to-moving-average method

Year/quarter		Actual value of petrol sales (000s of litres)	Trend value of petrol sales (centred moving averages – see Table 12.3)	Ratio $(Y/T_Y) \times 100$
		Y	T_Y	(%)
1992	Q1	9		
	Q2	11		
	Q3	15	12	125
	Q4	12	13.125	91
1993	Q1	11	14.625	75
	Q2	18	15.75	114
	Q3	20	18	111
	Q4	16	21.25	75
1994	Q1	25	24.25	103
	Q2	30	27.5	109
	Q3	32	29.625	108
	Q4	30	30.625	98
1995	Q1	28	32.25	87
	Q2	35	34	103
	Q3	40		
	Q4	36		

Calculation of seasonal index:

		Ratios $(T_Y \times 100)$		
Year	Q1	Q2	Q3	Q4
1992	–	–	125	91
1993	75	114	111	75
1994	103	109	108	98
1995	87	103	–	–
Average seasonal index	88	109	115	88	(Total = 400)*

*The four quarterly averages should sum to 400 to provide a seasonal index. If they do not they need to be adjusted proportionately to ensure that they do sum to 400.

each quarter, month, etc., over some given period of time. Using the multiplicative model, this is known as the *ratio-to-moving-average* method. The application of the method is set out in Table 12.4. The steps of the calculation procedure are:

1. Calculate the ratios of actual observations (Y) to their corresponding trend values (T_Y), i.e. Y/T_Y. This 'detrends' the data. We may note at

this point that the use of the moving average trend method (as opposed to the linear trend method) means that the trend values will not smooth out any cyclical movements. Thus, in effect, taking ratios as above also removes any cyclical effects as well as any trend. The rationale of the procedure, therefore, may be expressed as follows, using our original notation for the multiplicative model:

$$\frac{Y}{T \times C} \text{ is equivalent to } \frac{T \times S \times C \times R}{T \times C} = S \times R$$

The next step is to remove R from the 'detrended' series (with any cycles also now removed) and so to 'isolate' S.

2. To remove as much of R as possible from this series ($S \times R$), we calculate the average of the $S \times R$ values for the corresponding quarters of each year – see the bottom part of Table 12.4.

The seasonal index may be of interest in its own right. The index here shows, for example, that the petrol company can anticipate a fall in sales averaging 12 per cent below trend in the first quarter, a rise of 9 per cent above trend in the second quarter, a rise of 15 per cent above trend in the third quarter and a fall of 12 per cent in the fourth quarter. However, it is also used, of course, to produce a seasonally adjusted series by 'de-seasonalizing' the observed series, i.e. by calculating $(Y/S) \times 100$. This is shown in Table 12.5. Graphs to compare the actual (unadjusted) series and the seasonally adjusted series are shown in Figure 12.3 on page 226. Comparison of the two graphs reveals very clearly that seasonal factors mask a consistent underlying growth in petrol sales.

Measurement of cyclical variation (C)

Many sets of time series data in business are also affected by periodic upturns and downturns in business confidence and activity, commonly referred to as 'business cycles' or 'trade cycles'. These may occur with a varying degree of regularity over a number of years, say five from the peak of one cycle to the next. Their analysis tends to be of more interest to the government and to economists than to business managers generally. But in some industries in which the planning horizon is long (such as in the energy sectors), then attention to cyclical factors, especially those that may apply to these industries in particular, may be important.

The analysis of cycles simply involves the removal of S, T and R from a time series using the same methodology outlined above for analyzing

Table 12.5 Calculation of seasonally adjusted series for petrol sales

Year/quarter		Petrol sales (seasonally unadjusted) Y	Seasonal index (%) (see Table 12.4) S	Petrol sales (seasonally adjusted)* $(Y/S) \times 100$
1992	Q1	9	88	10
	Q2	11	109	10
	Q3	15	115	13
	Q4	12	88	14
1993	Q1	11	88	13
	Q2	18	109	17
	Q3	20	115	17
	Q4	16	88	18
1994	Q1	25	88	28
	Q2	30	109	28
	Q3	32	115	28
	Q4	30	88	34
1995	Q1	28	88	32
	Q2	35	109	32
	Q3	40	115	35
	Q4	36	88	41

*Rounded to nearest whole number.

seasonal variation. For this reason, and because of its more limited relevance in business than the analysis of trends and seasonal factors, we deal with the subject only briefly. Needless to say, cyclical analysis demands that the available time series covers a reasonably long period of time. The steps of the analysis are:

1. Find the trend values of the observed Y data, i.e. T_Y (using one of the methods explained earlier).
2. 'De-trend' the data, i.e. calculate Y/T_Y.
3. Where appropriate, 'de-seasonalize' the series by dividing by the seasonal index values (S) – normally this is not necessary because *annual* data only would be used for cyclical analysis.
4. Finally, remove as much of the random variation (R) as possible by a process of smoothing. This is achieved by taking moving averages.

The resultant information allows us then to plot the cyclical pattern of the original data and to measure the frequency (and amplitude) of the cycles.

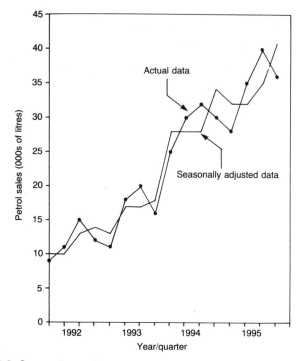

Figure 12.3 Comparison of seasonally adjusted and unadjusted petrol sales.

Random variation (R)

The term *random variation* is used to cover all types of variation other than trend, seasonal and cyclical movements. It covers all unpredictable movements such as the effect of strikes, natural disasters such as floods and famines, the effects of the Stock Exchange crash in October 1987, etc. It can be measured as the residual after the regular (trend, seasonal and cyclical) factors have been removed from a series, but there is little or no interest in such residuals in their own right and we devote no further attention to them.

Key learning points

Time series   A set of observations measured at successive points in time or over successive periods of time.

Trend (T)   The long-run movement in a time series.

Seasonal component (S)   The component of the time series model that shows a periodic pattern over 1 year or less.

Cyclical component (C)   The component of the time series model that results in periodic above-trend and below-trend behaviour of the time series lasting more than 1 year.

Random component (R)   The component of the time series model that reflects the random variation of the actual time series values beyond that which can be explained by the trend, cyclical and seasonal components.

Additive model

$$Y_t = T_t + S_t + C_t + R_t$$

Multiplicative model

$$Y_t = T_t \times S_t \times C_t \times R_t$$

Linear trend method   A method of forecasting which applies regression analysis to the time series data with time taken as the independent (i.e. explanatory) variable.

$$T_y = a + bX$$

Moving average method   A method of smoothing a time series by averaging successive groups of data points.

EXERCISES

1 Annual sales of fertilizer (thousands of tonnes) by a firm over the years 1986–95 are as follows:

Year:	1986	1987	1988	1989	1990	1991	1992	1993	1994	1995
Fertilizer:	3.9	3.9	3.6	4.8	4.5	5.3	5.5	6.4	7.0	7.1

(a) Calculate a linear trend of sales of fertilizer on time, with time measured in units of one year (1986 = 1).
(b) What is the annual increase in sales according to the regression equation?
(c) Predict sales for 1997.
(d) What assumptions relate to the answer to (c)?

2 Analyses of quarterly data on sales recorded over a period of 5 years gave the following linear trend equation and seasonal index:

$$Y_T = 120.48 - 1.2t$$

(where t is time measured in quarters and Q1 of year 1 = 1).

	Q1	Q2	Q3	Q4
Seasonal index:	111	95	84	110
Sales in year 6 were:	109	84	80	110

(a) Calculate a seasonally adjusted series for year 6.
(b) Produce forecasts for all four quarters of year 7 by using the trend and seasonal components.

3 A newly opened petrol filling station records sales over its first 12 months of operation as follows:

Month	Sales (thousands of litres)
January	74
February	84
March	88
April	92
May	90
June	67
July	80
August	81
September	73
October	86
November	81
December	70

Calculate a three-month moving average trend.

4 Quarterly figures of the consumption of gas in a factory from 1992 Q1 to 1995 Q3 are shown below:

	Q1	Q2	Q3	Q4
1992	29	22	17	29
1993	33	23	18	33
1994	41	27	22	37
1995	44	28	21	

(a) Calculate trend values using the moving average method.
(b) Compute the seasonal index.
(c) Comment on the size and direction of the seasonal movements indicated by the seasonal index.

Appendix A

Probability distribution tables

A1 Binomial probability distribution

This table shows the value of

$$P(X \text{ successes}) = C_X^n (p^X)(q^{n-X})$$

$$\text{where } C_X^n = \frac{n!}{X!(n-X)!}$$

for selected values of p and for $n = 1$ to 30. For values of p exceeding 0.5, the value of $P(X \text{ successes})$ can be obtained by substituting $q = (1-p)$ for p and by finding $P(n-X)$.

						p					
n	X	.05	.10	.15	.20	.25	.30	.35	.40	.45	.50
1	0	.9500	.9000	.8500	.8000	.7500	.7000	.6500	.6000	.5500	.5000
	1	.0500	.1000	.1500	.2000	.2500	.3000	.3500	.4000	.4500	.5000
2	0	.9025	.8100	.7225	.6400	.5625	.4900	.4225	.3600	.3025	.2500
	1	.0950	.1800	.2550	.3200	.3750	.4200	.4550	.4800	.4950	.5000
	2	.0025	.0100	.0225	.0400	.0625	.0900	.1225	.1600	.2025	.2500
3	0	.8574	.7290	.6141	.5120	.4219	.3430	.2746	.2160	.1664	.1250
	1	.1354	.2430	.3251	.3840	.4219	.4410	.4436	.4320	.4084	.3750
	2	.0071	.0270	.0574	.0960	.1406	.1890	.2389	.2880	.3341	.3750
	3	.0001	.0010	.0034	.0080	.0156	.0270	.0429	.0640	.0911	.1250
4	0	.8145	.6561	.5220	.4096	.3164	.2401	.1785	.1296	.0915	.0625
	1	.1715	.2916	.3685	.4096	.4219	.4116	.3845	.3456	.2995	.2500
	2	.0135	.0486	.0975	.1536	.2109	.2646	.3105	.3456	.3675	.3750
	3	.0005	.0036	.0115	.0256	.0469	.0756	.1115	.1536	.2005	.2500
	4	.0000	.0001	.0005	.0016	.0039	.0081	.0150	.0256	.0410	.0625

n	X	.05	.10	.15	.20	*p* .25	.30	.35	.40	.45	.50
5	0	.7738	.5905	.4437	.3277	.2373	.1681	.1160	.0778	.0503	.0312
	1	.2036	.3280	.3915	.4096	.3955	.3602	.3124	.2592	.2059	.1562
	2	.0214	.0729	.1382	.2048	.2637	.3087	.3364	.3456	.3369	.3125
	3	.0011	.0081	.0244	.0512	.0879	.1323	.1811	.2304	.2757	.3125
	4	.0000	.0004	.0022	.0064	.0146	.0284	.0488	.0768	.1128	.1562
	5	.0000	.0000	.0001	.0003	.0010	.0024	.0053	.0102	.0185	.0312
6	0	.7351	.5314	.3771	.2621	.1780	.1176	.0754	.0467	.0277	.0156
	1	.2321	.3543	.3993	.3932	.3560	.3025	.2437	.1866	.1359	.0938
	2	.0305	.0984	.1762	.2458	.2966	.3241	.3280	.3110	.2780	.2344
	3	.0021	.0146	.0415	.0819	.1318	.1852	.2355	.2765	.3032	.3125
	4	.0001	.0012	.0055	.0154	.0330	.0595	.0951	.1382	.1861	.2344
	5	.0000	.0001	.0004	.0015	.0044	.0102	.0205	.0369	.0609	.0938
	6	.0000	.0000	.0000	.0001	.0002	.0007	.0018	.0041	.0083	.0156
7	0	.6983	.4783	.3206	.2097	.1335	.0824	.0490	.0280	.0152	.0078
	1	.2573	.3720	.3960	.3670	.3115	.2471	.1848	.1306	.0872	.0547
	2	.0406	.1240	.2097	.2753	.3115	.3177	.2985	.2613	.2140	.1641
	3	.0036	.0230	.0617	.1147	.1730	.2269	.2679	.2903	.2918	.2734
	4	.0002	.0026	.0109	.0287	.0577	.0972	.1442	.1935	.2388	.2734
	5	.0009	.0002	.0012	.0043	.0115	.0250	.0466	.0774	.1172	.1641
	6	.0000	.0000	.0001	.0004	.0013	.0036	.0084	.0172	.0320	.0547
	7	.0000	.0000	.0000	.0000	.0001	.0002	.0006	.0016	.0037	.0078
8	0	.6634	.4305	.2725	.1678	.1001	.0576	.0319	.0168	.0084	.0039
	1	.2793	.3826	.3847	.3355	.2670	.1977	.1373	.0896	.0548	.0312
	2	.0515	.1488	.2376	.2936	.3115	.2965	.2587	.2090	.1569	.1094
	3	.0054	.0331	.0839	.1468	.2076	.2541	.2786	.2787	.2568	.2188
	4	.0004	.0046	.0815	.0459	.0865	.1361	.1875	.2322	.2627	.2734
	5	.0000	.0004	.0026	.0092	.0231	.0467	.0808	.1239	.1719	.2188
	6	.0000	.0000	.0002	.0011	.0038	.0100	.0217	.0413	.0703	.1094
	7	.0000	.0000	.0000	.0001	.0004	.0012	.0033	.0079	.0164	.0312
	8	.0000	.0000	.0000	.0000	.0000	.0001	.0002	.0007	.0017	.0039
9	0	.6302	.3874	.2316	.1342	.0751	.0404	.0207	.0101	.0046	.0020
	1	.2985	.3874	.3679	.3020	.2253	.1556	.1004	.0605	.0339	.0176
	2	.0629	.1722	.2597	.3020	.3003	.2668	.2162	.1612	.1110	.0703
	3	.0077	.0446	.1069	.1762	.2336	.2668	.2716	.2508	.2119	.1641
	4	.0006	.0074	.0283	.0661	.1168	.1715	.2194	.2508	.2600	.2461
	5	.0000	.0008	.0050	.0165	.0389	.0735	.1181	.1672	.2128	.2461
	6	.0000	.0001	.0006	.0028	.0087	.0210	.0424	.0743	.1160	.1641
	7	.0000	.0000	.0000	.0003	.0012	.0039	.0098	.0212	.0407	.0703
	8	.0000	.0000	.0000	.0000	.0001	.0004	.0013	.0035	.0083	.0716
	9	.0000	.0000	.0000	.0000	.0000	.0000	.0001	.0003	.0008	.0020

n	X	.05	.10	.15	.20	p .25	.30	.35	.40	.45	.50
10	0	.5987	.3487	.1969	.1074	.0563	.0282	.0135	.0060	.0025	.0010
	1	.3151	.3874	.3474	.2684	.1877	.1211	.0725	.0403	.0207	.0098
	2	.0746	.1937	.2759	.3020	.2816	.2335	.1757	.1209	.0763	.0439
	3	.0105	.0574	.1298	.2013	.2503	.2668	.2522	.2150	.1665	.1172
	4	.0010	.0112	.0401	.0881	.1460	.2001	.2377	.2508	.2384	.2051
	5	.0001	.0015	.0085	.0264	.0584	.1029	.1536	.2007	.2340	.2461
	6	.0000	.0001	.0012	.0055	.0162	.0368	.0689	.1115	.1596	.2051
	7	.0000	.0000	.0001	.0008	.0031	.0090	.0212	.0425	.0746	.1172
	8	.0000	.0000	.0000	.0001	.0004	.0014	.0043	.0106	.0229	.0439
	9	.0000	.0000	.0000	.0000	.0000	.0001	.0005	.0016	.0042	.0098
	10	.0000	.0000	.0000	.0000	.0000	.0000	.0000	.0001	.0003	.0010
11	0	.5688	.3138	.1673	.0859	.0422	.0198	.0088	.0036	.0014	.0005
	1	.3293	.3835	.3248	.2362	.1549	.0932	.0518	.0266	.0125	.0054
	2	.0867	.2131	.2866	.2953	.2581	.1998	.1395	.0887	.0513	.0269
	3	.0137	.0710	.1517	.2215	.2581	.2568	.2254	.1774	.1259	.0806
	4	.0014	.0158	.0536	.1107	.1721	.2201	.2428	.2365	.2060	.1611
	5	.0001	.0025	.0132	.0388	.0803	.1321	.1830	.2207	.2360	.2256
	6	.0000	.0003	.0023	.0097	.0268	.0566	.0985	.1471	.1931	.2256
	7	.0000	.0000	.0003	.0017	.0064	.0173	.0379	.0701	.1128	.1611
	8	.0000	.0000	.0000	.0002	.0011	.0037	.0102	.0234	.0462	.0806
	9	.0000	.0000	.0000	.0000	.0001	.0005	.0018	.0052	.0126	.0269
	10	.0000	.0000	.0000	.0000	.0000	.0000	.0002	.0007	.0021	.0054
	11	.0000	.0000	.0000	.0000	.0000	.0000	.0000	.0000	.0002	.0005
12	0	.5404	.2824	.1422	.0687	.0317	.0138	.0057	.0022	.0008	.0002
	1	.3413	.3766	.3012	.2062	.1267	.0712	.0368	.0174	.0075	.0029
	2	.0988	.2301	.2924	.2835	.2323	.1678	.1088	.0639	.0339	.0161
	3	.0173	.0852	.1720	.2362	.2581	.2397	.1954	.1419	.0923	.0537
	4	.0021	.0213	.0683	.1329	.1936	.2311	.2367	.2128	.1700	.1208
	5	.0002	.0038	.0193	.0532	.1032	.1585	.2039	.2270	.2225	.1934
	6	.0000	.0005	.0040	.0155	.0401	.0792	.1281	.1766	.2124	.2256
	7	.0000	.0000	.0006	.0033	.0115	.0291	.0591	.1009	.1489	.1934
	8	.0000	.0000	.0001	.0005	.0024	.0078	.0199	.0420	.0762	.1208
	9	.0000	.0000	.0000	.0001	.0004	.0015	.0048	.0125	.0277	.0537
	10	.0000	.0000	.0000	.0000	.0000	.0002	.0008	.0025	.0068	.0161
	11	.0000	.0000	.0000	.0000	.0000	.0000	.0001	.0003	.0010	.0029
	12	.0000	.0000	.0000	.0000	.0000	.0000	.0000	.0000	.0001	.0002
13	0	.5133	.2542	.1209	.0550	.0238	.0097	.0037	.0013	.0004	.0001
	1	.3512	.3672	.2774	.1787	.1029	.0540	.0259	.0113	.0045	.0016
	2	.1109	.2448	.2937	.2680	.2059	.1388	.0836	.0453	.0220	.0095
	3	.0214	.0997	.1900	.2457	.2517	.2181	.1651	.1107	.0660	.0349
	4	.0028	.0277	.0838	.1535	.2097	.2337	.2222	.1845	.1350	.0873

n	X	.05	.10	.15	.20	*p* .25	.30	.35	.40	.45	.50
13	5	.0003	.0055	.0266	.0691	.1258	.1803	.2154	.2214	.1989	.1571
	6	.0000	.0008	.0063	.0230	.0559	.1030	.1546	.1968	.2169	.2095
	7	.0000	.0001	.0011	.0058	.0186	.0442	.0833	.1312	.1775	.2095
	8	.0000	.0000	.0001	.0011	.0047	.0142	.0336	.0656	.1089	.1571
	9	.0000	.0000	.0000	.0001	.0009	.0034	.0101	.0243	.0495	.0873
	10	.0000	.0000	.0000	.0000	.0001	.0006	.0022	.0065	.0162	.0349
	11	.0000	.0000	.0000	.0000	.0000	.0001	.0003	.0012	.0036	.0095
	12	.0000	.0000	.0000	.0000	.0000	.0000	.0000	.0001	.0005	.0016
	13	.0000	.0000	.0000	.0000	.0000	.0000	.0000	.0000	.0000	.0001
14	0	.4877	.2288	.1028	.0440	.0178	.0068	.0024	.0008	.0002	.0001
	1	.3593	.3559	.2539	.1539	.0832	.0407	.0181	.0073	.0027	.0009
	2	.1229	.2570	.2912	.2501	.1802	.1134	.0634	.0317	.0141	.0056
	3	.0259	.1142	.2056	.2501	.2402	.1943	.1366	.0845	.0462	.0222
	4	.0037	.0348	.0998	.1720	.2202	.2290	.2022	.1549	.1040	.0611
	5	.0004	.0078	.0352	.0860	.1468	.1963	.2178	.2066	.1701	.1222
	6	.0000	.0013	.0093	.0322	.0734	.1262	.1759	.2066	.2088	.1833
	7	.0000	.0002	.0019	.0092	.0280	.0618	.1082	.1574	.1952	.2095
	8	.0000	.0000	.0003	.0020	.0082	.0232	.0510	.0918	.1398	.1833
	9	.0000	.0000	.0000	.0003	.0018	.0066	.0183	.0408	.0762	.1222
	10	.0000	.0000	.0000	.0000	.0003	.0014	.0049	.0136	.0312	.0611
	11	.0000	.0000	.0000	.0000	.0000	.0002	.0010	.0033	.0093	.0222
	12	.0000	.0000	.0000	.0000	.0000	.0000	.0001	.0005	.0019	.0056
	13	.0000	.0000	.0000	.0000	.0000	.0000	.0000	.0001	.0002	.0009
	14	.0000	.0000	.0000	.0000	.0000	.0000	.0000	.0000	.0000	.0001
15	0	.4633	.2059	.0874	.0352	.0134	.0047	.0016	.0005	.0001	.0000
	1	.3658	.3432	.2312	.1319	.0668	.0305	.0126	.0047	.0016	.0005
	2	.1348	.2669	.2856	.2309	.1559	.0916	.0476	.0219	.0090	.0032
	3	.0307	.1285	.2184	.2501	.2252	.1700	.1110	.0634	.0318	.0139
	4	.0049	.0428	.1156	.1876	.2252	.2186	.1792	.1268	.0780	.0417
	5	.0006	.0105	.0449	.1032	.1651	.2061	.2123	.1859	.1404	.0916
	6	.0000	.0019	.0132	.0430	.0917	.1472	.1906	.2066	.1914	.1527
	7	.0000	.0003	.0030	.0138	.0393	.0811	.1319	.1771	.2013	.1964
	8	.0000	.0000	.0005	.0035	.0131	.0348	.0710	.1181	.1647	.1964
	9	.0000	.0000	.0001	.0007	.0034	.0116	.0298	.0612	.1048	.1527
	10	.0000	.0000	.0000	.0001	.0007	.0030	.0096	.0245	.0515	.0916
	11	.0000	.0000	.0000	.0000	.0001	.0006	.0024	.0074	.0191	.0417
	12	.0000	.0000	.0000	.0000	.0000	.0001	.0004	.0016	.0052	.0139
	13	.0000	.0000	.0000	.0000	.0000	.0000	.0001	.0003	.0010	.0032
	14	.0000	.0000	.0000	.0000	.0000	.0000	.0000	.0000	.0001	.0005
	15	.0000	.0000	.0000	.0000	.0000	.0000	.0000	.0000	.0000	.0000
16	0	.4401	.1853	.0743	.0281	.0100	.0033	.0010	.0003	.0001	.0000
	1	.3706	.3294	.2097	.1126	.0535	.0228	.0087	.0030	.0009	.0002

						p					
n	X	.05	.10	.15	.20	.25	.30	.35	.40	.45	.50
16	2	.1463	.2745	.2775	.2111	.1336	.0732	.0353	.0150	.0056	.0018
	3	.0359	.1423	.2285	.2463	.2079	.1465	.0888	.0468	.0215	.0085
	4	.0061	.0514	.1311	.2001	.2252	.2040	.1553	.1014	.0572	.0278
	5	.0008	.0137	.0555	.1201	.1802	.2099	.2008	.1623	.1123	.0667
	6	.0001	.0028	.0180	.0550	.1101	.1649	.1982	.1983	.1684	.1222
	7	.0000	.0004	.0045	.0197	.0524	.1010	.1524	.1889	.1969	.1746
	8	.0000	.0001	.0009	.0055	.0197	.0487	.0923	.1417	.1812	.1964
	9	.0000	.0000	.0001	.0012	.0058	.0185	.0442	.0840	.1318	.1746
	10	.0000	.0000	.0000	.0002	.0014	.0056	.0167	.0392	.0755	.1222
	11	.0000	.0000	.0000	.0000	.0002	.0013	.0049	.0142	.0337	.0667
	12	.0000	.0000	.0000	.0000	.0000	.0002	.0011	.0040	.0115	.0278
	13	.0000	.0000	.0000	.0000	.0000	.0000	.0002	.0008	.0029	.0085
	14	.0000	.0000	.0000	.0000	.0000	.0000	.0000	.0001	.0005	.0018
	15	.0000	.0000	.0000	.0000	.0000	.0000	.0000	.0000	.0001	.0002
	16	.0000	.0000	.0000	.0000	.0000	.0000	.0000	.0000	.0000	.0000
17	0	.4181	.1668	.0631	.0225	.0075	.0023	.0007	.0002	.0000	.0000
	1	.3741	.3150	.1893	.0957	.0426	.0169	.0060	.0019	.0005	.0001
	2	.1575	.2800	.2673	.1914	.1136	.0581	.0260	.0102	.0035	.0010
	3	.0415	.1556	.2359	.2393	.1893	.1245	.0701	.0341	.0144	.0052
	4	.0076	.0605	.1457	.2093	.2209	.1868	.1320	.0796	.0411	.0182
	5	.0010	.0175	.0668	.1361	.1914	.2081	.1849	.1379	.0875	.0472
	6	.0001	.0039	.0236	.0680	.1276	.1784	.1991	.1839	.1432	.0944
	7	.0000	.0007	.0065	.0267	.0668	.1201	.1685	.1927	.1841	.1484
	8	.0000	.0001	.0014	.0084	.0279	.0644	.1134	.1606	.1883	.1855
	9	.0000	.0000	.0003	.0021	.0093	.0276	.0611	.1070	.1540	.1855
	10	.0000	.0000	.0000	.0004	.0025	.0095	.0263	.0571	.1008	.1484
	11	.0000	.0000	.0000	.0001	.0005	.0026	.0090	.0242	.0525	.0944
	12	.0000	.0000	.0000	.0000	.0001	.0006	.0024	.0021	.0215	.0472
	13	.0000	.0000	.0000	.0000	.0000	.0001	.0005	.0021	.0068	.0182
	14	.0000	.0000	.0000	.0000	.0000	.0000	.0001	.0004	.0016	.0052
	15	.0000	.0000	.0000	.0000	.0000	.0000	.0000	.0001	.0003	.0010
	16	.0000	.0000	.0000	.0000	.0000	.0000	.0000	.0000	.0000	.0001
	17	.0000	.0000	.0000	.0000	.0000	.0000	.0000	.0000	.0000	.0000
18	0	.3972	.1501	.0536	.0180	.0056	.0016	.0004	.0001	.0000	.0000
	1	.3763	.3002	.1704	.0811	.0338	.0126	.0042	.0012	.0003	.0001
	2	.1683	.2835	.2556	.1723	.0958	.0458	.0190	.0069	.0022	.0006
	3	.0473	.1680	.2406	.2297	.1704	.1046	.0547	.0246	.0095	.0031
	4	.0093	.0700	.1592	.2153	.2130	.1681	.1104	.0614	.0291	.0117
	5	.0014	.0218	.0787	.1507	.1988	.2017	.1664	.1146	.0666	.0327
	6	.0002	.0052	.0301	.0816	.1436	.1873	.1941	.1655	.1181	.0708
	7	.0000	.0010	.0091	.0350	.0820	.1376	.1792	.1892	.1657	.1214
	8	.0000	.0002	.0022	.0120	.0376	.0811	.1327	.1734	.1864	.1669
	9	.0000	.0000	.0004	.0033	.0139	.0386	.0794	.1284	.1694	.1855

n	X	.05	.10	.15	.20	p .25	.30	.35	.40	.45	.50
18	10	.0000	.0000	.0001	.0008	.0042	.0149	.0385	.0771	.1248	.1669
	11	.0000	.0000	.0000	.0001	.0010	.0046	.0151	.0374	.0742	.1214
	12	.0000	.0000	.0000	.0000	.0002	.0012	.0047	.0145	.0354	.0708
	13	.0000	.0000	.0000	.0000	.0000	.0002	.0012	.0044	.0134	.0327
	14	.0000	.0000	.0000	.0000	.0000	.0000	.0002	.0011	.0039	.0117
	15	.0000	.0000	.0000	.0000	.0000	.0000	.0000	.0002	.0009	.0031
	16	.0000	.0000	.0000	.0000	.0000	.0000	.0000	.0000	.0001	.0006
	17	.0000	.0000	.0000	.0000	.0000	.0000	.0000	.0000	.0000	.0001
	18	.0000	.0000	.0000	.0000	.0000	.0000	.0000	.0000	.0000	.0000
19	0	.3774	.1351	.0456	.0144	.0042	.0011	.0003	.0001	.0000	.0000
	1	.3774	.2852	.1529	.0685	.0268	.0093	.0029	.0008	.0002	.0000
	2	.1787	.2852	.2428	.1540	.0803	.0358	.0138	.0046	.0013	.0003
	3	.0533	.1796	.2428	.2182	.1517	.0869	.0422	.0175	.0062	.0018
	4	.0112	.0798	.1714	.2182	.2023	.1491	.0909	.0467	.0203	.0074
	5	.0018	.0266	.0907	.1636	.2023	.1916	.1468	.0933	.0497	.0222
	6	.0002	.0069	.0374	.0955	.1574	.1916	.1844	.1451	.0949	.0518
	7	.0000	.0014	.0122	.0443	.0974	.1525	.1844	.1797	.1443	.0961
	8	.0000	.0002	.0032	.0166	.0487	.0981	.1489	.1797	.1771	.1442
	9	.0000	.0000	.0007	.0051	.0198	.0514	.0980	.1464	.1771	.1762
	10	.0000	.0000	.0001	.0013	.0066	.0220	.0528	.0976	.1449	.1762
	11	.0000	.0000	.0000	.0003	.0018	.0077	.0233	.0532	.0970	.1442
	12	.0000	.0000	.0000	.0000	.0004	.0022	.0083	.0237	.0529	.0961
	13	.0000	.0000	.0000	.0000	.0001	.0005	.0024	.0085	.0233	.0518
	14	.0000	.0000	.0000	.0000	.0000	.0001	.0006	.0024	.0082	.0222
	15	.0000	.0000	.0000	.0000	.0000	.0000	.0001	.0005	.0022	.0074
	16	.0000	.0000	.0000	.0000	.0000	.0000	.0000	.0001	.0005	.0018
	17	.0000	.0000	.0000	.0000	.0000	.0000	.0000	.0000	.0001	.0003
	18	.0000	.0000	.0000	.0000	.0000	.0000	.0000	.0000	.0000	.0000
	19	.0000	.0000	.0000	.0000	.0000	.0000	.0000	.0000	.0000	.0000
20	0	.3585	.1216	.0388	.0115	.0032	.0008	.0002	.0000	.0000	.0000
	1	.3774	.2702	.1368	.0576	.0211	.0068	.0020	.0005	.0001	.0000
	2	.1887	.2852	.2293	.1369	.0669	.0278	.0100	.0031	.0008	.0002
	3	.0596	.1901	.2428	.2054	.1339	.0716	.0323	.0123	.0040	.0011
	4	.0133	.0898	.1821	.2182	.1897	.1304	.0738	.0350	.0139	.0046
	5	.0022	.0319	.1028	.1746	.2023	.1789	.1272	.0746	.0365	.0148
	6	.0003	.0089	.0454	.1091	.1686	.1916	.1712	.1244	.0746	.0370
	7	.0000	.0020	.0160	.0545	.1124	.1643	.1844	.1659	.1221	.0739
	8	.0000	.0004	.0046	.0222	.0609	.1144	.1614	.1797	.1623	.1201
	9	.0000	.0001	.0011	.0074	.0271	.0654	.1158	.1597	.1771	.1602
	10	.0000	.0000	.0002	.0020	.0099	.0308	.0686	.1171	.1593	.1762
	11	.0000	.0000	.0000	.0005	.0030	.0120	.0336	.0710	.1185	.1602

n	X	.05	.10	.15	.20	p .25	.30	.35	.40	.45	.50
20	12	.0000	.0000	.0000	.0001	.0008	.0039	.0136	.0355	.0727	.1201
	13	.0000	.0000	.0000	.0000	.0002	.0010	.0045	.0146	.0366	.0739
	14	.0000	.0000	.0000	.0000	.0000	.0002	.0012	.0049	.0150	.0370
	15	.0000	.0000	.0000	.0000	.0000	.0000	.0003	.0013	.0049	.0148
	16	.0000	.0000	.0000	.0000	.0000	.0000	.0000	.0003	.0013	.0046
	17	.0000	.0000	.0000	.0000	.0000	.0000	.0000	.0000	.0002	.0011
	18	.0000	.0000	.0000	.0000	.0000	.0000	.0000	.0000	.0000	.0002
	19	.0000	.0000	.0000	.0000	.0000	.0000	.0000	.0000	.0000	.0000
	20	.0000	.0000	.0000	.0000	.0000	.0000	.0000	.0000	.0000	.0000
25	0	.2774	.0718	.0172	.0038	.0008	.0001	.0000	.0000	.0000	.0000
	1	.3650	.1994	.0759	.0236	.0063	.0014	.0003	.0000	.0000	.0000
	2	.2305	.2659	.1607	.0708	.0251	.0074	.0018	.0004	.0001	.0000
	3	.0930	.2265	.2174	.1358	.0641	.0243	.0076	.0019	.0004	.0001
	4	.0269	.1384	.2110	.1867	.1175	.0572	.0224	.0071	.0018	.0004
	5	.0060	.0646	.1564	.1960	.1645	.1030	.0506	.0199	.0063	.0016
	6	.0010	.0239	.0920	.1633	.1828	.1472	.0908	.0442	.0172	.0053
	7	.0001	.0072	.0441	.1108	.1654	.1712	.1327	.0800	.0381	.0143
	8	.0000	.0018	.0175	.0623	.1241	.1651	.1607	.1200	.0701	.0322
	9	.0000	.0004	.0058	.0294	.0781	.1336	.1635	.1511	.1084	.0609
	10	.0000	.0000	.0016	.0118	.0417	.0916	.1409	.1612	.1419	.0974
	11	.0000	.0000	.0004	.0040	.0189	.0536	.1034	.1465	.1583	.1328
	12	.0000	.0000	.0000	.0012	.0074	.0268	.0650	.1140	.1511	.1550
	13	.0000	.0000	.0000	.0003	.0025	.0115	.0350	.0760	.1236	.1550
	14	.0000	.0000	.0000	.0000	.0007	.0042	.0161	.0434	.0867	.1328
	15	.0000	.0000	.0000	.0000	.0002	.0013	.0064	.0212	.0520	.0974
	16	.0000	.0000	.0000	.0000	.0000	.0004	.0021	.0088	.0266	.0609
	17	.0000	.0000	.0000	.0000	.0000	.0001	.0006	.0031	.0115	.0322
	18	.0000	.0000	.0000	.0000	.0000	.0000	.0001	.0009	.0042	.0143
	19	.0000	.0000	.0000	.0000	.0000	.0000	.0000	.0002	.0013	.0053
	20	.0000	.0000	.0000	.0000	.0000	.0000	.0000	.0000	.0001	.0016
	21	.0000	.0000	.0000	.0000	.0000	.0000	.0000	.0000	.0000	.0004
	22	.0000	.0000	.0000	.0000	.0000	.0000	.0000	.0000	.0000	.0001
30	0	.2146	.0424	.0076	.0012	.0002	.0000	.0000	.0000	.0000	.0000
	1	.3389	.1413	.0404	.0093	.0018	.0003	.0000	.0000	.0000	.0000
	2	.2586	.2277	.1034	.0337	.0086	.0018	.0003	.0000	.0000	.0000
	3	.1270	.2361	.1703	.0785	.0269	.0072	.0015	.0003	.0000	.0000
	4	.0451	.1771	.2028	.1325	.0604	.0208	.0056	.0012	.0002	.0000

n	X	.05	.10	.15	.20	p .25	.30	.35	.40	.45	.50
	5	.0124	.1023	.1861	.1723	.1047	.0464	.0157	.0041	.0008	.0001
	6	.0027	.0474	.1368	.1795	.1455	.0829	.0353	.0115	.0029	.0006
	7	.0005	.0180	.0828	.1538	.1662	.1219	.0652	.0263	.0081	.0019
	8	.0001	.0058	.0420	.1106	.1593	.1501	.1009	.0505	.0191	.0055
	9	.0000	.0016	.0181	.0676	.1298	.1573	.1328	.0823	.0382	.0133
	10	.0000	.0004	.0067	.0365	.0909	.1416	.1502	.1152	.0656	.0280
	11	.0000	.0001	.0022	.0161	.0551	.1103	.1471	.1396	.0976	.0509
	12	.0000	.0000	.0006	.0064	.0291	.0749	.1254	.1474	.1265	.0806
	13	.0000	.0000	.0001	.0022	.0134	.0444	.0935	.1360	.1433	.1115
	14	.0000	.0000	.0000	.0007	.0054	.0231	.0611	.1101	.1424	.1354
	15	.0000	.0000	.0000	.0002	.0019	.0106	.0351	.0783	.1242	.1445
	16	.0000	.0000	.0000	.0000	.0006	.0042	.0177	.0489	.0953	.1354
	17	.0000	.0000	.0000	.0000	.0002	.0015	.0079	.0269	.0642	.1115
	18	.0000	.0000	.0000	.0000	.0000	.0005	.0031	.0129	.0379	.0806
	19	.0000	.0000	.0000	.0000	.0000	.0001	.0010	.0054	.0196	.0509
	20	.0000	.0000	.0000	.0000	.0000	.0000	.0003	.0020	.0088	.0280
	21	.0000	.0000	.0000	.0000	.0000	.0000	.0001	.0006	.0034	.0133
	22	.0000	.0000	.0000	.0000	.0000	.0000	.0000	.0002	.0012	.0055
	23	.0000	.0000	.0000	.0000	.0000	.0000	.0000	.0000	.0003	.0019
	24	.0000	.0000	.0000	.0000	.0000	.0000	.0000	.0000	.0001	.0006
	25	.0000	.0000	.0000	.0000	.0000	.0000	.0000	.0000	.0000	.0001

This table is taken from *Tables of the Binomial Probability Distribution*, Applied Mathematics Series, US Department of Commerce, 1950, by courtesy of the National Institute of Standards and Technology (formerly the National Bureau of Standards).

A2 Poisson probability distribution

This table shows the value of

$$P(X) = \frac{(e^{-\mu})\,\mu^{x}}{X!}$$

for selected values of X and for $\mu = .005$ to 10.0.

X	.005	.01	.02	.03	.04	.05	.06	.07	.08	.09
0	.9950	.9900	.9802	.9704	.9608	.9512	.9418	.9324	.9231	.9139
1	.0050	.0099	.0192	.0291	.0384	.0476	.0565	.0653	.0738	.0823
2	.0000	.0000	.0002	.0004	.0008	.0012	.0017	.0023	.0030	.0037
3	.0000	.0000	.0000	.0000	.0000	.0000	.0000	.0001	.0001	.0001

X	0.1	0.2	0.3	0.4	0.5	0.6	0.7	0.8	0.9	1.0
0	.9048	.8187	.7408	.6703	.6065	.5488	.4966	.4493	.4066	.3679
1	.0905	.1637	.2222	.2681	.3033	.3293	.3476	.3595	.3659	.3679
2	.0045	.0164	.0333	.0536	.0758	.0988	.1217	.1438	.1647	.1839
3	.0002	.0011	.0033	.0072	.0126	.0198	.0284	.0383	.0494	.0613
4	.0000	.0001	.0002	.0007	.0016	.0030	.0050	.0077	.0111	.0153
5	.0000	.0000	.0000	.0001	.0002	.0004	.0007	.0012	.0020	.0031
6	.0000	.0000	.0000	.0000	.0000	.0000	.0001	.0002	.0003	.0005
7	.0000	.0000	.0000	.0000	.0000	.0000	.0000	.0000	.0000	.0001

X	1.1	1.2	1.3	1.4	1.5	1.6	1.7	1.8	1.9	2.0
0	.3329	.3012	.2725	.2466	.2231	.2019	.1827	.1653	.1496	.1353
1	.3662	.3614	.3543	.3452	.3347	.3230	.3106	.2975	.2842	.2707
2	.2014	.2169	.2303	.2417	.2510	.2584	.2640	.2678	.2700	.2707
3	.0738	.0867	.0998	.1128	.1255	.1378	.1496	.1607	.1710	.1804
4	.0203	.0260	.0324	.0395	.0471	.0551	.0636	.0723	.0812	.0902
5	.0045	.0062	.0084	.0111	.0141	.0176	.0216	.0260	.0309	.0361
6	.0008	.0012	.0018	.0026	.0035	.0047	.0061	.0078	.0098	.0120
7	.0001	.0002	.0003	.0005	.0008	.0011	.0015	.0020	.0027	.0034
8	.0000	.0000	.0001	.0001	.0001	.0002	.0003	.0005	.0006	.0009
9	.0000	.0000	.0000	.0000	.0000	.0000	.0001	.0001	.0001	.0002

X	2.1	2.2	2.3	2.4	2.5	2.6	2.7	2.8	2.9	3.0
0	.1225	.1108	.1003	.0907	.0821	.0743	.0672	.0608	.0550	.0498
1	.2572	.2438	.2306	.2177	.2052	.1931	.1815	.1703	.1596	.1494
2	.2700	.2681	.2652	.2613	.2565	.2510	.2450	.2384	.2314	.2240
3	.1890	.1966	.2033	.2090	.2138	.2176	.2205	.2225	.2237	.2240
4	.0992	.1082	.1169	.1254	.1336	.1414	.1488	.1557	.1622	.1680

X	2.1	2.2	2.3	2.4	2.5	μ 2.6	2.7	2.8	2.9	3.0
5	.0417	.0476	.0538	.0602	.0668	.0735	.0804	.0872	.0940	.1008
6	.0146	.0174	.0206	.0241	.0278	.0319	.0362	.0407	.0455	.0504
7	.0044	.0055	.0068	.0083	.0099	.0118	.0139	.0163	.0188	.0216
8	.0011	.0015	.0019	.0025	.0031	.0038	.0047	.0057	.0068	.0081
9	.0003	.0004	.0005	.0007	.0009	.0011	.0014	.0018	.0022	.0027
10	.0001	.0001	.0001	.0002	.0002	.0003	.0004	.0005	.0006	.0008
11	.0000	.0000	.0000	.0000	.0000	.0001	.0001	.0001	.0002	.0002
12	.0000	.0000	.0000	.0000	.0000	.0000	.0000	.0000	.0000	.0001

X	3.1	3.2	3.3	3.4	3.5	3.6	3.7	3.8	3.9	4.0
0	.0450	.0408	.0369	.0334	.0302	.0273	.0247	.0224	.0202	.0183
1	.1397	.1304	.1217	.1135	.1057	.0984	.0915	.0850	.0789	.0733
2	.2165	.2087	.2008	.1929	.1850	.1771	.1692	.1615	.1539	.1465
3	.2237	.2226	.2209	.2186	.2158	.2125	.2087	.2046	.2001	.1954
4	.1734	.1781	.1823	.1858	.1888	.1912	.1931	.1944	.1951	.1954
5	.1075	.1140	.1203	.1264	.1322	.1377	.1429	.1477	.1522	.1563
6	.0555	.0608	.0662	.0716	.0771	.0826	.0881	.0936	.0989	.1402
7	.0246	.0278	.0312	.0348	.0385	.0425	.0466	.0508	.0551	.0595
8	.0095	.0111	.0129	.0148	.0169	.0191	.0215	.0241	.0269	.0298
9	.0033	.0040	.0047	.0056	.0066	.0076	.0089	.0102	.0116	.0132
10	.0010	.0013	.0016	.0019	.0023	.0028	.0033	.0039	.0045	.0053
11	.0003	.0004	.0005	.0006	.0007	.0009	.0011	.0013	.0016	.0019
12	.0001	.0001	.0001	.0002	.0002	.0003	.0003	.0004	.0005	.0006
13	.0000	.0000	.0000	.0000	.0001	.0001	.0001	.0001	.0002	.0002
14	.0000	.0000	.0000	.0000	.0000	.0000	.0000	.0000	.0000	.0001

X	4.1	4.2	4.3	4.4	4.5	4.6	4.7	4.8	4.9	5.0
0	.0166	.0150	.0136	.0123	.0111	.0101	.0091	.0082	.0074	.0067
1	.0679	.0630	.0583	.0540	.0500	.0462	.0427	.0395	.0365	.0337
2	.1393	.1323	.1254	.1188	.1125	.1063	.1005	.0948	.0894	.0842
3	.1904	.1852	.1798	.1743	.1687	.1631	.1574	.1517	.1460	.1404
4	.1951	.1944	.1933	.1917	.1898	.1875	.1849	.1820	.1789	.1755
5	.1600	.1633	.1662	.1687	.1708	.1725	.1738	.1747	.1753	.1755
6	.1093	.1143	.1191	.1237	.1281	.1323	.1362	.1398	.1432	.1462
7	.0640	.0686	.0732	.0778	.0824	.0869	.0914	.0959	.1002	.1044
8	.0328	.0360	.0393	.0428	.0463	.0500	.0537	.0575	.0614	.0653
9	.0150	.0168	.0188	.0209	.0232	.0255	.0280	.0307	.0334	.0363
10	.0061	.0071	.0081	.0092	.0104	.0118	.0132	.0147	.0164	.0181
11	.0023	.0027	.0032	.0037	.0043	.0049	.0056	.0064	.0073	.0082
12	.0008	.0009	.0011	.0014	.0016	.0019	.0022	.0026	.0030	.0034
13	.0002	.0003	.0004	.0005	.0006	.0007	.0008	.0009	.0011	.0013
14	.0001	.0001	.0001	.0001	.0002	.0002	.0003	.0003	.0004	.0005
15	.0000	.0000	.0000	.0000	.0001	.0001	.0001	.0001	.0001	.0002

μ

X	5.1	5.2	5.3	5.4	5.5	5.6	5.7	5.8	5.9	6.0
0	.0061	.0055	.0050	.0045	.0041	.0037	.0033	.0030	.0027	.0025
1	.0311	.0287	.0265	.0244	.0225	.0207	.0191	.0176	.0162	.0149
2	.0793	.0746	.0701	.0659	.0618	.0580	.0544	.0509	.0477	.0446
3	.1348	.1293	.1239	.1185	.1133	.1082	.1033	.0985	.0938	.0892
4	.1719	.1681	.1641	.1600	.1558	.1515	.1472	.1428	.1383	.1339
5	.1753	.1748	.1740	.1728	.1714	.1697	.1678	.1656	.1632	.1606
6	.1490	.1515	.1537	.1555	.1571	.1584	.1594	.1601	.1605	.1606
7	.1086	.1125	.1163	.1200	.1234	.1267	.1298	.1326	.1353	.1377
8	.0692	.0731	.0771	.0810	.0849	.0887	.0925	.0962	.0998	.1033
9	.0392	.0423	.0454	.0486	.0519	.0552	.0586	.0620	.0654	.0688
10	.0200	.0220	.0241	.0262	.0285	.0309	.0334	.0359	.0386	.0413
11	.0093	.0104	.0116	.0129	.0143	.0157	.0173	.0190	.0207	.0225
12	.0039	.0045	.0051	.0058	.0065	.0073	.0082	.0092	.0102	.0113
13	.0015	.0018	.0021	.0024	.0028	.0032	.0036	.0041	.0046	.0052
14	.0006	.0007	.0008	.0009	.0011	.0013	.0015	.0017	.0019	.0022
15	.0002	.0002	.0003	.0003	.0004	.0005	.0006	.0007	.0008	.0009
16	.0001	.0001	.0001	.0001	.0001	.0002	.0002	.0002	.0003	.0003
17	.0000	.0000	.0000	.0000	.0000	.0001	.0001	.0001	.0001	.0001

X	6.1	6.2	6.3	6.4	6.5	6.6	6.7	6.8	6.9	7.0
0	.0022	.0020	.0018	.0017	.0015	.0014	.0012	.0011	.0010	.0009
1	.0137	.0126	.0116	.0106	.0098	.0090	.0082	.0076	.0070	.0064
2	.0417	.0390	.0364	.0340	.0318	.0296	.0276	.0258	.0240	.0223
3	.0848	.0806	.0765	.0726	.0688	.0652	.0617	.0584	.0552	.0521
4	.1294	.1249	.1205	.1162	.1118	.1076	.1034	.0992	.0952	.0912
5	.1579	.1549	.1519	.1487	.1454	.1420	.1385	.1349	.1314	.1277
6	.1605	.1601	.1595	.1586	.1575	.1562	.1546	.1529	.1511	.1490
7	.1399	.1418	.1435	.1450	.1462	.1472	.1480	.1486	.1489	.1490
8	.1066	.1099	.1130	.1160	.1188	.1215	.1240	.1263	.1284	.1304
9	.0723	.0757	.0791	.0825	.0858	.0891	.0923	.0954	.0985	.1014
10	.0441	.0469	.0498	.0528	.0558	.0588	.0618	.0649	.0679	.0710
11	.0245	.0265	.0285	.0307	.0330	.0353	.0377	.0401	.0426	.0452
12	.0124	.0137	.0150	.0164	.0179	.0194	.0210	.0227	.0245	.0264
13	.0058	.0065	.0073	.0081	.0089	.0098	.0108	.0119	.0130	.0142
14	.0025	.0029	.0033	.0037	.0041	.0046	.0052	.0058	.0064	.0071
15	.0010	.0012	.0014	.0016	.0018	.0020	.0023	.0026	.0029	.0033
16	.0004	.0005	.0005	.0006	.0007	.0008	.0010	.0011	.0013	.0014
17	.0001	.0002	.0002	.0002	.0003	.0003	.0004	.0004	.0005	.0006
18	.0000	.0001	.0001	.0001	.0001	.0001	.0001	.0002	.0002	.0002
19	.0000	.0000	.0000	.0000	.0000	.0000	.0000	.0001	.0001	.0001

X	7.1	7.2	7.3	7.4	7.5	μ 7.6	7.7	7.8	7.9	8.0
0	.0008	.0007	.0007	.0006	.0006	.0005	.0005	.0004	.0004	.0003
1	.0059	.0054	.0049	.0045	.0041	.0038	.0035	.0032	.0029	.0027
2	.0208	.0194	.0180	.0167	.0156	.0145	.0134	.0125	.0116	.0107
3	.0492	.0464	.0438	.0413	.0389	.0366	.0345	.0324	.0305	.0286
4	.0874	.0836	.0799	.0764	.0729	.0696	.0663	.0632	.0602	.0573
5	.1241	.1204	.1167	.1130	.1094	.1057	.1021	.0986	.0951	.0916
6	.1468	.1445	.1420	.1394	.1367	.1339	.1311	.1282	.1252	.1221
7	.1489	.1486	.1481	.1474	.1465	.1454	.1442	.1428	.1413	.1396
8	.1321	.1337	.1351	.1363	.1373	.1382	.1388	.1392	.1395	.1396
9	.1042	.1070	.1096	.1121	.1144	.1167	.1187	.1207	.1224	.1241
10	.0740	.0770	.0800	.0829	.0858	.0887	.0914	.0941	.0967	.0993
11	.0478	.0504	.0531	.0558	.0585	.0613	.0640	.0667	.0695	.0722
12	.0283	.0303	.0323	.0344	.0366	.0388	.0411	.0434	.0457	.0481
13	.0154	.0168	.0181	.0196	.0211	.0227	.0243	.0260	.0278	.0296
14	.0078	.0086	.0095	.0104	.0113	.0123	.0134	.0145	.0157	.0169
15	.0037	.0041	.0046	.0051	.0057	.0062	.0069	.0075	.0083	.0090
16	.0016	.0019	.0021	.0024	.0026	.0030	.0033	.0037	.0041	.0045
17	.0007	.0008	.0009	.0010	.0012	.0013	.0015	.0017	.0019	.0021
18	.0003	.0003	.0004	.0004	.0005	.0006	.0006	.0007	.0008	.0009
19	.0001	.0001	.0001	.0002	.0002	.0002	.0003	.0003	.0003	.0004
20	.0000	.0000	.0001	.0001	.0001	.0001	.0001	.0001	.0001	.0002
21	.0000	.0000	.0000	.0000	.0000	.0000	.0000	.0000	.0001	.0001

X	8.1	8.2	8.3	8.4	8.5	8.6	8.7	8.8	8.9	9.0
0	.0003	.0003	.0002	.0002	.0002	.0002	.0002	.0002	.0001	.0001
1	.0025	.0023	.0021	.0019	.0017	.0016	.0014	.0013	.0012	.0011
2	.0100	.0092	.0086	.0079	.0074	.0068	.0063	.0058	.0054	.0050
3	.0269	.0252	.0237	.0222	.0208	.0195	.0183	.0171	.0160	.0150
4	.0544	.0517	.0491	.0466	.0443	.0420	.0398	.0377	.0357	.0337
5	.0882	.0849	.0816	.0784	.0752	.0722	.0692	.0663	.0635	.0607
6	.1191	.1160	.1128	.1097	.1066	.1034	.1003	.0972	.0941	.0911
7	.1378	.1358	.1338	.1317	.1294	.1271	.1247	.1222	.1197	.1171
8	.1395	.1392	.1388	.1382	.1375	.1366	.1356	.1344	.1332	.1318
9	.1256	.1269	.1280	.1290	.1299	.1306	.1311	.1315	.1317	.1318
10	.1017	.1040	.1063	.1084	.1104	.1123	.1140	.1157	.1172	.1186
11	.0749	.0776	.0802	.0828	.0853	.0878	.0902	.0925	.0948	.0970
12	.0505	.0530	.0555	.0579	.0604	.0629	.0654	.0679	.0703	.0728
13	.0315	.0334	.0354	.0374	.0395	.0416	.0438	.0459	.0481	.0504
14	.0182	.0196	.0210	.0225	.0240	.0256	.0272	.0289	.0306	.0324
15	.0098	.0107	.0116	.0126	.0136	.0147	.0158	.0169	.0182	.0194
16	.0050	.0055	.0060	.0066	.0072	.0079	.0086	.0093	.0101	.0109

X	8.1	8.2	8.3	8.4	8.5	μ 8.6	8.7	8.8	8.9	9.0
17	.0024	.0026	.0029	.0033	.0036	.0040	.0044	.0048	.0053	.0058
18	.0011	.0012	.0014	.0015	.0017	.0019	.0021	.0024	.0026	.0029
19	.0005	.0005	.0006	.0007	.0008	.0009	.0010	.0011	.0012	.0014
20	.0002	.0002	.0002	.0003	.0003	.0004	.0004	.0005	.0005	.0006
21	.0001	.0001	.0001	.0001	.0001	.0002	.0002	.0002	.0002	.0003
22	.0000	.0000	.0000	.0000	.0001	.0001	.0001	.0001	.0001	.0001

X	9.1	9.2	9.3	9.4	9.5	9.6	9.7	9.8	9.9	10.0
0	.0001	.0001	.0001	.0001	.0001	.0001	.0001	.0001	.0001	.0000
1	.0010	.0009	.0009	.0008	.0007	.0007	.0006	.0005	.0005	.0005
2	.0046	.0043	.0040	.0037	.0034	.0031	.0029	.0027	.0025	.0023
3	.0140	.0131	.0123	.0115	.0107	.0100	.0093	.0087	.0081	.0076
4	.0319	.0302	.0285	.0269	.0254	.0240	.0226	.0213	.0201	.0189
5	.0581	.0555	.0530	.0506	.0483	.0460	.0439	.0418	.0398	.0378
6	.0881	.0851	.0822	.0793	.0764	.0736	.0709	.0682	.0656	.0631
7	.1145	.1118	.1091	.1064	.1037	.1010	.0982	.0955	.0928	.0901
8	.1302	.1286	.1269	.1251	.1232	.1212	.1191	.1170	.1148	.1126
9	.1317	.1315	.1311	.1306	.1300	.1293	.1284	.1274	.1263	.1251
10	.1198	.1210	.1219	.1228	.1235	.1241	.1245	.1249	.1250	.1251
11	.0991	.1012	.1031	.1049	.1067	.1083	.1098	.1112	.1125	.1137
12	.0752	.0776	.0799	.0822	.0844	.0866	.0888	.0908	.0928	.0948
13	.0526	.0549	.0572	.0594	.0617	.0640	.0662	.0685	.0707	.0729
14	.0342	.0361	.0380	.0399	.0419	.0439	.0459	.0479	.0500	.0521
15	.0208	.0221	.0235	.0250	.0265	.0281	.0297	.0313	.0330	.0347
16	.0118	.0127	.0137	.0147	.0157	.0168	.0180	.0192	.0204	.0217
17	.0063	.0069	.0075	.0081	.0088	.0095	.0103	.0111	.0119	.0128
18	.0032	.0035	.0039	.0042	.0046	.0051	.0055	.0060	.0065	.0071
19	.0015	.0017	.0019	.0021	.0023	.0026	.0028	.0031	.0034	.0037
20	.0007	.0008	.0009	.0010	.0011	.0012	.0014	.0015	.0017	.0019
21	.0003	.0003	.0004	.0004	.0005	.0006	.0006	.0007	.0008	.0009
22	.0001	.0001	.0002	.0002	.0002	.0002	.0003	.0003	.0004	.0004
23	.0000	.0001	.0001	.0001	.0001	.0001	.0001	.0001	.0002	.0002
24	.0000	.0000	.0000	.0000	.0000	.0000	.0000	.0001	.0001	.0001

A3 Standard normal distribution

The entries in this table are the probabilities that a random variable having the standard normal distribution assumes a value between 0 and z_1; the probability is represented by the area under the curve (the shaded area). Areas for negative values of z are obtained by symmetry.

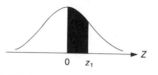

	Second decimal place in z									
z	0.00	0.01	0.02	0.03	0.04	0.05	0.06	0.07	0.08	0.09
0.0	0.0000	0.0040	0.0080	0.0120	0.0160	0.0199	0.0239	0.0279	0.0319	0.0359
0.1	0.0398	0.0438	0.0478	0.0517	0.0557	0.0596	0.0636	0.0675	0.0714	0.0753
0.2	0.0793	0.0832	0.0871	0.0910	0.0948	0.0987	0.1026	0.1064	0.1103	0.1141
0.3	0.1179	0.1217	0.1255	0.1293	0.1331	0.1368	0.1406	0.1443	0.1480	0.1517
0.4	0.1554	0.1591	0.1628	0.1664	0.1700	0.1736	0.1772	0.1808	0.1844	0.1879
0.5	0.1915	0.1950	0.1985	0.2019	0.2054	0.2088	0.2123	0.2157	0.2190	0.2224
0.6	0.2257	0.2291	0.2324	0.2357	0.2389	0.2422	0.2454	0.2486	0.2517	0.2549
0.7	0.2580	0.2611	0.2642	0.2673	0.2704	0.2734	0.2764	0.2794	0.2823	0.2852
0.8	0.2881	0.2910	0.2939	0.2967	0.2995	0.3023	0.3051	0.3078	0.3106	0.3133
0.9	0.3159	0.3186	0.3212	0.3238	0.3264	0.3289	0.3315	0.3340	0.3365	0.3389
1.0	0.3413	0.3438	0.3461	0.3485	0.3508	0.3531	0.3554	0.3577	0.3599	0.3621
1.1	0.3643	0.3665	0.3686	0.3708	0.3729	0.3749	0.3770	0.3790	0.3810	0.3830
1.2	0.3849	0.3869	0.3888	0.3907	0.3925	0.3944	0.3962	0.3980	0.3997	0.4015
1.3	0.4032	0.4049	0.4066	0.4082	0.4099	0.4115	0.4131	0.4147	0.4162	0.4177
1.4	0.4192	0.4207	0.4222	0.4236	0.4251	0.4265	0.4279	0.4292	0.4306	0.4319
1.5	0.4332	0.4345	0.4357	0.4370	0.4382	0.4394	0.4406	0.4418	0.4429	0.4441
1.6	0.4452	0.4463	0.4474	0.4484	0.4495	0.4505	0.4515	0.4525	0.4535	0.4545
1.7	0.4554	0.4564	0.4573	0.4582	0.4591	0.4599	0.4608	0.4616	0.4625	0.4633
1.8	0.4641	0.4649	0.4656	0.4664	0.4671	0.4678	0.4686	0.4693	0.4699	0.4706
1.9	0.4713	0.4719	0.4726	0.4732	0.4738	0.4744	0.4750	0.4756	0.4761	0.4767
2.0	0.4772	0.4778	0.4783	0.4788	0.4793	0.4796	0.4803	0.4808	0.4812	0.4817
2.1	0.4821	0.4826	0.4830	0.4834	0.4838	0.4842	0.4846	0.4850	0.4854	0.4857
2.2	0.4861	0.4864	0.4868	0.4871	0.4875	0.4878	0.4881	0.4884	0.4887	0.4890
2.3	0.4893	0.4896	0.4898	0.4901	0.4904	0.4906	0.4909	0.4911	0.4913	0.4916
2.4	0.4918	0.4920	0.4922	0.4925	0.4927	0.4929	0.4931	0.4932	0.4934	0.4936
2.5	0.4938	0.4940	0.4941	0.4943	0.4945	0.4946	0.4948	0.4949	0.4951	0.4952
2.6	0.4953	0.4955	0.4956	0.4957	0.4959	0.4960	0.4961	0.4962	0.4963	0.4974
2.7	0.4965	0.4966	0.4967	0.4968	0.4969	0.4970	0.4971	0.4972	0.4973	0.4974
2.8	0.4974	0.4975	0.4976	0.4977	0.4977	0.4978	0.4979	0.4979	0.4980	0.4981
2.9	0.4981	0.4982	0.4982	0.4983	0.4984	0.4984	0.4985	0.4985	0.4986	0.4986
3.0	0.4987	0.4987	0.4987	0.4988	0.4988	0.4989	0.4989	0.4989	0.4990	0.4990
3.1	0.4990	0.4991	0.4991	0.4991	0.4992	0.4992	0.4992	0.4992	0.4993	0.4993
3.2	0.4993	0.4993	0.4994	0.4994	0.4994	0.4994	0.4994	0.4995	0.4995	0.4995
3.3	0.4995	0.4995	0.4995	0.4996	0.4996	0.4996	0.4996	0.4996	0.4996	0.4997
3.4	0.4997	0.4997	0.4997	0.4997	0.4997	0.4997	0.4997	0.4997	0.4997	0.4998
3.5	0.4998									
4.0	0.49997									
4.5	0.499997									
5.0	0.4999997									

A4   *t* distribution

Entries in the table give t_α values, where α is the area or probability in the upper tail of the *t* distribution. For example, with 10 degrees of freedom and an area of .05 in the upper tail, $t_{.05} = 1.812$.

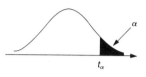

Degrees of freedom	$t_{.100}$	$t_{.050}$	$t_{.025}$	$t_{.010}$	$t_{.005}$
1	3.078	6.314	12.706	31.821	63.657
2	1.886	2.920	4.303	6.965	9.925
3	1.638	2.353	3.182	4.541	5.841
4	1.533	2.132	2.776	3.747	4.604
5	1.476	2.015	2.571	3.365	4.032
6	1.440	1.943	2.447	3.143	3.707
7	1.415	1.895	2.365	2.998	3.499
8	1.397	1.860	2.306	2.896	3.355
9	1.383	1.833	2.262	2.821	3.250
10	1.372	1.812	2.228	2.764	3.169
11	1.363	1.796	2.201	2.718	3.106
12	1.356	1.782	2.179	2.681	3.055
13	1.350	1.771	2.160	2.650	3.012
14	1.345	1.761	2.145	2.624	2.977
15	1.341	1.753	2.131	2.602	2.947
16	1.337	1.746	2.120	2.583	2.921
17	1.333	1.740	2.110	2.567	2.898
18	1.330	1.734	2.101	2.552	2.878
19	1.328	1.729	2.093	2.539	2.861
20	1.325	1.725	2.086	2.528	2.845
21	1.323	1.721	2.080	2.518	2.831
22	1.321	1.717	2.074	2.508	2.819
23	1.319	1.714	2.069	2.500	2.808
24	1.318	1.711	2.064	2.492	2.797
25	1.316	1.708	2.060	2.485	2.787
26	1.315	1.706	2.056	2.479	2.779
27	1.314	1.703	2.052	2.473	2.771
28	1.313	1.701	2.048	2.467	2.763
29	1.311	1.699	2.045	2.462	2.756
30	1.310	1.697	2.042	2.457	2.750
40	1.303	1.684	2.021	2.423	2.704
60	1.296	1.671	2.000	2.390	2.660
120	1.289	1.658	1.980	2.358	2.617
∞	1.282	1.645	1.960	2.326	2.576

Reproduced from *Biometrika Tables for Statisticians*, Cambridge University Press: Cambridge, 1954, by permission of the Biometrika trustees.

A5 χ^2 distribution

Entries in the table give χ^2_α, where α is the area or probability in the tail of the distribution (the shaded area). For example, with 10 degrees of freedom and $\alpha = 0.05$, $\chi^2_\alpha = 18.307$.

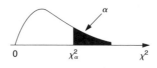

Degrees of freedom	$\chi^2_{.995}$	$\chi^2_{.990}$	$\chi^2_{.975}$	$\chi^2_{.950}$	$\chi^2_{.900}$
1	0.0000393	0.0001571	0.0009821	0.0039321	0.0157908
2	0.0100251	0.0201007	0.0506356	0.102587	0.210720
3	0.0717212	0.114832	0.215795	0.351846	0.584375
4	0.206990	0.297110	0.484419	0.710721	1.063623
5	0.411740	0.554300	0.831211	1.145476	1.61031
6	0.675727	0.872085	1.237347	1.63539	2.20413
7	0.989265	1.239043	1.68987	2.16735	2.83311
8	1.344419	1.646482	2.17973	2.73264	3.48954
9	1.734926	2.087912	2.70039	3.32511	4.16816
10	2.15585	2.55821	3.24697	3.94030	4.86518
11	2.60321	3.05347	3.81575	4.57481	5.57779
12	3.07382	3.57056	4.40379	5.22603	6.30380
13	3.56503	4.10691	5.00874	5.89186	7.04150
14	4.07468	4.66043	5.62872	6.57063	7.78953
15	4.60094	5.22935	6.26214	7.26094	8.54675
16	5.14224	5.81221	6.90766	7.96164	9.31223
17	5.69724	6.40776	7.56418	8.67176	10.0852
18	6.26481	7.01491	8.23075	9.39046	10.8649
19	6.84398	7.63273	8.90655	10.1170	11.6509
20	7.43386	8.26040	9.59083	10.8508	12.4426
21	8.03366	8.89720	10.28293	11.5913	13.2396
22	8.64272	9.54249	10.9823	12.3380	14.0415
23	9.26042	10.19567	11.6885	13.0905	14.8479
24	9.88623	10.8564	12.4011	13.8484	15.6587
25	10.5197	11.5240	13.1197	14.6114	16.4734
26	11.1603	12.1981	13.8439	15.3791	17.2919
27	11.8076	12.8786	14.5733	16.1513	18.1138
28	12.4613	13.5648	15.3079	16.9279	18.9392
29	13.1211	14.2565	16.0471	17.7083	19.7677
30	13.7867	14.9535	16.7908	18.4926	20.5992
40	20.7065	22.1643	24.4331	26.5093	29.0505
50	27.9907	29.7067	32.3574	34.7642	37.6886
60	35.5346	37.4848	40.4817	43.1879	46.4589
70	43.2752	45.4418	48.7576	51.7393	55.3290
80	51.1720	53.5400	57.1532	60.3915	64.2778
90	59.1963	61.7541	65.6466	69.1260	73.2912
100	67.3276	70.0648	74.2219	77.9295	82.3581

Degrees of freedom	$\chi^2_{.100}$	$\chi^2_{.050}$	$\chi^2_{.025}$	$\chi^2_{.010}$	$\chi^2_{.005}$
1	2.70554	3.84146	5.02389	6.63490	7.87944
2	4.60517	5.99147	7.37776	9.21034	10.5966
3	6.25139	7.81473	9.34840	11.3449	12.8381
4	7.77944	9.48773	11.1433	13.2767	14.8602
5	9.23635	11.0705	12.8325	15.0863	16.7496
6	10.6446	12.5916	14.4494	16.8119	18.5476
7	12.0170	14.0671	16.0128	18.4753	20.2777
8	13.3616	15.5073	17.5346	20.0902	21.9550
9	14.6837	16.9190	19.0228	21.6660	23.5893
10	15.9871	18.3070	20.4831	23.2093	25.1882
11	17.2750	19.6751	21.9200	24.7250	26.7569
12	18.5494	21.0261	23.3367	26.2170	28.2995
13	19.8119	22.3621	24.7356	27.6883	29.8194
14	21.0642	23.6848	26.1190	29.1413	31.3193
15	22.3072	24.9958	27.4884	30.5779	32.8013
16	23.5418	26.2962	28.8454	31.9999	34.2672
17	24.7690	27.5871	30.1910	33.4087	35.7185
18	25.9894	28.8693	31.5264	34.8053	37.1564
19	27.2036	30.1435	32.8523	36.1908	38.5822
20	28.4120	31.4104	34.1696	37.5662	39.9968
21	29.6151	32.6705	35.4789	38.9321	41.4010
22	30.8133	33.9244	36.7807	40.2894	42.7956
23	32.0069	35.1725	38.0757	41.6384	44.1813
24	33.1963	36.4151	39.3641	42.9798	45.5585
25	34.3816	37.6525	40.6465	44.3141	46.9278
26	35.5631	38.8852	41.9232	45.6417	48.2899
27	36.7412	40.1133	43.1944	46.9630	49.6449
28	37.9159	41.3372	44.4607	48.2782	50.9933
29	39.0875	42.5569	45.7222	49.5879	52.3356
30	40.2560	43.7729	46.9792	50.8922	53.6720
40	51.8050	55.7585	59.3417	63.6907	66.7659
50	63.1671	67.5048	71.4202	76.1539	79.4900
60	74.3970	79.0819	83.2976	88.3794	91.9517
70	85.5271	90.5312	95.0231	100.425	104.215
80	96.5782	101.879	106.629	112.329	116.321
90	107.565	113.145	118.136	124.116	128.229
100	118.498	124.342	129.561	135.807	140.169

A6 F distribution

The table shows values of F for various degrees of freedom, v_1 and v_2, from 1 to ∞, and for $\alpha = 0.05$ and $\alpha = 0.01$.

(a) $\alpha = 0.05$

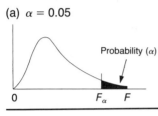

Probability (α)

0 F_α F

Denominator degrees of freedom (v_2)	Numerator degrees of freedom (v_1)								
	1	2	3	4	5	6	7	8	9
1	161.4	199.5	215.7	224.6	230.2	234.0	236.8	238.9	240.5
2	18.51	19.00	19.16	19.25	19.30	19.33	19.35	19.37	19.38
3	10.13	9.55	9.28	9.12	9.01	8.94	8.89	8.85	8.81
4	7.71	6,94	6.59	6.39	6.26	6.16	6.09	6.04	6.00
5	6.61	5.79	5.41	5.19	5.05	4.95	4.88	4.82	4.77
6	5.99	5.14	4.76	4.53	4.39	4.28	4.21	4.15	4.10
7	5.59	4.74	4.35	4.12	3.97	3.87	3.79	3.73	3.68
8	5.32	4.46	4.07	3.84	3.69	3.58	3.50	3.44	3.39
9	5.12	4.26	3.86	3.63	3.48	3.37	3.29	3.23	3.18
10	4.96	4.10	3.71	3.48	3.33	3.22	3.14	3.07	3.02
11	4.84	3.98	3.59	3.36	3.20	3.09	3.01	2.95	2.90
12	4.75	3.89	3.49	3.26	3.11	3.00	2.91	2.85	2.80
13	4.67	3.81	3.41	3.18	3.03	2.92	2.83	2.77	2.71
14	4.60	3.74	3.34	3.11	2.96	2.85	2.76	2.70	2.65
15	4.54	3.68	3.29	3.06	2.90	2.79	2.71	2.64	2.59
16	4.49	3.63	3.24	3.01	2.85	2.74	2.66	2.59	2.54
17	4.45	3.59	3.20	2.96	2.81	2.70	2.61	2.55	2.49
18	4.41	3.55	3.16	2.93	2.77	2.66	2.58	2.51	2.46
19	4.38	3.52	3.13	2.90	2.74	2.63	2.54	2.48	2.42
20	4.35	3.49	3.10	2.87	2.71	2.60	2.51	2.45	2.39
21	4.32	3.47	3.07	2.84	2.68	2.57	2.49	2.42	2.37
22	4.30	3.44	3.05	2.82	2.66	2.55	2.46	2.40	2.34
23	4.28	3.42	3.03	2.80	2.64	2.53	2.44	2.37	2.32
24	4.26	3.40	3.01	2.78	2.62	2.51	2.42	2.36	2.30
25	4.24	3.39	2.99	2.76	2.60	2.49	2.40	2.34	2.28
26	4.23	3.37	2.98	2.74	2.59	2.47	2.39	2.32	2.27
27	4.21	3.35	2.96	2.73	2.57	2.46	2.37	2.31	2.25
28	4.20	3.34	2.95	2.71	2.56	2.45	2.36	2.29	2.24
29	4.18	3.33	2.93	2.70	2.55	2.43	2.35	2.28	2.22
30	4.17	3.32	2.92	2.69	2.53	2.42	2.33	2.27	2.21
40	4.08	3.23	2.84	2.61	2.45	2.34	2.25	2.18	2.12
60	4.00	3.15	2.76	2.53	2.37	2.25	2.17	2.10	2.04
120	3.92	3.07	2.68	2.45	2.29	2.17	2.09	2.02	1.96
∞	3.84	3.00	2.60	2.37	2.21	2.10	2.01	1.94	1.88

10	12	15	Numerator degrees of freedom (v_1) 20	24	30	40	60	120	∞
241.9	243.9	245.9	248.0	249.1	250.1	251.1	252.2	253.3	254.3
19.40	19.41	19.43	19.45	19.45	19.46	19.47	19.48	19.49	19.50
8.79	8.74	8.70	8.66	8.64	8.62	8.59	8.57	8.55	8.53
5.96	5.91	5.86	5.80	5.77	5.75	5.72	5.69	5.66	5.63
4.74	4.68	4.62	4.56	4.53	4.50	4.46	4.43	4.40	4.36
4.06	4.00	3.94	3.87	3.84	3.81	3.77	3.74	3.70	3.67
3.64	3.57	3.51	3.44	3.41	3.38	3.34	3.30	3.27	3.23
3.35	3.28	3.22	3.15	3.12	3.08	3.04	3.01	2.97	2.93
3.14	3.07	3.01	2.94	2.90	2.86	2.83	2.79	2.75	2.71
2.98	2.91	2.85	2.77	2.74	2.70	2.66	2.62	2.58	2.54
2.85	2.79	2.72	2.65	2.61	2.57	2.53	2.49	2.45	2.40
2.75	2.69	2.62	2.54	2.51	2.47	2.43	2.38	2.34	2.30
2.67	2.60	2.53	2.46	2.42	2.38	2.34	2.30	2.25	2.21
2.60	2.53	2.46	2.39	2.35	2.31	2.27	2.22	2.18	2.13
2.54	2.48	2.40	2.33	2.29	2.25	2.20	2.16	2.11	2.07
2.49	2.42	2.35	2.28	2.24	2.19	2.15	2.11	2.06	2.01
2.45	2.38	2.31	2.23	2.19	2.15	2.10	2.06	2.01	1.96
2.41	2.34	2.27	2.19	2.15	2.11	2.06	2.02	1.97	1.92
2.38	2.31	2.23	2.16	2.11	2.07	2.03	1.98	1.93	1.88
2.35	2.28	2.20	2.12	2.08	2.04	1.99	1.95	1.90	1.84
2.32	2.25	2.18	2.10	2.05	2.01	1.96	1.92	1.87	1.81
2.30	2.23	2.15	2.07	2.03	1.98	1.94	1.89	1.84	1.78
2.27	2.20	2.13	2.05	2.01	1.96	1.91	1.86	1.81	1.76
2.25	2.18	2.11	2.03	1.98	1.94	1.89	1.84	1.79	1.73
2.24	2.16	2.09	2.01	1.96	1.92	1.87	1.82	1.77	1.71
2.22	2.15	2.07	1.99	1.95	1.90	1.85	1.80	1.75	1.69
2.20	2.13	2.06	1.97	1.93	1.88	1.84	1.79	1.73	1.67
2.19	2.12	2.04	1.96	1.91	1.87	1.82	1.77	1.71	1.65
2.18	2.10	2.03	1.94	1.90	1.85	1.81	1.75	1.70	1.64
2.16	2.09	2.01	1.93	1.89	1.84	1.79	1.74	1.68	1.62
2.08	2.00	1.92	1.84	1.79	1.74	1.69	1.64	1.58	1.51
1.99	1.92	1.84	1.75	1.70	1.65	1.59	1.53	1.47	1.39
1.91	1.83	1.75	1.66	1.61	1.55	1.50	1.43	1.35	1.25
1.83	1.75	1.67	1.57	1.52	1.46	1.39	1.32	1.22	1.00

(b) $\alpha = 0.01$

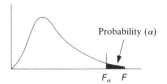

Probability (α)

F_α F

Denominator degrees of freedom (v_2)	Numerator degrees of freedom (v_1)								
	1	2	3	4	5	6	7	8	9
1	4,052	4,999.5	5,403	5,625	5,764	5,859	5,928	5,982	6,022
2	98.50	99.00	99.17	99.25	99.30	99.33	99.36	99.37	99.39
3	34.12	30.82	29.46	28.71	28.24	27.91	27.67	27.49	27.35
4	21.20	18.00	16.69	15.98	15.52	15.21	14.98	14.80	14.66
5	16.26	13.27	12.06	11.39	10.97	10.67	10.46	10.29	10.16
6	13.75	10.92	9.78	9.15	8.75	8.47	8.26	8.10	7.98
7	12.25	9.55	8.45	7.85	7.46	7.19	6.99	6.84	6.72
8	11.26	8.65	7.59	7.01	6.63	6.37	6.18	6.03	5.91
9	10.56	8.02	6.99	6.42	6.06	5.80	5.61	5.47	5.35
10	10.04	7.56	6.55	5.99	5.64	5.39	5.20	5.06	4.94
11	9.65	7.21	6.22	5.67	5.32	5.07	4.89	4.74	4.63
12	9.33	6.93	5.95	5.41	5.06	4.82	4.64	4.50	4.39
13	9.07	6.70	5.74	5.21	4.86	4.62	4.44	4.30	4.19
14	8.86	6.51	5.56	5.04	4.69	4.46	4.28	4.14	4.03
15	8.68	6.36	5.42	4.89	4.56	4.32	4.14	4.00	3.89
16	8.53	6.23	5.29	4.77	4.44	4.20	4.03	3.89	3.78
17	8.40	6.11	5.18	4.67	4.34	4.10	3.93	3.79	3.68
18	8.29	6.01	5.09	4.58	4.25	4.01	3.84	3.71	3.60
19	8.18	5.93	5.01	4.50	4.17	3.94	3.77	3.63	3.52
20	8.10	5.85	4.94	4.43	4.10	3.87	3.70	3.56	3.46
21	8.02	5.78	4.87	4.37	4.04	3.81	3.64	3.51	3.40
22	7.95	5.72	4.82	4.31	3.99	3.76	3.59	3.45	3.35
23	7.88	5.66	4.76	4.26	3.94	3.71	3.54	3.41	3.30
24	7.82	5.61	4.72	4.22	3.90	3.67	3.50	3.36	3.26
25	7.77	5.57	4.68	4.18	3.85	3.63	3.46	3.32	3.22
26	7.72	5.53	4.64	4.14	3.82	3.59	3.42	3.29	3.18
27	7.68	5.49	4.60	4.11	3.78	3.56	3.39	3.26	3.15
28	7.64	5.45	4.57	4.07	3.75	3.53	3.36	3.23	3.12
29	7.60	5.42	4.54	4.04	3.73	3.50	3.33	3.20	3.09
30	7.56	5.39	4.51	4.02	3.70	3.47	3.30	3.17	3.07
40	7.31	5.18	4.31	3.83	3.51	3.29	3.12	2.99	2.89
60	7.08	4.98	4.13	3.65	3.34	3.12	2.95	2.82	2.72
120	6.85	4.79	3.95	3.48	3.17	2.96	2.79	2.66	2.56
∞	6.63	4.61	3.78	3.32	3.02	2.80	2.64	2.51	2.41

Numerator degrees of freedom (v_1)									
10	12	15	20	24	30	40	60	120	∞
6,056	6,106	6,157	6,209	6,235	6,261	6,287	6,313	6,339	6,366
99.40	99.42	99.43	99.45	99.46	99.47	99.47	99.48	99.49	99.50
27.23	27.05	26.87	26.69	26.60	26.50	26.41	26.32	26.22	26.13
14.55	14.37	14.20	14.02	13.93	13.84	13.75	13.65	13.56	13.46
10.05	9.89	9.72	9.55	9.47	9.38	9.29	9.20	9.11	9.02
7.87	7.72	7.56	7.40	7.31	7.23	7.14	7.06	6.97	6.88
6.62	6.47	6.31	6.16	6.07	5.99	5.91	5.82	5.74	5.65
5.81	5.67	5.52	5.36	5.28	5.20	5.12	5.03	4.95	4.86
5.26	5.11	4.96	4.81	4.73	4.65	4.57	4.48	4.40	4.31
4.85	4.71	4.56	4.41	4.33	4.25	4.17	4.08	4.00	3.91
4.54	4.40	4.25	4.10	4.02	3.94	3.86	3.78	3.69	3.60
4.30	4.16	4.01	3.86	3.78	3.70	3.62	3.54	3.45	3.36
4.10	3.96	3.82	3.66	3.59	3.51	3.43	3.34	3.25	3.17
3.94	3.80	3.66	3.51	3.43	3.35	3.27	3.18	3.09	3.00
3.80	3.67	3.52	3.37	3.29	3.21	3.13	3.05	2.96	2.87
3.69	3.55	3.41	3.26	3.18	3.10	3.02	2.93	2.84	2.75
3.59	3.46	3.31	3.16	3.08	3.00	2.92	2.83	2.75	2.65
3.51	3.37	3.23	3.08	3.00	2.92	2.84	2.75	2.66	2.57
3.43	3.30	3.15	3.00	2.92	2.84	2.76	2.67	2.58	2.49
3.37	3.23	3.09	2.94	2.86	2.78	2.69	2.61	2.52	2.42
3.31	3.17	3.03	2.88	2.80	2.72	2.64	2.55	2.46	2.36
3.26	3.12	2.98	2.83	2.75	2.67	2.58	2.50	2.40	2.31
3.21	3.07	2.93	2.78	2.70	2.62	2.54	2.45	2.35	2.26
3.17	3.03	2.89	2.74	2.66	2.58	2.49	2.40	2.31	2.21
3.13	2.99	2.85	2.70	2.62	2.54	2.45	2.36	2.27	2.17
3.09	2.96	2.81	2.66	2.58	2.50	2.42	2.33	2.23	2.13
3.06	2.93	2.78	2.63	2.55	2.47	2.38	2.29	2.20	2.10
3.03	2.90	2.75	2.60	2.52	2.44	2.35	2.26	2.17	2.06
3.00	2.87	2.73	2.57	2.49	2.41	2.33	2.23	2.14	2.03
2.98	2.84	2.70	2.55	2.47	2.39	2.30	2.21	2.11	2.01
2.80	2.66	2.52	2.37	2.29	2.20	2.11	2.02	1.92	1.80
2.63	2.50	2.35	2.20	2.12	2.03	1.94	1.84	1.73	1.60
2.47	2.34	2.19	2.03	1.95	1.86	1.76	1.66	1.53	1.38
2.32	2.18	2.04	1.88	1.79	1.70	1.59	1.47	1.32	1.00

Appendix B

Computer software for statistical analysis

Computer software packages are widely used nowadays to perform various statistical analysis procedures. When used properly, they can save considerable time and effort and decrease the likelihood of human error. The purpose of this appendix is to provide a brief overview of three packages which are in widespread use, namely:

- MINITAB
- SAS (Statistical Analysis System)
- SPSSX (Statistical Package for the Social Sciences)

MINITAB

MINITAB is a very 'user-friendly' and flexible statistical package. It has been designed especially for those who have no previous experience of computers. It is widely available for use on personal computers (in both WINDOWS and non-WINDOWS versions) as well as mainframe computers and may be used interactively, i.e. results are displayed straightaway on screen and, if required, further analysis can be carried out. The package has many capabilities, covering most of the topics dealt with in this book. It is also useful in more advanced statistical analysis and is used extensively in business, industry and government. Knowledge of MINITAB also provides a helpful introduction to the other statistical packages noted below as well as more specialized programs.

Further information about the MINITAB system may be obtained from:
MINITAB, Inc.,
3081 Enterprise Drive,
State College,
PA 16801-2756,
USA.

References

1. B. F. Ryan and B. L. Joiner, *Minitab Handbook*, 3rd edn, Duxbury Press: Belmont, CA, 1994.

2. R. L. Schaefer and R. B. Anderson, *The Student Edition of Minitab: Statistical Software*, Addison-Wesley: Reading, MA; Benjamin/Cummings: Melo Park, CA, 1989. (This is a student edition of the MINITAB package, comprising software plus users' manual. The student edition is a scaled-down version of the full program. Further details are available from: MINITAB Inc, 3081 Enterprise Drive, State College, PA 16801-2756, USA.)

SAS and SPSSX

These are both large-scale, general-purpose statistical packages, available in both PC and mainframe versions. They are, however, capable of handling much larger data sets than MINITAB and the range of diagnostic tests and statistical procedures they contain is much more extensive.

References

1. *SAS Introductory Guide for Personal Computers Version*, 6th edn, SAS Institute: Cary, NC, 1990.

2. *SAS User's Guide: Statistics Version*, 5th edn, SAS Institute: Cary, NC, 1990.

3. Norusis, Marija, *SPSS/PC for the IBM PC/XT/AT*, SPSS Inc.: Chicago, 1990.

4. Norusis, Marija, *SPSSX Introductory Statistics Guide*, McGraw-Hill: New York, 1990.

Appendix C

Sources of business and economic statistics

This appendix gives details of the following:

☐ The principal sources of the main business and economic statistics for the United Kingdom.

☐ The principal international sources.

☐ Guides to statistical sources.

UK sources

General UK sources

Annual Abstract of Statistics (HMSO) and *Monthly Digest of Statistics* (HMSO): statistics covering a wide range of business, economic and other topics.

Economic Trends and *Economic Trends Annual Supplement* (HMSO, annually): the principal economic series (output, employment, prices, etc.). The *Annual Supplement* presents long-run quarterly figures for the main series.

Regional Trends (HMSO, annually): brings together the main statistics available on a regional basis.

Social Trends (HMSO, annually): brings together key social and demographic series.

United Kingdom Balance of Payments – the 'CSO Pink Book' (HMSO, annually): details of visible and invisible trade, investment and other capital transactions.

United Kingdom National Accounts – the 'CSO Blue Book' (HMSO, annually): detailed estimates of national production, income and expenditure; value-added by industry, capital investment and financial accounts.

Specific UK sources

Labour statistics

Employment Gazette (HMSO, monthly): employment, unemployment, hours worked, earnings, labour costs, retail prices, industrial disputes.

Labour Force Survey Quarterly Bulletin (HMSO, quarterly): data on employment, unemployment and the labour force analyzed by a wide range of factors.
New Earnings Survey (HMSO, annually): detailed data on earnings by industry, occupation, region, etc.

Production and sales

Reports on the Census of Production – Business Monitor PA series (HMSO, annually): data (in separate parts for each industry) on sales, purchases, stocks, capital expenditure, employment, wages and salaries.
UK Markets (Taylor Nelson AGB, annual and quarterly series of reports): UK manufacturer sales for each of 4,800 products, export/import and net supply.

Finance

Financial Statistics (HMSO, monthly): key financial and monetary statistics of the UK.

Prices

Retail Price Index: *Employment Gazette* (HMSO, monthly) and the general sources listed above.
Wholesale Price Indexes: *Price Index Numbers for Current Cost Accounting* (HMSO, annually) and *Business Monitor MM17* (HMSO, monthly) and the general sources listed above.
Inflation Report (Bank of England, quarterly): analyses of inflation trends and prospects.

Housing and construction

Housing and Construction Statistics (HMSO, annually and quarterly): data on a wide range of housing and construction topics.

Foreign trade

Overseas Trade Statistics of the UK (HMSO, annually and monthly): detailed statistics of imports and exports.
Overseas Trade Analysed in Terms of Industries – Business Monitor MQ10 (HMSO, quarterly): imports and exports by industry.

Transport

Transport Statistics, Great Britain (HMSO, annually): collected series on transport topics.

International sources

There is a very large number of sources of international data. A comprehensive guide arranged according to subject is:

Instat – International Statistics Sources: A Subject Guide to Sources of International Comparative Statistics by M. C. Fleming and J. G. Nellis, London: Routledge, 1995.

The main organizations producing international statistics are: the United Nations (UN), the International Labour Organization (ILO) – both of which cover all countries – the Organization for Economic Co-operation and Development (OECD) – covering Western European countries, Turkey, Canada, USA, Japan, Australia and New Zealand – and Eurostat – covering countries in the EU and, occasionally, the USA and Japan.

Non-EU sources

General
  UN Statistical Year Book (UN, New York, annually): wide range of data for all countries.

Labour
  Yearbook of Labour Statistics (ILO, Geneva, annually): wide range of data on employment, unemployment, earnings, etc.

National Accounts
  UN National Accounts Statistics (UN, New York, annually) and *National Accounts* (OECD, Paris, annually): national production, income, expenditure, capital formation, etc.

EU sources

A very wide range of statistics publications is issued by the Statistical Office of the European Communities (Eurostat) in Luxembourg. Selected titles are listed below. Their titles generally indicate their coverage and in these cases no further detail is given.

  Basic Statistics of the Community (annually).
  Industry Statistical Year Book (annually).
  Industrial Trends: Monthly Statistics (monthly): indices for industrial production, employment, wages and salaries, imports and exports.
  Industrial Production: Quarterly Statistics (quarterly): industrial production by product.
  Structure and Activity of Industry (annually).
  Earnings: Industry and Services (half-yearly): earnings by industry.
  Labour Force Survey (annually).
  National Accounts – 3 volumes (annually).
  External Trade Statistical Year Book (annually).

Guides to sources

United Kingdom
  Government Statistics: A brief guide to sources (Information Services Division, Cabinet Office, London, free).
  Guide to Official Statistics, CSO (HMSO, occasional).

Review of UK Statistical Sources: a series of volumes providing comprehensive guides to sources and critical appraisals of the nature of the data available. A select list of titles of relevance in a business context is given below. Volumes 1–5 were published by Heinemann Educational Books, London, volumes 6–22 were published by Pergamon Press, Oxford, and volumes 23–29 were published by Chapman & Hall, London.

Volume 3: *Housing in Great Britain and Housing in Northern Ireland* (1974).
Volume 5: *General Sources of Statistics* (1976).
Volume 7: *Road Passenger Transport and Road Goods Transport* (1978).
Volume 10: *Ports and Inland Waterways and Civil Aviation* (1979).
Volume 11: *Coal, Gas, Electricity* (1980).
Volume 12: *Construction and the Related Professions* (1980).
Volume 13: *Wages and Earnings* (1980).
Volume 14: *Rail and Sea Transport* (1981).
Volume 16: *Iron and Steel, Shipbuilding* (1984).
Volume 17: *Water Industry and Weather* (1985).
Volume 18: *Posts and Telecommunications* (1986).
Volume 19: *Intellectual Property Rights* (1986).
Volume 21: *Financial Statistics* (1987).
Volume 22: *Printing and Publishing* (1987).
Volume 23: *Local Government* (1988).
Volume 24: *Agriculture* (1988).
Volume 26: *International Aspects of UK Economic Activities* (1991).
Volume 27: *Research and Development* (1993).
Volume 28: *The Food Industries* (1993).
Volume 29: *Distribution* (1992).

International

M. C. Fleming and J. G. Nellis, *Instat – International Statistics Sources: A Subject Guide to Sources of International Comparative Statistics*, Routledge: London, 1995.
R. Bean, *International Labour Statistics: A handbook, guide and recent trends*, Routledge: London, 1989.
Eurostat Catalogue: publications and electronic services (free from Eurostat and from the Office for Official Publications of the European Communities, Luxembourg).

Appendix D

References for further reading

General introductory references

Ehrenberg, A. S. C., *A Primer in Data Reduction*, John Wiley & Sons: Chichester, 1982.

Huff, Darrell, *How to Lie With Statistics*, Penguin Books: London, 1973.

Kennedy, Gavin, *Invitation to Statistics*, Martin Robertson: Oxford, 1983.

Reichmann, W. J., *The Use and Abuse of Statistics*, Penguin Books: London, 1964.

Rowntree, Derek, *Statistics Without Tears*, Penguin Books: London, 1984.

Sprent, Peter, *Understanding Data*, Penguin Books: London, 1988.

Technical references

Anderson, David R., Sweeney, Dennis J. and Williams, Thomas A., *Statistics for Business and Economics*, 5th edn, West Publishing Co.: St Paul, 1993.

Fleming, Michael C. and Nellis, Joseph G., *Principles of Applied Statistics*, Routledge: London, 1994.

Groebner, David F. and Shannon, Patrick W., *Business Statistics: A decision-making approach*, 2nd edn, Merrill Publishing Co.: Columbus, 1985.

Kenkel, James L., *Introductory Statistics for Management and Economics*, 2nd edn, Duxbury Press: Boston, 1984.

Kvanli, Alan H., Guynes, Stephen C. and Pavur, Robert J., *Introduction to Business Statistics: A computer integrated approach*, 3rd edn, West Publishing Co.: St Paul, 1992.

Mendenhall, William, Reinmuth, James E., Beaver, Robert and Duhan, Dale, *Statistics for Management and Economics*, 5th edn, Duxbury Press: Boston, 1986.

Moskowitz, Herbert and Wright, Gordon P., *Statistics for Management and Economics*, Merrill Publishing Co.: Columbus, 1985.

Ott, Lyman and Hildebrand, David K., *Statistical Thinking for Managers*, Duxbury Press: Boston, 1983.

Toh, R. S. and Hu, M. Y., *Basic Business Statistics: An Intuitive Approach*, West Publishing: St Paul, MN, 1991.

Tufte, E. R., *The Visual Display of Quantitative Information*, Graphics Press UK: Godalming, 1989.

Solutions to exercises

CHAPTER 3

1 (a) 66. (b) 64. (c) 72.
  (d) 42. (e) $Q_1 = 58$, (f) 14.
  (g) 7. $Q_3 = 72$. (h) 9.2.
  (i) 126.14 (j) 11.23.

2 (a) (i) £61.6. (ii) £55. (iii) £46.
    (iv) £33.03. (v) $Q_1 = £34.6$, (vi) £23.8.
       $Q_3 = £82.2$.

3 30.525%.

4 £16.28.

5 2.77%.

6 34.49%.

7 14.2 years.

8 (a) Coefficient of variation: males = 11.4%, females = 7.5%; therefore answer is 'Yes'.

  (b) Coefficient of variation: weights = 20%, heights = 7.5%; therefore answer is 'Yes'.

9 (a) 2.9. (b) 2.55.

CHAPTER 4

1 (a) Laspeyres: 162.50 Paasche: 160.75.
  (b) Laspeyres: 162.50 Paasche: 165.72.

2 (a) £1860.03. (b) 55%.

3 (a) 153.33. (b) 154.45.

4 6.3%.

5 £5713.72.

6 (a) 87.5p.   (b) £4375.43.

7 (a) Craftsmen 133.33%; labourers 118.75%; drivers 121.05%.
(b) 124.5.

CHAPTER 5

1 (a) 0.091.   (b) 0.125.   (c) 0.273.

2 (b) 0.8.   (c) 0.2.

3 (a) 0.1346.   (b) 0.9375.   (c) 0.1333.

4 (a) 8/15.   (b) 2/15   (c) 2/3.
(d) 0 (since only two are selected!).

5 120 (permutations).

6 (a) 11/24.   (b) 1/4.   (c) 1/24.

7 (a) 0.001.   (b) 0.032.   (c) 0.999.

8 (a) 0.15.   (b) 0.4.

CHAPTER 6

1 (a) 0.9606.   (b) 0.9994.   (c) 0.999996.

2 (a) 5.   (b) 4.

3 (a) 0.1585.   (b) 0.5941.   (c) 0.1094.
(d) 0.9688.

4 (a) 0.9138.   (b) 0.0862.

5 (a) 0.1179.   (b) 0.1755.   (c) 0.068.
(d) Mean = 5 per hour; standard deviation = $\sqrt{\text{mean}}$ = 2.236.

6 0.055.

7 (a) 0.8754.   (b) 0.2650.

8 (a) 0.4332.   (b) 0.1359.   (c) 0.84.
(d) 0.1587.   (e) 0.6826.   (f) 0.8664.

9 (a) 0.6902.   (b) 0.1056.   (c) 0.0228.
(d) £108.40.

10 (a) 0.5643.   (b) 31.3 cm.

11 (a) 0.0228.   (b) 0.2857.   (c) 9.522, i.e. 9 workers.

12 15.69 oz.

CHAPTER 7

1 (a) 4.

(b) 3.83.

(Note, the finite population correction (fpc) factor is applied here because sample size n is large relative to the population size N.)

(c) 2.

(Note, it is not specified whether sampling is with or without replacement; it must be assumed, therefore, that sampling is *without* replacement since this is the normal practice. The fpc factor cannot be applied as the actual population size is not specified, but since it is said to be large, it may be assumed that the sampling fraction is small and thus application of the fpc factor would be of little practical importance.)

2 (a) 0.0951.   (b) 0.9955.

3 (a) 0.1335.

(b) 0.2895. (Note that (a) involves a sampling distribution of means while (b) does not.)

4 0.0918.

5 (a) 14,000 miles (since the sample mean provides an unbiased point estimate of the population mean μ).

(b) 14,000 $\pm$ 1960 miles

(c) 68.26%.

(d) 96.04 (rounded up to 97).

6 £1.95 $\pm$ 10p.

7 (c) -1.363.

8 (a) 0.025.   (b) 0.025.   (c) 0.85.

(d) 0.15.

9 4.6 $\pm$ 0.4 years.

10 (a) 8900 $\pm$ 277 hours.   (b) 8900 $\pm$ 227 hours.

CHAPTER 8

1 (a) Two-tailed; H_0: $\mu = \mu_0$, H_1: $\mu \neq \mu_0$.

(b) One-tailed; H_0: $\mu = 5$, H_1: $\mu > 5$.

(c) One-tailed; H_0: $\mu = \mu_0$, H_1: $\mu < \mu_0$.

(d) Two-tailed; H_0: $\mu = \mu_0$, H_1: $\mu \neq \mu_0$.

(e) One-tailed; H_0: $\mu = \mu_0$, H_1: $\mu < \mu_0$.

2 (a) ± 1.96.   (b) $+1.645$ or -1.645.   (c) ± 1.645.

(d) $+2.33$ or -2.33.   (e) ± 2.575.   (f) -1.645.

(g) $+1.28$.

3 (a) 76.08 and 83.92. Region of acceptance lies between these critical values.

(b) 76.71 and 83.29. Region of acceptance is given by values greater than 76.71 (for $Z = -1.645$) or values less than 83.29 (for $Z = +1.645$).

4 Yes. H_0 ($\mu = 15000$) rejected ($Z = -6.7$; $Z_{\alpha/2} = \pm1.96$).

5 No. H_0 ($\mu = 4700$) accepted ($Z = 2.05$; $Z_\alpha = +2.33$).

6 Yes. H_0 ($\mu = 12.8$) rejected ($Z = -3.283$; $Z_\alpha = -1.645$).

7 3.647.

8 Yes. H_0 ($\mu = 307.8$) rejected ($Z = 6.72$; $Z_{\alpha/2} = \pm1.96$).

9 $\sigma_{\bar{x}} = \sigma/\sqrt{n} = 0.16/\sqrt{4} = 0.08$.
Warning limits are: $\mu \pm 2\sigma_{\bar{x}} = 5 \pm 2(0.08) = 4.84$ to 5.16.
Control limits are: $\mu \pm 3\sigma_{\bar{x}} = 5 \pm 3(0.08) = 4.76$ to 5.24.
The fourth sample should be taken as a warning as the means falls outside the warning limits, but in itself should not be regarded as serious. The seventh and eighth sample means, however, both fall outside the control limits and action is therefore required to investigate why the process is out of control.

10 Yes. H_0 ($\mu = 100$) rejected ($t = 6.7$; $t_{\alpha/2} = \pm2.093$ with $20 - 1$ df).

11 Yes. H_0 ($\mu = 40$) accepted ($t = -1.414$; $t_{\alpha/2} = \pm2.776$ with $5 - 1$ df).

12 Yes. H_0 ($\mu_1 - \mu_2 = 0$) rejected ($Z = 2.53$; $Z_{\alpha/2} = \pm1.96$).

13 No. ($Z_\alpha = \pm2.58$).

14 No. H_0 ($\mu_1 - \mu_2 = 0$) accepted ($t = -1.65$; $t_{\alpha/2} = \pm2.101$ with $n_1 + n_2 - 2$ df).

15 Yes. H_0 ($\mu_1 - \mu_2 = 10,000$) accepted ($Z = -1.75$; $Z_{\alpha/2} = \pm2.58$).

CHAPTER 9

1 Reject H_0, i.e. conclude that pattern of sales has changed ($x^2 = 22$; $x^2_{0.01} = 9.210$ with $k - 1 = 2$ df).

2 Accept H_0, i.e. performance not significantly different ($x^2 = 1.91$; $x^2_{0.05} = 3.84$ with $k - 1 = 1$ df).

3 Accept H_0, i.e. distribution does not differ significantly from a normal distribution ($x^2 = 7.24$; $x^2_{0.05} = 7.81$ with $k - 3 = 3$ df).

4 Accept H_0, i.e. no significant relationship between brand preferences and socio-economic group ($x^2 = 1.576$; $x^2_{0.05} = 5.991$ with $(r - 1)(c - 1) = 2$ df).

5 Accept H_0, i.e. no significant relationship ($x^2 = 0.17$; $x^2_{0.05} = 9.488$ with $(r - 1)(c - 1) = 4$ df).

CHAPTER 10

1 (a) $a = 34.3$; $b = 4.46$.
(b) Yes. H_0 ($B = 0$) is rejected ($t = 7.69$; $t_{0.05} = 1.895$ with $9 - 2 = 7$ df).

(c) $r = 0.946$.

(d) $1 - 0.895 = 0.105$, i.e. 10.5%.

(e) £34.3 + £4.46 × 10 = £78.90, say £79.

2 (a) $a = 41.9$; $b = -2.47$.

(b) Significantly less than zero ($t = -6.98$; $t_{0.05} = -1.86$ with $10 - 2 = 8$ df).

(c) $r = -0.927$.

(d) 85.9%.

(e) $41.9 - 2.47 \times 12 = 12.3$ thousand litres (approximately), say 12 thousand litres.

3 (a) $a = 10.188$; $b = -0.14143$. Assembly times are *negatively* related to aptitude scores.

(b) $r = -0.916$. Significantly less than zero ($t = -6.46$; $t_{0.05} = -1.86$ with $10 - 2 = 8$ df).

(c) Higher scores on the aptitude test are significantly related to *lower* assembly times.

CHAPTER 11

1 (a) $Y_c = 16.4 + 0.931X_1 - 0.074X_2$.

(b) Sales of cars increase by 0.931 on average for each year of experience of the salesperson but decrease by 0.074 on average as the age of the salesperson increases.

(c) Yes (the p value for the F statistic of 5.05 is 0.044 which is less than 0.05).

(d) X_1 significant; p value = $0.016 < 0.05$ (H_0: $B_1 = 0$; H_1: $B_1 > 0$).
X_2 not significant: p value = $0.554 > 0.05$ (H_0: $B_2 = 0$; H_1: $B_2 < 0$).

(e) 59.1% (=R^2).

(f) $Y_c = 16.4 + 0.931(10) - 0.074(20)$.
$= 16.4 + 9.31 - 1.48 = 24.23$ (say 24 cars).

2 (a) 6.

(b) $B_1 > 0$, $B_2 > 0$, $B_3 < 0$, $B_4 < 0$.

(c) B_1: Yes. B_2: Yes. B_3: No. B_4: No.

(d) The F statistic (4288.09) has a p value of 0.011 which is less than the significance level of 5 per cent ($\alpha = 0.05$). The conclusion is, therefore, that the explanatory variables *as a set* significantly affect profits.

(e) B_1: Yes (p value = $0.038 < 0.05$).
B_2: Yes (p value = $0.019 < 0.05$).
B_3: No (p value = $0.156 > 0.05$).
B_4: No (p value = $0.123 > 0.05$).

CHAPTER 12

1 (a) $a = 2.95$; $b = 0.408$.   (b) 408 tonnes.   (c) 7.855 thousand tonnes.

(d) That trend observed over the period 1986–95 will continue to hold up to 1997.

2 (a) 98.20, 88.42, 95.24, 90.91.

(b) 100.43, 84.82, 73.99, 95.57.

3

Feb	Mar	Apr	May	June	July	Aug	Sept	Oct	Nov
82	88	90	83	79	76	78	80	80	79

4 (a)

	Q1	Q2	Q3	Q4
1992			24.75	25.375
1993	25.625	26.25	27.75	29.25
1994	30.25	31.25	32.125	32.625
1995	32.625			

(b) Q1 132.77; Q2 86.80; Q3 67.18; Q4 113.25.

(c) Seasonal movements in the first and fourth quarters are 32.75 per cent and 13.25 per cent above trend respectively, on average, while in the second and third quarters they are 13.19 per cent and 32.81 per cent below trend respectively on average.

Index